I0761065

Humor in the Historical Works of Tacitus

Humor in the Historical Works of Tacitus

Emma Warhover

UNIVERSITY OF MICHIGAN PRESS
ANN ARBOR

Published in the United States of America by the
University of Michigan Press
First published March 2026

A CIP catalog record for this book is available from the British Library.

Library of Congress Cataloging-in-Publication Data

Names: Warhover, Emma, 1993– author | Michigan Publishing (University of Michigan) publisher
Title: Humor in the historical works of Tacitus / Emma Warhover.
Description: Ann Arbor [Michigan] : University of Michigan Press, 2026. | Includes bibliographical references (pages 175–184) and index.
Identifiers: LCCN 2025033288 (print) | LCCN 2025033289 (ebook) | ISBN 9780472133680 hardcover | ISBN 9780472222506 ebook
Subjects: LCSH: Tacitus, Cornelius—Criticism and interpretation | Tacitus, Cornelius—Humor | Wit and humor, Ancient—Authorship | Historiography—Rome
Classification: LCC PA6747 .W37 2026 (print) | LCC PA6747 (ebook)
LC record available at https://lccn.loc.gov/2025033288
LC ebook record available at https://lccn.loc.gov/2025033289

DOI: https://doi.org/10.3998/mpub.14461360

Cover illustration: "Tarquinius Superbus Makes Himself King," by John Leech, from Gilbert à Beckett, *The Comic History of Rome* (London, 1851). Courtesy Wikimedia Commons.

The authorized representative in the EU for product safety and compliance is Easy Access System Europe, Mustamäe tee 50, 10621 Tallinn, Estonia, gpsr.requests@easproject.com

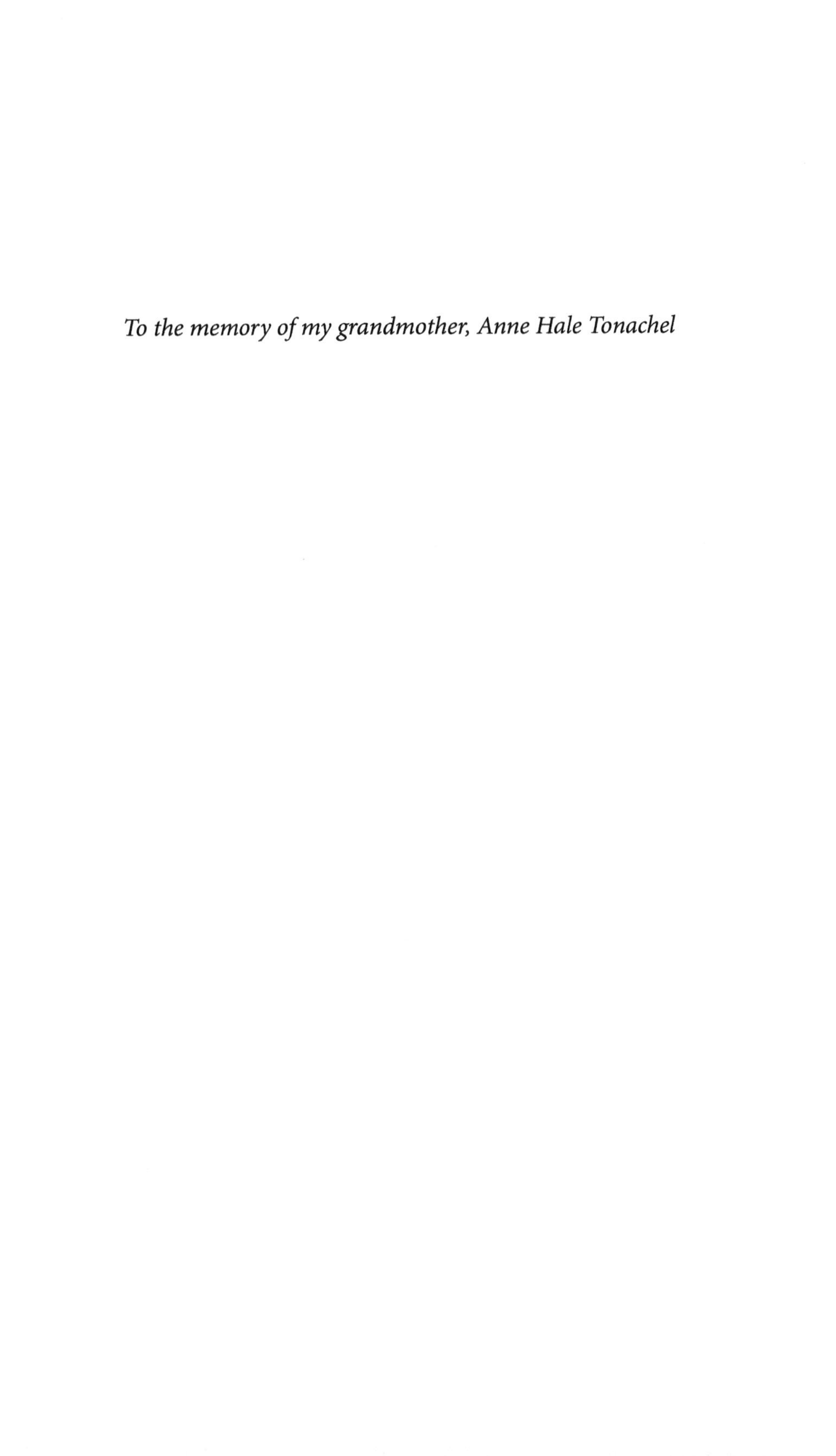

To the memory of my grandmother, Anne Hale Tonachel

Contents

Acknowledgments ix

Introduction 1

ONE Flattery Will Get You Everywhere: Otho and Humor in *Histories* 1 15

TWO Humor as Precedent: The Trial of Libo Drusus 47

THREE The Wedding of Messalina and Silius 71

FOUR Humor in Nero's Consolidation of Power 95

FIVE Humor as a Tool of Nero's Power 133

Conclusion 169

Bibliography 175

Index Locorum 185

General Index 191

Digital materials related to this title can be found on
the Fulcrum platform via the following citable URL:
https://doi.org/10.3998/mpub.14461360

Acknowledgments

This book began as a dissertation under the direction of James Rives, whose mentorship, encouragement, and willingness to read messy drafts allowed the project to develop from idea to actual scholarly work. The members of my dissertation committee—Cynthia Damon, Robert Babcock, Emily Baragwanath—all provided valuable suggestions for both the dissertation and later stages of the project. A separate thanks must fly to Sharon James, whose sudden death in 2023 deprived us all of her intellect and determination.

I thank my colleagues at the temporary positions I have held while in the process of improving and revising this book. My supervisors Sanjaya Thakur, Melissa Morison, and Chuck Pazdernik have all encouraged me to keep up with scholarship while teaching full-time, and indeed all my colleagues in the Classics departments at first Colorado College and then Grand Valley State University have been generous with advice and support, including the small but necessary help of simply being interested in my research. Thanks especially to Ben Howland for being a great fellow-toiler in the 4–4 teaching grind.

The Meeting on Ancient Satire, Comedy, and Humor (MASCH) reviewed a chapter of this work back in 2023; thanks to them for helping me gather confidence that other scholars would be interested in this project and for inviting me to share in their discussions of humor in the ancient world. I am especially grateful to T. H. M. Gellar-Goad for serving as the respondent when MASCH critiqued my chapter.

My friends Jonathan Fifer, Sophie Hao, and Paul Liu have listened to me alternately rejoice and fret about this project and have offered their delight and reassurance in return. All three are excellent people, and I would have been lucky to know just one of them.

Finally, my thanks to my parents, Eliza Tonachel and Bob Warhover. They gave me the commitment to education, sense of humor, and stubborn attitude without which this project would never have begun. I love you, mom and dad.

Introduction

Humor serves many purposes besides amusement. Although fun and entertainment are naturally and correctly thought of as the primary functions of humor, it can also be turned toward serious purposes, and it often is. Irony, satire, sarcasm, and even ridicule use the techniques of humorous composition to criticize, insult, expose hypocrisy, accumulate social cachet, and to perform other functions that have less to do with entertainment than with controlling the impression that an audience will take from a narrative. Therefore, it need not come as a surprise that Cornelius Tacitus, an eminently serious ancient historian, employed humorous techniques in service of his historical and literary aims.

Previous scholarship on Tacitus has rarely emphasized his subtle use of humor, although many of its constituent parts have been studied extensively. Tacitus' work is suffused with irony, end-of-the-sentence surprises (rendered through appendix sentences and *variatio*), and other elements of the distinctive style by which he keeps his readers disconcerted.[1] I argue that many of the recognized features of Tacitus' style are in fact conducive to humor in addition to their other effects. The appendix sentence, for example, is structurally similar to

---

1. Much has been written on Tacitean style. Oakley (2009) provides a summary. See also comments in Leeman (1963, 337–55); Martin (1981, 214–35); von Albrecht (1989, 136–59); Damon (2003, 12–20); and Ash (2007, 14–21). Direct discussion of humor is less usual, but it does exist. For example, Dickison (1977) and Fraser (2007) argue that specific passages in Tacitus depend on humor. Plass (1988) is perhaps the fullest treatment of Tacitus' use of humor. Many other scholars acknowledge in passing that something in Tacitus is "funny" (e.g., Haynes 2003, 107 on Vitellius). Scholarship therefore acknowledges isolated jokes but has less often considered that these darkly humorous moments accumulate into a pillar of Tacitus' rhetorical program.

a punchline and can be employed for humorous effect.[2] Irony, although not identical to humor, commonly creates humor, and Tacitus' use of antithesis is similarly conducive to humor. By recognizing elements of Tacitus' work as humorous, we can recognize another basis for Tacitus' techniques of subtle implication[3] and connect Tacitus to ancient rhetorical recommendations on the uses of humor.

An important precedent for my study is Paul Plass' *Wit and the Writing of History: The Rhetoric of Historiography in Imperial Rome* (1988). Plass examines the works of Suetonius, Cassius Dio, Seneca, and especially Tacitus for humorous moments and concludes that humor is a tool for discussing "political irrationality," that is, decisions that disregard practical or realistic concerns and instead treat political power as the only factor worth considering (1988, 103). Wit allows authors to "point to deeper uncertainty about political reality and pretense" (1988, 8). Plass' contribution is enormous, and I have noted his insights frequently. His approach to humor, however, differs slightly from mine, and his broad focus did not allow for in-depth analysis. Plass identified a significant catalogue of humorous sentences and phrases in ancient Roman historical writing and named the purpose of humor in many of these passages. I agree with Plass' determination that these passages use humor and extend my analysis into the episodes that surround Plass' humorous snippets, which are often revealed to be punchlines—merely the most humorous sentence in a paragraph or an episode in which Tacitus has constructed a pervasive humorous contrast. By narrowing my attention to a few episodes and studying the role of humor in those episodes, I advance an interpretation of Tacitus' particular use of humor that focuses the broader scope of Plass' work.

---

2. Tacitus' use of epigrams performs a similar function, to present a twisted logic that interprets events instead of simply narrating them (Plass 1988, 11–13).

3. In an early comment on the rhetorical effects of Tacitus' style, Inez Ryberg noted Tacitus' tendency to imply rather than provide evidence for many of his interpretations of historical events. For Ryberg, Tacitus' implications help him avoid responsibility for historical interpretations that he espouses without evidence (1942, 383). In her study of the effect of Tacitus' literary style on his historical narrative, Bessie Walker (1952) provides a framework for understanding Tacitus through his rhetorical techniques as well as his subject matter. Ellen O'Gorman describes Tacitus as a participant in a tradition of "sceptical history," in which the historian represents both truths and false appearances as equally relevant to understanding the past (2000, 3). Tacitus' style facilitates this ironic double vision; *variatio* and information-laden subordinate clauses keep truth and falsehood rhetorically balanced with each other so a reader cannot discard one and keep the other (O'Gorman 2000, 4–6). O'Gorman's focus is on irony, which is not necessarily humorous but does often contribute to humor. Holly Haynes asserts that Tacitus illustrates history "as much in how he makes you feel as in the content he relates" and that this is connected to a sense of uncertainty "as to whether there is a joke or not" (2012, 295).

Because the terminology associated with humor varies widely, I will first define the terms I employ in my analysis. I follow modern anglophone scholarship in calling the phenomenon I study "humor." The word "humor" often has a more lighthearted connotation than seems appropriate for the material I discuss. Because my analysis applies to a range of phenomena, however, I employ "humor" as an umbrella term to include everything from carefree joking to sordid irony.[4] Other terms are sometimes applicable, but I only occasionally find it useful to employ more specific terminology. If I understand a phrase as humorous, it need not also be called witty—it may be witty, but identifying it as wit merely invites quibbling over terminology.[5] I use other terms in specific contexts. "Absurdity" or "absurd" applies to circumstances that produce humor by straining credulity. I use "joke" to indicate a short passage with a punchline. (Tacitus was not in the business of writing jokes, but I use the word occasionally to describe a structure that contains a sentence or two leading up to a humorous surprise at the end.[6]) In some cases, I use the Latin term *sententia*, which can indicate humor but does not necessarily do so. I use "comedy" to refer only to the theatrical genre exemplified in Latin by Plautus and Terence. "Satire" also refers exclusively to the literary genre. I restrict "mockery" and "ridicule" to describing events that occur within the text, not because Tacitus never uses humor to criticize anyone,[7] but because "mockery" implies a direct relationship between the person making the joke and the target that does not exist between a historian and historical figures.

Humor is even more difficult to define than to name. Time and culture make profound changes to humor, so a modern definition will not necessarily illuminate ancient Roman humor. Ancient sources can better indicate what Tacitus would have thought about humor, and luckily two significant discussions survive in the works of Cicero and Quintilian. Tacitus distinguished him-

---

4. "Humor" is also used to describe less conventionally pleasant discourse, as in, "dark humor" and "sick humor." "Humor" is used as an umbrella term in virtually every modern study that I have consulted, and at least one study has shown that "humor" is the preferred general term in colloquial English (Apte 1985, 206–10).
5. "Wit" is Paul Plass' preferred term in part because he looks at short passages that illustrate Tacitus' or a character's perspective and because it describes pithy epigrams (Plass 1988, 6–7). Because I look at longer passages, and because I suspect that everything Tacitus wrote was calculated to demonstrate his perspective in one way or another, Plass' term is not ideal for my project.
6. Many such passages could just as accurately be described as *inconcinnitas* or *variatio*, but neither of these terms necessarily imply humor.
7. Indeed, Martin likens Tacitus' criticisms of society to Juvenal's, although Martin sees Tacitus as more involved in the political system he criticized than Juvenal was with the phenomena he criticized (1981, 38).

self as an orator before turning to historical writing, and the influence of oratory on Roman historical writing is well documented.[8] Cicero's lengthiest discussion of humor is at *De Oratore* 2.216–2.290. Quintilian's discussion of humor is found in section 6.3 of his *Institutio Oratoria*. Their theories would have been known to Tacitus, and although he has a deserved reputation for departing from earlier styles (Martin 1981, 214–15), Cicero's and Quintilian's advice is rarely so dogmatic as to be inapplicable to Tacitean technique. In addition, both authors give practical advice on using humor in a way that does not violate elite Roman decorum, a major concern for Tacitus.

Cicero's and Quintilian's practical advice on humor, therefore, provides an ancient Roman perspective on humor and a series of characteristics that are likely to represent humor when they appear in Tacitus. For example, both Cicero and Quintilian say that *gravitas* enhances humor. Cicero claims that "there is no category of jokes that is not also a source for earnest and serious things"[9] (*nullum genus est ioci, quo non ex eodem severa et gravia sumantur*, 2.250).[10] Similarly, Quintilian says that *severitas* makes a speaker more appealing when he is making a joke (6.3.26). These observations demonstrate that seriousness and humor could reinforce each other in Roman rhetoric. Cicero and Quintilian also agree that orators should not use humor when alleging a

8. The relationship between rhetoric and historiography has recently been at the center of controversies on the use of *inventio* in history (see Damon 2007 for a summary), but the ancient connections between history and rhetoric go back at least to Thucydides' famous comment on his method for composing speeches (Thuc. 1.22.1). A. J. Woodman's *Rhetoric in Classical Historiography: Four Studies* (1988) remains an essential text on *inventio* in ancient historiography, as it illuminates both Tacitus' attention to and departure from principles of historiography as described by Cicero. A connection between Tacitus and Quintilian is also likely. Cicero was an important part of Roman education by Tacitus' time (Keeline 2018, 2–4; see also Bonner 1977, 288–308 for Cicero's influence on oratory), and Quintilian was granted a salary by Vespasian and employed as a tutor to Domitian's heirs (Jerome in Shanz and Hosius 1959, 745–47). There is also evidence for a connection between Tacitus and Quintilian; in a letter, Pliny the younger mentions that he had been Quintilian's student (6.6.3), and other letters confirm that Pliny was acquainted with Tacitus (1.6, 6.16, 6.20, 7.20, 7.33). Mendell is all but certain that Tacitus was Quintilian's student (1957, 20, 73). Although no immediate connection can be confirmed, Tacitus would likely have been familiar with the rhetorical theories put forward by one of the most famous orators of the previous generation.

9. Translations of *De Oratore* are from May and Wisse (2001) unless otherwise noted. This translation is modified from May and Wisse, who have the less general "thoughts" instead of "things."

10. Cicero's rhetorical works have also been studied for their use of humor. Of special interest is the *Pro Caelio*, in which Cicero's client appears somewhat akin to a comedic *adulescens* and Cicero's enemy, Clodius Pulcher, and his sister, Clodia, are the targets of frequent zingers. Scholarship on humor in this speech includes Geffcken (1995); Volpe (1977); and Leigh (2004). Hughes discusses Cicero's engagement with humor more generally (1997, 193–96). Fantham surveys Cicero's use of humor in his orations (2004, 199–208). In 1896, at least one scholar had already concluded that humor was, in Cicero's opinion, necessary for good oratory (Brugnola 1896, 6). Quintilian even defends Cicero from the accusation of being too prone to humor (6.3.4–5).

serious crime, nor when pity is called for (*De Orat.* 2.237, *Inst.* 6.3.31). Crucially, they make their recommendations based not on what is funniest but on what uses of humor are consistent with an orator's dignity.[11] I argue that Tacitus uses humor for the same purposes an orator would. Although humor may be diverting, it mainly serves a point.

Both Cicero and Quintilian cite examples of humor that illustrate fraught power dynamics, a parallel with the humor used by Tacitus. For example, Cicero quotes an exchange between L. Licinius Crassus and another lawyer, L. Aelius Lamia, whose body was in some way unusual (*deformis*, *De Orat.* 2.262):

> The fellow made a nuisance of himself by his interruptions, and Crassus said, "Let's hear the pretty boy." When the laughter had subsided, Lamia replied, "I could not mold my bodily appearance myself, but I could mold my own talents." So then Crassus said, "Let's hear the accomplished speaker," and the laughter was even more uproarious.

> *qui cum interpellaret odiose, "audiamus" inquit "pulchellum puerum" Crassus; cum esset adrisum, "non potui mihi" inquit Lamia "formam ipse fingere, ingenium potui": tum hic "audiamus" inquit "disertum": multo etiam adrisum est vehementius.*

Here, Crassus uses a joke to shift the debate from any substantive question into a credibility contest. Lamia's appearance was irrelevant, as Lamia pointed out, but it was apparent and therefore admitted no denial. Because Lamia was manifestly not a "pretty boy," Crassus could imply that he was not an "accomplished speaker" either. By using humor, Crassus conjured a reason for the audience to disregard Lamia, without directly impugning his argument. Laughter is one result of Crassus' joking, but it is valued mainly as a sign that Crassus had controlled the audience's reactions.[12] Among other examples, this demonstrates the calculation with which Roman orators employed humor to direct an audience's attention and sympathies.

Quintilian, who practiced oratory during the imperial period, adds examples that illustrate the careful use of humor by *equites* speaking to emperors. In

---

11. Cicero draws a contrast between an orator and a clown or actor (*sannio* or *mimus*), acknowledging that the *sannio* is extremely funny, but not in the way that an orator should be (*De Orat.* 2.251).
12. Corbeill argues that Romans in the late Republic considered bodily flaws to be reliable indices of personal flaws (1996, 15–16). Crassus' jokes, therefore, would have been considered relatively substantive in their context. Nevertheless, Crassus' jokes are diversionary in that they distract the audience from Lamia's point.

one example, "A Roman *eques* was drinking in the theatre, and Augustus sent him a messenger to say 'If I want lunch, I go home.' 'Of course,' said the *eques*, 'you are not afraid of losing your place'"[13] (*Hinc eques Romanus, ad quem in spectaculis bibentem cum misisset Augustus qui ei diceret: 'ego si prandere volo, domum eo,' 'tu enim' inquit 'non times ne locum perdas,'* 6.3.63). Although Augustus is the emperor, the *eques* delivers a humorous rebuke and wins the argument without being punished. Quintilian does not advertise the *eques*' criticism of Augustus but nevertheless reveals that humor can offer a way to talk back to power while simultaneously allowing the emperor to save face.[14] This exchange channels the tension between the reality of Augustus' political dominance (especially his attempts to legislate morality) and the official fiction that he was merely *primus inter pares*. Humor reveals the contrast between what is true and what is held to be true, but it does not disrupt the social and political forces that require falsehoods to be considered true.[15] This type of cautious humor appears frequently in Tacitus' comments on emperors, in which he uses humor to expose the persistent incongruities between official policy and actual practice.

In addition, the humor employed by Quintilian's *eques* has an unanswerable quality that an outright insult would not have shared. Calling direct attention to Augustus' flaws would have kept the conversation focused on moral censure, an arena that Augustus dominated. By diverting the conversation to the power differential between the interlocutors, the *eques* corners Augustus, leaving him with no palatable answer. Humor therefore provides an opportunity for covert but persuasive criticism, as it will in Tacitus.

Cicero and Quintilian also provide examples of practical strategies for cre-

---

13. Translations of Quintilian are from Russell's 2001 Loeb edition unless otherwise indicated.
14. Irony is often "face-saving" in that both parties may leave the exchange without social damage, and the ironic quip forestalls a reply (Barbe 1995, 10, 20–22).
15. These ancient examples of humor accord with the modern theory that political humor is unlikely to spur political change. The real-life impact and purpose of political humor is controversial. In a much-cited article, Antonin Obrdlik described the "gallows humor" of Nazi-occupied Czechoslovakia as "an index of strength or morale on the part of oppressed peoples" and as a challenge to oppressors (1942, 709). Cynthia Willett opines that modern American political humor can be both coercive and liberating (2008, 3–4). Tsakona and Popa note that political messages communicated with humor may be taken less seriously by an audience or understood as a sign of the speaker's inability to be serious about serious topics (2011, 11). Popa's, Watters', and Mascha's essays in the same volume explore modern Romanian and Italian examples of the impact of humor on politics. In their view, humor cannot introduce new ideas but rather "recycles and reinforces dominant values and views on politics" (2011, 2). Elliott Oring argues that political humor is often treated as distinct from other types of humor, but that it rarely advocates for change or affords protection from retribution (2016, 109–28).

ating appropriate humor in formal Latin prose. Cicero cites irony (*dissimulatio*, 2.269)[16] as one of the many factors that can contribute to humor and adds that "insinuation" (*significatio*, 2.268)[17] and "calling something disgraceful by an honorable name" (*cum honesto verbo vitiosa res appellatur*, 2.272) are related methods for creating humor. Another relative is what Cicero calls *subabsurda dicendo*, the technique of pretending to believe something while communicating that in fact you do not believe it (2.289).[18] All the above techniques are related to irony. In addition, Cicero and Quintilian identify ambiguity as a possible source of humor (*De Orat.* 2.250, *Inst.* 6.3.47–49; 6.3.62). Cicero also includes false praise and euphemisms.[19] Irony, ambiguity, deception, false praise, and euphemisms are all present in Tacitus, where they may contribute to humor, just as Cicero and Quintilian recommend.

Cicero and Quintilian also provide caveats about the use of humor, detailing which types of humor are inappropriate and circumstances that are not suitable for humor. Cicero cautions against indecency, including *obscenitas* (2.252), while Quintilian makes disapproving references to the humor of *scurrae* and mimes (6.3.8).[20] Quintilian generally recommends against punning on people's names (6.3.53–54), although Cicero recommends it (2.220, 2.257), so taste differs.[21] Cicero and Quintilan also remind orators to limit their use of

16. *Dissimulatio* ordinarily means "deception" but refers to irony in this context (Leeman et al. 1989, 2.269; May and Wisse 2001n262). Deception, however, does also play a role in humor in Tacitus.
17. May and Wisse say *significatio* means implying more than was actually said (2001, *ad loc*), as do Leeman et al. (1989, *ad loc*). They compare its use here to clearer explanations of the same term that appear at *De Orat.* 2.270, 3.220; *Rhetorica ad Herennium* 4.67; and Quintilian *Inst.* 9.2.3.
18. Cicero's definition of *subabsurda* fits neatly with Braester's modern definition of irony, which claims that all ironic discourse has a literal meaning, a concealed (ironic) meaning, and a third meaning in which the first two are combined (1992, 75). It also bears a resemblance to Haiman on sarcasm: "quotation—of prior words [. . .] in itself functions as a telltale index of the speaker's disrespect for both the repeated message and the person who first uttered it" (1990, 191). Barbe says irony depends on an audience's perception of a speaker and often on shared knowledge and context (1995, 11–13).
19. Crassus calling Lamia a "pretty boy" (2.262) is an example of false praise. Scipio's comment on a "diligent" (in fact, lazy or cowardly) centurion (2.272) is an example of a euphemism.
20. *Scurrae* may refer to amateur jokesters or to professional or semiprofessional comedians who may have resembled the parasites of Roman comedy. In his study of *urbanitas*, Ramage argues that although early references to *scurrilitas* associate it with urbanity, it develops a sense of inappropriateness as early as Plautus (Ramage 1973, 30–31). Ramage also contends that as time went on, *scurrilitas* became codified as unsuitable behavior. By the imperial period, *scurrae* are mentioned less often in surviving texts, although they are occasionally included in the entourages of emperors and aristocrats (Ash 2007, 2.87.2). Cicero also mentions the humor of *scurrae* as inappropriate for an orator because such humor is imprecise and could rebound on its user as easily as on its targets (*De Orat.* 2.244–245).
21. Tacitus' *Dialogus* includes a pun on Aper's name (at 11.1, discussed by Mayer 2001, *ad loc*). Wood-

humor (*De Orat.* 2.221, *Inst.* 6.3.26–28). These rules of decorum apply in Tacitus' historical works, where humor is restrained and careful.

Taken together, the evidence of Cicero and Quintilian presents a coherent judgment on humor in rhetoric. They differ on individual points, and Quintilian is more cautious about the danger of addressing a powerful audience. Generally, however, Quintilian's opinions on humor are consistent with Cicero's, whom he credits with special excellence in humor (6.3.3). Their agreement strongly suggests an enduring model of humor in Roman rhetoric, one that Tacitus would have employed in his writing.[22] Even the differences between Cicero and Quintilian, namely the latter's greater attention to the tastes of the powerful, evince continuity more than difference; technique may be modified, but principles remain the same. This model of humor provides a baseline for the use of humor in Roman rhetorical genres, which had considerable differences from humor elsewhere.

Other Roman historians, also influenced by rhetoric, may follow these principles, too. Plass (1988) discusses humor in Suetonius, Cassius Dio, and Seneca in addition to Tacitus. Ridley, making the case that Livy's humorlessness has been greatly exaggerated, finds wryly humorous episodes in Livy and suggests that at least two of Sallust's pointed insults are humorous (2017, 99–109, 92). *Variatio* is typical of Sallust as well as Tacitus, and Scafuro has connected Livy's account of the Bacchanalia scandal in Book 39 to the tropes of New Comedy (1989, 119). Rhetorical techniques for creating humor would have been available to all the Roman historians and may have influenced historiography where appropriate. Tacitus, however, offers a particular opportunity because of his documented engagement with irony, concealment, strong contrast, and even drama.

Although Roman rhetoricians are adamant that the orator should not imitate the humor of comic performers, Tacitus was greatly influenced by ancient tragedy, as Francesca Santoro L'Hoir has shown in *Tragedy, Rhetoric, and the*

man and Martin note a play on Labeo Antistius' name at *An.* 3.75.1 (1996, *ad loc*), which they understand as part of a tradition of etymologizing puns. Whitmarsh understands *tacere* at *Agricola* 2.4 as a pun on Tacitus' own name (2006, 310–11). Ash notes a pun on Valens' name in *Histories* 2.93.2, when the Vitellians grow stronger (*convaluerunt*) at his arrival (2017, 200). Joseph sees "etymological wordplay" when Tacitus says Agrippina's name was "increased" (*augetur*) to Augusta at *An.* 12.26.1 (2023, 321). Tacitus probably agreed with Cicero about punning on names.

22. The *Rhetorica ad Herennium*, a rhetorical manual that dates to the early first century BCE, provides a much more succinct comment on humor that nevertheless corresponds to later advice. The anonymous author recommends provoking laughter to reengage a disengaged audience (1.10), another benefit mentioned by Quintilian (*Inst.* 6.3.1).

Historiography of Tacitus' "Annales" (2006).[23] According to Santoro L'Hoir, Tacitus and other orators of his era studied and imitated many literary genres, especially theatrical ones (2006, 7). In the *Annals*, Tacitus used a consistent pattern of tragic vocabulary and motifs to convey the iniquity of the Julio-Claudians (Santoro L'Hoir 2006, 16–17). Santoro L'Hoir finds numerous parallels to Aeschylean tragedy, beginning in the very first chapters of the *Annals*. By the Neronian books, however, tragic performance has been "concretized" and Nero's self-presentation as an actor is relatively easy to understand, compared to the dangerously veiled wishes of Tiberius (2006, 43–44).

Santoro L'Hoir's work builds on that of Shadi Bartsch, who argued in *Actors in the Audience* that Nero's public performances confused the boundary between performer and spectator and that phenomenon bled into contemporary politics (1994, 2–3). Nero's forays into tragic performance were infamous, and Suetonius and Cassius Dio also exploited the slippage between Nero's stage performances and his imperial persona (1994, 40–46). Nero aspired to be a serious artist, and many of the roles he took were overtly tragic, but ancient historians emphasized the bizarre ironies of his stage career. For example, Suetonius dwells on Nero's performance as the matricidal Orestes as a case of life imitating art, although Nero had already killed Agrippina before he portrayed Orestes (Bartsch 1994, 42–43).

The connection between Tacitus and tragedy is therefore well established. Comedy is a less obvious influence. With some exceptions,[24] the instances of humor I discuss do not, in my opinion, draw on comedy.[25] Nevertheless, Tacitean humor often arises from performance and its contrast with reality, or from discrepancies between what is believed and what is true. Bartsch's work underlies my analysis of Nero because she describes the essentially absurd dynamic typical of Nero's court. Theatricality can be disastrous, tyrannical, and laugh-

---

23. Other major analyses of Tacitus and tragedy include Marchetta (2004) and Galtier (2011). Nero is Tacitus' most obviously theatrical subject, and shorter studies have dealt with his relationship to tragedy and theater generally (Leigh 2017 surveys Nero's reputation for performance; Schmitzer 2005 discusses the death of Britannicus). Tacitus' use of tragedy is especially prominent in his treatment of Nero, but subtler uses of tragedy appear even in his treatment of Vespasian (Haynes 2022). Feldherr—although his focus is on Livy—describes the slippage between ancient history and theater (1998, 168) and analyzes Livy's use of tragic conventions in his treatment of Tarquinius Superbus (187–93).

24. Dickison (1977) finds evidence of comic archetypes in Tacitus' portrayal of Claudius, discussed further in chapter 3 of this book.

25. I also spend little time on satire, although it was an active humorous genre in Tacitus' time. Other scholarship has productively compared Tacitus to the satirists, including Plass (1995) and Nappa (2010), who compare Tacitus to Martial and Juvenal, respectively.

able all at once. Santoro L'Hoir points out tragic vocabulary and motifs in several of the episodes that I call humorous (most notably the deaths of Agrippina and Britannicus), and although her tragic interpretation is persuasive, several of the characteristics she examines may point to humor as well. She identifies "equivocation and irony," an "atmosphere of secrecy and innuendo," and "contrasting abstract terms" as typical of Tacitus' engagement with tragedy (2006, 39–40). Irony, innuendo, and contrast have powerful humorous applications, and where Santoro L'Hoir's analysis brings out the tragic structures in Tacitus, I emphasize connections to humor. Theatricality, deception, and hypocrisy can create both humor and tragedy, occasionally even in the same passage.

The connection between humor and tragedy can become uncomfortable in Tacitus' historical works. Some passages that I have identified as humorous are also disturbing, and many are theatrical. Nero's murder of his mother Agrippina, for example, has attracted scholarly attention for its use of tragedy,[26] yet Tacitus also dwells on the preposterous details of Nero's plan and his agents' incompetence. Tacitus presents Nero's matricide as a tragic horror and his incompetence as a comic one. Tacitean humor is not "comic relief" as it does not comfort the reader. Rather, it demonstrates the fissures that power creates between truth and perception.

The association between humor and strong contrasts is particularly significant. This association is supported by modern humor theory, especially Victor Raskin and Salvatore Attardo's script theory of humor, which I have consulted for help in identifying ancient humor. Script theory was advanced first in Raskin's 1985 book *Semantic Mechanisms of Humor* and has been periodically developed ever since, most notably by Salvatore Attardo. Raskin and Attardo together updated the theory and christened it the General Theory of Verbal Humor in a 1991 article.[27] The essential premise of their theory is that humor is created by the intersection of two opposed "scripts." Because each script consists of a set of associations based on cultural conditioning and individual knowledge, this insight is applicable to a wide range of cultures. In my analysis of Tacitus, I have treated script theory's central hypothesis as a foundation for identifying humor; when two opposed scripts overlap, their intersection creates humor.[28] When scripts overlap without being opposed, they can create one of

26. Santoro L'Hoir (2006, 89–92); Marchetta (2004, 97–586).

27. Attardo has further explored these theories in *Linguistic Theories of Humor* (1994) and *Humorous Texts: A Semantic and Pragmatic Analysis* (2001).

28. Attardo has also posited the existence of a "logical mechanism," a rhetorical figure or twist in

several nonhumorous literary figures. When they are opposed but do not overlap, they create conflict. In "plain narrative," scripts neither overlap nor oppose each other (Attardo 1994, 204).

The simplicity of script theory's central hypothesis belies the many years of productive scholarly debate it has produced. Raskin and Attardo's theory has been adapted, critiqued, tested, and expanded almost continuously since its publication. One important interlocutor is Elliott Oring, who was one of the original readers of the 1991 article that introduced the General Theory of Verbal Humor (Attardo and Raskin 1991, 333). Oring has continued to criticize the theory, often for vagueness and an inability to deliver on its linguistic claims.[29] Oring's own model of humor centers on "appropriate incongruity," which means that jokes must include incongruity that simultaneously seems suitable.[30] Appropriate incongruity aims to contextualize jokes as much as it attempts to explain their mechanical operation (2019, 166). Although I am not certain that Oring's "appropriateness" is any better defined than script theory's "opposition,"[31] it is a useful tool for tying the abstractions of script theory back into a particular culture. Neither theory is designed to be employed in the context of ancient philology, but each provides necessary structure for understanding humor. I rely more heavily on Attardo and Raskin's theories because they provide specific tools for analyzing humor, but Oring's work has influenced my assessment of the links between humor and meaning.

Script theory is well suited to Roman historiography, a genre in which character traits and patterns of events repeat frequently and can even become for-

---

reasoning that helps bring opposed scripts together (1994, 225–26). Although this element of the theory has been hotly debated, I find it useful to identify not only the scripts involved in humor, but the reasoning implied within jokes. Script theory also resembles Arthur Koestler's "bisociation" theory of humor, which he described in *Insight and Outlook* (1949) and *The Act of Creation* (1964, 27–50). Koestler's theory refers to "logical chains" (1949, 25–26) that have much in common with scripts and must intersect to create humor.

29. His 2011 articles "Parsing the Joke: The General Theory of Verbal Humor and Appropriate Incongruity" and "Still Further Thoughts on Logical Mechanisms: A Response to Christian F. Hempelmann and Salvatore Attardo" directly address flaws in script theory as does "Oppositions, Overlaps, and Ontologies: The General Theory of Verbal Humor Revisited" (2019).

30. Appropriate incongruity is explained in detail in *Jokes and Their Relations* (1992, 1–15) and appears frequently in Oring's other work on humor.

31. Raskin originally described opposition by using examples of broad categories (true/false, good/bad, death/life) but also acknowledged that much humor relies on narrower categories like "obscene/non-obscene" or even "money/no money" (1985, 113–14). Such oppositions do appear in jokes, but the "thing/not thing" model of script opposition leaves much unilluminated. I have used some of Raskin's original opposed pairs (real/unreal especially) and also striven to identify the oppositions particular to Tacitus—imperial/enslaved, for example.

mulaic.[32] Roman readers would have recognized a tyrant by his cruelty and emotionality, for example, and would likely have extrapolated further tyrannical traits. The "tyrant" script might overlap with any number of noncontradictory scripts, and contradictory scripts can be accommodated within the same narrative episode without necessarily overlapping. When scripts both overlap and contradict each other, however, humor is created. Tacitus' portrayal of the emperor Otho provides an example of this contrast. As I argue in chapter 1, Otho behaves like a usurper, but fails to wield any practical power. The conflict between his dual, incompatible roles as emperor and private citizen creates a humorous tone in Tacitus' account of his short principate. Similar discrepancies between appearance and reality animate much of Tacitus' work (Martin 1981, 10, 215, 235), and when Tacitus focuses on these contrasts, he takes advantage of humor to illuminate their importance.

Contrast alone, however, cannot entirely explain Tacitus' use of humor. Although contrast is central to the script theory of humor and to my identification of humor in Tacitus, the binding power of humor is equally significant, especially when apparently contradictory ideas are shown to reinforce each other. Tacitus frequently maintains ambiguity even when he presents incompatible alternatives; truths cannot be comprehended without lies, and vice versa. O'Gorman has proposed that Tacitus' program of irony confounds simplistic "decoding" and requires readers to grapple with more complex questions of meaning (2000, 10–11). Under ironic conditions, truth may not even supersede falsehood (2000, 3–4). Humor, although not identical to irony, performs a similar function.[33] We cannot "get" the joke without recognizing a central contrast, but nor can we get it without understanding the overlap between contrasting elements. Humor weds discrepancy to congruity and therefore not only preserves ambiguity but also crystalizes associations between apparently divergent ideas and does so in a pithy and memorable way (Plass 1988, 64). Humor and irony share these functions, but where irony is widespread and unobtrusive, humor is pointed and emphatic.[34]

---

32. One drawback of these modern theories is that they are calibrated for the analysis of short jokes, a format not often found in Tacitus. I have therefore drawn on work by Wladyslaw Chlopicki (1997 and 2000), who proposes methods for applying these theories to short stories. (Attardo has also adapted script theory to analyze an Oscar Wilde short story [2001, 163–201], but that approach focused on locating and analyzing short jokes, which does not work as well for Tacitus.) Often, I have also applied ideas meant for short jokes to longer passages and found that the effect is still productive.

33. For the connection between humor and irony, see also Plass (1988, 4).

34. Although I have adopted this distinction to explain my focus on humor (and my belief that the

Tacitus' use of humor is, I argue, best detected with the script theory of humor, which provides a framework for recognizing humorous discourse, and best understood through Roman rhetorical theory. Tacitus uses humor not for its own sake, but to illustrate the inconsistencies and absurdities of the historical material that he treats.[35] His use of humorous techniques takes its cue from Roman rhetorical theory in that the jokes are calculated to persuade the audience without offending them and can be recognized by comparison to the techniques that Cicero and Quintilian suggest were meant to create humor. Tacitus' use of humor can be observed in many of the unusual elements of his style and contributes to the complex network of implication that underlies his historical writing.

His use of humor does not transform his works into comedies, however. Their serious content and arguments are ample evidence of their gravity. Instead, Tacitus uses humor sarcastically, to sharpen criticisms of his villains and to highlight the differences between actual behavior and correct behavior. As Cicero declared, every category of joke can give rise also to serious matters (*De Orat.* 2.250). By recognizing Tacitus' purposeful and subtle use of humor, we can understand how it contributes to his complex, manipulative literary technique, especially how he advances his apparently unfounded implications. Tacitus' use of humor also emphasizes themes within episodes or narrative arcs. By examining some of the most prominent examples of these phenomena, I hope to show that humor is an important part of Tacitus' rhetorical strategy, and that consciously studying it advances our understanding of Tacitus' style and meaning, while also showing that humor, often considered a plaything, is a tool of rhetoric.[36]

My argument addresses the *Histories* and *Annals* in the order in which Tacitus wrote them. Chapter 1 comprises my analysis of Tacitus' use of humor in his characterization of the emperor Otho. I argue that Tacitus establishes a com-

---

phenomenon I have identified is indeed humor), humor and irony are often so closely intertwined that a strong division between them is purposeless. One modern study of irony lists its potential functions as "humor, status elevation, aggression, and emotional control" (Dews et al. 1995, 348–50), which are functions of humor as well, so even irony that does not qualify as humor may function similarly.

35. Plass 1988, 6, 20. Put another way: "in this setting [the early Principate] incongruity helps shape our perception of historical reality itself" (1988, 26). Martin, too, connects Tacitus' unique style to his "acute sensitivity for the disparity between men's professions and their actions, and still more between their professed and their real motives" and cites his use of appendix sentences as a symptom of his portrayal of political psychology (1981, 215).

36. Working on Claudius' reign, Dickison concluded that Tacitus attempted to provoke "not laughter which is relatively purposeless but one which is directed at an end, namely criticism" (1977, 646–47).

plex tension between Otho's precarious role as emperor and his persistent inability to maintain authority over his followers. I track Tacitus' use of this motif from Otho's accession to his downfall and demonstrate why humor was an effective rhetorical tool for this purpose. Otho's characterization relies heavily on this set of contradictions in his behavior, which both describes Tacitus' most biting criticisms of the emperor and conforms to Raskin and Attardo's definition of humor.

Chapter 2 examines the case of Libo Drusus, who was, according to Tacitus, the first victim of Tiberius' *maiestas* trials. I argue that humor is essential to Tacitus' characterization of Libo. Modern historians speculate that Libo was probably guilty of treason (or at least subversion), but Tacitus minimizes Libo's potential threat by portraying him as humorously incompetent and his trial as a farce with a tragic ending. Tacitus does not glorify Libo, who remains a secondary target of his contempt, but he suggests that the Senate's reaction to him was disproportionate. In doing so, Tacitus establishes a negative impression of the *maiestas* trials by playing up their contradictions while also deflecting attention from Libo's possible guilt.

In chapter 3, I examine an episode that has already been noted for its use of the tropes of ancient comedy; the empress Messalina's marriage to Silius (concurrent with her marriage to Claudius) is presented as ludicrous, in part to show contempt for the power wielded by women and freedmen in Claudius' principate. The episode also presents a case study in how Tacitus alternates between humor and outrage at the goings-on of the imperial court.

In chapter 4, I argue that Tacitus presents Nero's rise to power as synonymous with the rise of absurdity in Rome's governing elite. Nero does increasingly scandalous things and gives flagrantly transparent excuses for them. Instead of undermining Nero's authority, his ridiculous behavior confirms his waxing power when others are forced to take his risible excuses seriously. Nero's behavior becomes increasingly ridiculous and increasingly criminal until both his power and his laughability culminate in the murder of Agrippina.

My discussion of Nero continues in chapter 5, in which I examine his decline in power through the lens of the same humor and absurdity that originally fueled his rise. Although absurdity propelled Nero to power, it proves inviable in the long term. Nero continues to behave in absurd ways, but others in his orbit realize that they, too, can manipulate the absurdities Nero has unleashed, and he loses control of his own fictions. Consequently, others are able to usurp the bizarre logic of his principate and use it in their favor.

ONE

Flattery Will Get You Everywhere

Otho and Humor in *Histories* 1

In this chapter, I discuss Tacitus' portrayal of Otho in the first book of the *Histories*. I argue that Tacitus uses humor in his representation of Otho in Book 1, and that humor plays an essential part in constructing an image of the principate as shaped by deviousness and contradiction. Humor helps to illustrate the delicate balance between the authority of an emperor and the demands of his partisans.

Tacitus develops the humorous element of Otho's character gradually. At Otho's introduction, Tacitus presents embryonic elements of humor that he expands upon after Otho decides to make himself emperor. I identify a pervasive opposition between private and public action, and between power and powerlessness, as the humorous contrast that animates Tacitus' treatment of Otho. I argue that Tacitus' use of humor becomes more pronounced as Otho encourages his followers during his revolt and when the Senate and people flock to congratulate him on becoming emperor. Otho's lack of control over his ostensible subjects becomes increasingly obvious as he gains greater official power. The humorous tone reaches its peak when Otho makes a speech to appease his troops, who have rushed the palace in a brief, confused mutiny. This is when Otho is most clearly beholden to his troops, yet he insists that they respect the façade of his authority.

Tacitus repeatedly points out that Otho struggles to behave like an emperor. At first, Otho presents himself as an emperor despite not being one, and later he cannot exercise imperial power despite his official position as emperor. Other emperors in Tacitus are caught between public and personal concerns, but Otho is an especially humorous example because he attempts to fulfill both official and private roles in the same way at the same time. Technically, Otho wields imperial power, but he obeys the advice of councilors in his own household on major political decisions and never manages to control the army that he supposedly commands. This characterization of Otho dramatizes a series of contradictions[1] that Tacitus associates with the principate. Humor is crucial to Tacitus' portrayal of Otho because it permits contradictory ideas to overlay each other without canceling each other out. Instead of presenting a single interpretation, humor combines two ideas without eliminating either.[2] This model of humor aligns with Raskin's script theory, which hypothesizes that humor consists of opposed, overlapping "scripts," or groups of preset linguistic expectations (Raskin 1985, 99). In Tacitus, opposed scripts litter the narrative and occasionally overlap to create humor that highlights the importance of these contrasts to the narrative.[3] Tacitus uses humorous contrasts to illustrate the idiosyncratic reasoning that the emperors create and that later afflicts them. I identify "official" and "private" as the main contrast in Tacitus' initial treatment of Otho, and "powerful" and "powerless" as central after Otho has become emperor. Using these contradictory ideas, Tacitus creates tension in Otho's character and with the powerful/powerless contrast he implies that self-contradiction is an endemic problem of the principate.

Tacitus' Introduction of Otho

When Tacitus first introduces Otho as Titus Vinius' friend and prospective son-in-law (1.13.2),[4] he emphasizes his similarity to Nero: "Otho had led an irre-

1. Ash argues that Otho's contradictions are common to other sources' portrayals of him and that Tacitus worked to synthesize contemporary, partisan reports of Otho's conduct into a coherent whole (1999, 83–86). Although I argue that Tacitus purposefully emphasizes the contradictions in his portrayal of Otho, contradiction does seem to have been an important part of his portrayal by other historians, too. Tacitus does not necessarily increase the total number of contradictions in his treatment of Otho, but he focuses on a few significant contradictions that also promote humor.
2. In this way, Tacitus' humor functions like his use of irony, by presenting contradictory meanings but refusing to anoint one as truth (O'Gorman 2000, 10–11).
3. Script theory does not require that the opposed scripts remain in tension after the joke is over, but because most jokes have "background incongruities" which would be impossible to resolve, Attardo, Hempelmann, and Di Maio acknowledge that nearly all jokes remain unresolved (2002, 27–28). The consistent presence of opposed ideas in Tacitus also resonates with Koestler's "logical chains," which operate throughout a text but only occasionally join to create humor (1949, 25–26). Because Tacitus' works are more complex than the jokes used to build script theory, I consider all Tacitean humor at best partially resolved. As O'Gorman argues, Tacitean irony cannot and should not be decoded as certainly meaning one thing or another, because it is meant to force readers to draw their own conclusions (2000, 11–12).
4. This is an inauspicious start. The reference to a son-in-law and father-in-law evokes Caesar's civil war with Pompey (Damon 2003, *ad loc*).

sponsible boyhood and a dissolute youth, and endeared himself to Nero by competing with him in luxury"[5] (*Otho pueritiam incuriose, adulescentiam petulanter egerat, gratus Neroni aemulatione luxus*, 1.13.3). This description contains no undeniable signs of humor,[6] but suggests that Otho could have become a second Nero.[7] A second Nero would have been a disaster and especially incongruent as a successor to Galba, who cultivated a reputation for old-fashioned sternness. During Nero's reign, Otho attained favor because he was serious about frivolity, and this same quality ruins his reputation with Galba.[8] The humor here turns on the contrast between the qualities considered virtues by Nero and Galba. In addition, Otho appears unreliable but ambitious, as evidenced by the increasing levels of effort (*incuriose*, *petulanter*, *aemulatione*) that he devotes to inane activities.

Tacitus also summarizes Otho's relationship with his wife Poppaea Sabina, whom Tacitus calls "the imperial whore" (*principale scortum*, 1.13.3). "Imperial whore" strikes a contrast between high and low diction (Damon 2003, *ad loc*), a frequent feature of humorous texts,[9] and is another example of conjoined opposites associated with Nero. "Empress" and "whore" ought to be mutually exclusive occupations, but because Nero made Poppaea empress, she was an empress even if she did not behave like one.[10] By connecting Otho and Nero at Otho's first appearance, Tacitus establishes Otho's connections to the Julio-Claudian principate (particularly Nero) and foregrounds the nexus of contradictions that emperors create when they attempt to serve their own desires and cultivate a favorable public image at the same time.

Tacitus further emphasizes the contradictions fostered by Nero in narrating how Nero sent Otho to govern Lusitania because he suspected that Otho had

---

5. Unless otherwise indicated, translations of the *Histories* are quoted from Levene's revision of Fyfe (1997). Sometimes, as here, I have modified vocabulary.
6. Tacitus omits details that could contribute to humor, like the extravagances reported by Plutarch and Pliny the Elder (Damon 2003, 13.3) which could have been laughable for being far outside normal limits. Cicero mentions that inflating a description beyond belief can be a source of humor (*De Orat.* 2.267). Otho's luxury may not have been truly impossible to maintain, but could have been surprising enough to be humorous, yet Tacitus chose to ignore that material.
7. Nero looms over Tacitus' narrative of the year 69 and serves as a comparandum for all the aspiring emperors (Haynes 2003, 40), but Otho is the only one of them who was Nero's personal associate.
8. *Aemulatione luxus* describes the relationship between Otho and Nero (1.13.3). *Aemulatio* can be a good quality in the proper context—Cicero calls it ambiguous, with positive and negative senses (*Tusc.* 4.17–4.18)—but *luxus* is not a quality worth competing over. Part of the danger of Nero's rule was that he misapplied imperial power to frivolous arenas.
9. Attardo finds switching between high- and low-register words particularly prevalent in "literary humor" (1994, 230–31).
10. Tacitus returns to the empress-whore dichotomy in the character of Messalina, in whose characterization he also uses humor (discussed in chapter 3).

been having sex with Poppaea, to whom he was married at the time (1.13.3). In typical circumstances, a sexual relationship between husband and wife would be normal, but not under Nero's rule (Plass 1988, 61–62).[11] Furthermore, Otho is sent to Lusitania not to be governor but "under cover of a governorship" (*specie legationis*, 1.13.3). This last detail reiterates that Nero appointed Otho out of an ulterior motive (Damon 2003, *ad loc*). Tacitus made Nero's true purpose clear in the first part of the sentence, before the appearance of *specie*. *Specie legationis* reminds Tacitus' readers that Nero lied publicly to conceal his unscrupulous private decisions. Because Tacitus has already shown that Nero intended to separate Otho and Poppaea, *specie* highlights another discrepancy, that Nero treated his excuses as credible even when his real reasons were obvious.[12] Tacitus presents Nero's lie as an example of the way an emperor can warp reality; the emperor dictates what people are supposed to do and believe, and everybody obeys the emperor without actually believing the things that they are required to profess. The contradictions of Nero's principate prepare the ground for humor by establishing a situation in which conflicting ideas not only can but must go together.[13] As a second Nero, Otho will require his supporters to accept contradictions.

Section 1.13 lays a foundation for Tacitus' humorous characterization of Otho. Tacitus' description of Nero's contradictory commands fosters cynical amusement at the flaws of his rule, and by extension the flaws of his crony, Otho. The fact that the emperor picks his friends for their skill in luxury, that a married couple is banned from sex, that a husband tolerates his wife's affair, and that a "whore" is empress together create a strong contrast between Roman ideals and Neronian reality. Such a contrast conforms to ancient ideas about the

11. Tacitus' version of the Nero-Poppaea-Otho love triangle in the *Histories* is abbreviated compared to versions found in other sources (Damon 2003, *ad loc*), and the time frame is distorted as well. Tacitus inserts a subordinate clause about Nero getting rid of Octavia between a clause where Nero marries Poppaea to Otho and one where Nero sends Otho to govern Lusitania. This sequence clashes with Tacitus' chronology in the *Annals*, where Nero sends Otho to Lusitania at 13.46.3 and does not banish Octavia until 14.60.1. The version in the *Histories* implies a different (and incorrect) order of events that temporarily obfuscates the fact that Otho was married to Poppaea when Nero objected to their relationship. By obscuring that fact, the *Histories* narrative bends the truth to make Nero's claim seem more reasonable. In addition, the *Histories* version emphasizes the similarity between Otho and Nero because they work together to obtain Poppaea, while the version in the *Annals* concentrates on Poppaea herself (Ash 1999, 91).

12. Transparent deception can contribute to humor. Cicero and Quintilian both identify *dissimulatio* as a potential source of humor (*De Orat.* 2.269; *Inst.* 9.2.14). Quintilian also includes obvious lies as one method for creating humor (6.3.70). Raskin classifies humor as a form of "non-*bona-fide*" communication, a category that also embraces outright falsehoods (Raskin 1985, 100–101).

13. Contradiction is a central feature of Nero's principate, as I discuss in chapters 4 and 5.

humorous use of irony and lying. Tacitus associates Otho with a set of motifs that will contribute to more humor later.

Much of Otho's first appearance is tied to a description of the upside-down world of Nero's principate, with an emphasis on the twisted logic it encouraged. Tacitus presents Nero's court as dangerous in part because Nero demands that his courtiers believe things that are absurd. This portrayal of Nero promotes a humorous tone without compromising the sense that Nero was dangerous. Tacitus presents his readers with bizarre examples of Nero's commands to demonstrate the paradoxes of imperial power, and these commands lead to an illogical but carefully patterned system of contradictions. Several sentences end in ironic surprises (*aemulatione luxus*, *specie legationis*), and *principale scortum* has its contradiction built in. Tacitus uses irony to illustrate what power looked like under Nero and what it might also become under Otho. The contrasts in this paragraph suggest that Otho's rule will promote contradictions, like Nero's did.

Tacitus repeats Otho's connection to Nero once more before this section is over. Continuing with Otho's history, he says that Otho governed Lusitania without any major disasters[14] and allied with Galba decisively (1.13.4). Once removed from Nero's court, Otho displayed political aptitude and ambition.[15] But even while recounting Otho's alliance with Galba against Nero, Tacitus reiterates Otho's similarity to Nero. According to Tacitus, Otho attracted Nero's former courtiers by his resemblance to Nero: "the court supported him as a second Nero" (*prona in eum aula Neronis ut similem*, 1.13.4). The placement of *similem* at the end of the sentence strengthens the connection between them (Perkins 1993, 850). In this way, Tacitus reminds his readers that Otho appeared similar enough to Nero that he attracted support from Nero's allies. Tacitus also suggests that Otho's similarity to Nero was a political advantage instead of a demerit; a substantial faction still favored Neronian customs. Throughout Book 1, Tacitus' characterization of Otho draws on parallels to Nero and to the court over which he presided.

---

14. Tacitus says Otho governed "in a friendly manner" (*comiter*, 1.13.4). *Comiter* could be a positive characterization or could indicate that Otho was over-friendly (Damon 2003, *ad loc*; compare also Santoro L'Hoir (2006, 135–36) on Tacitus' attribution of *comitas* to Germanicus). I follow Syme in accepting an overtly positive significance to *comiter* here because a negative reading would be at odds with Tacitus' later comments on Otho at *Annals* 13.46.3 (1958, 545). The negative reading would also contradict a parallel passage in Suetonius (*Otho* 3).
15. Volunteering to lead a revolt against an emperor might demonstrate imprudence, but because the emperor in question was Nero, Tacitus does not criticize Otho for his eagerness to rebel.

Otho's Revolt

Tacitus begins to use humor to highlight the contradictions in Otho's character during Otho's revolt against Galba. As the revolt begins, Otho has fallen out of favor with Galba and is frantically planning his next move (1.21). Having established Otho's similarity to Nero, Tacitus now illustrates Otho's character in terms of its contradictory "official" and "private" elements. The passage gradually accumulates factors that lead to humor by setting up the official/private contrast that defines Otho's character. Otho reflects[16] that "his extravagance was burdensome for an emperor, and his poverty was all but unendurable for a private person" (*luxuria etiam principi onerosa, inopia uix priuato toleranda*, 1.21.1).[17] Otho seems to be considering becoming emperor to solve his financial problems, but personal luxury is hardly more appropriate when it eats up public funds than when it consumes personal wealth. Otho is unsuited to lead either a private or an official life. The former is financially impossible, and the latter would be inappropriate. The official/private contrast continues to be relevant, and often humorous, up to the end of Book 1. One key element of humor here is that Otho can find no sensible solution to his problem. Becoming emperor would not dispel Otho's insolvency, as his expenditure was still "burdensome for an emperor." On the other hand, "poverty [. . .] unendurable for a private person" is a weak basis on which to become emperor, as it is a reason to desire power, not a means to acquire it. Otho's impossible situation foreshadows the opposition between power and powerlessness that will dominate his principate, because although he becomes emperor, he never fills that role securely. The inconsistency in Otho's position gives rise to humor because it requires two conflicting ideas to operate at once; Otho must become emperor because he cannot remain a private citizen, but he should not become emperor because he is unsuitable as a leader.

Although Tacitus initially expresses the private/official contrast without much humor, he expands on the contrast to portray Otho as humorously

16. Although much of the passage is focalized through him, Otho is not the grammatical subject. Instead, Tacitus credits several abstract concepts with goading him (*nulla spes, omne in turbido consilium, multa simul exstimulabant*, 1.21.1). Tacitus' syntax implies that Otho did not control his own thought process.

17. I have altered the translation of *onerosa* from "would have ruined an emperor" to "was burdensome," which more closely imitates the Latin sentence structure. Heubner understands the contrast between *principi* and *priuato* as an indication that the two states are coexistent (1963, 1.21.1). I agree but stress that although they coexist in Otho, *princeps* and *priuatus* are not compatible roles.

trapped between being an emperor and being a private citizen. First, Tacitus makes Otho seem ridiculous by showing that he deferred to the opinions of his household while attempting to become emperor. As he dithers, Otho comes up with a few good reasons to take the principate; he could already be in danger of Galba's anger, and if he will die for treason anyway, he may as well die trying to become emperor (1.21.2). After Otho decides to risk it, his freedmen usurp the spotlight. Otho's authority over his own decisions is diminished when Tacitus describes the role his household played in his revolt. Although Otho came up with reasons to attempt a coup, his household seals the decision. Tacitus implies that Otho had not actually made up his mind by the end of section 21, because his slaves and freedmen persuade him as if he is undecided.[18] By elaborating on the extent to which Otho was influenced by his household, Tacitus suggests that Otho relied on the decision of his subordinates in the moment when he considered taking imperial authority. Such a blatant incongruity lends itself to humor, which Tacitus exploits in the following passage.

Paragraphs 21 and 22 are a Tacitean weighted alternative writ large. On the one hand, Otho believed that he decided on rebellion himself; on the other hand, he was persuaded by members of his household. Many of Tacitus' alternatives are weighted in favor of the second option,[19] including here, where Tacitus insinuates that Otho was a follower in his own rebellion. Tacitus is the only ancient source to suggest that Otho might have been responsible for his own decision. Other sources do not enlarge upon Otho's reasoning (Keitel 1991, 2783).[20] By raising the possibility that Otho could have made up his own mind, Tacitus emphasizes Otho's eventual cession of responsibility. Section 22 portrays the future emperor as indecisive and his plans as haphazard. It also contains significant ingredients of humor, establishing humorous motifs that will reappear in later episodes. Two key phrases, Tacitus' ironic appraisal of Otho's

18. Tacitus implicitly criticizes Otho for needing to be persuaded by his freedmen's petty arguments after he had already framed the decision as a choice between life and death. The slaves' and freedmen's appeals to Otho cast doubt on his professed intention to seek glory (1.21.2). If he believed his choice was between death and empire, he would not require further persuasion.

19. Whitehead finds emphasis on the second element in an alternative to be more than ten times as frequent as emphasis on the first element, although he finds that most Tacitean alternatives have no clear emphasis (1979, 478–93). Develin notes that on average, the second part of a weighted alternative is more likely to be presented as true and is also usually the more sinister of the two (1983, 86). The same point is common anecdotally, for example Martin (1981, 122, 222).

20. I take Keitel's point that Otho is unusually decisive here, but I contend that Tacitus does not make Otho entirely responsible for the decision, and that treating his decision at greater length draws attention also to his wavering.

household and his jab at the role of astrologers, qualify as jokes and have an outsize impact on Tacitus' characterization of Otho.

The appeals of Otho's slaves and freedmen emphasize the conflation of his private role and (prospective) official role. Tacitus pointedly remarks that Otho's slaves are "treated more permissively than is typical in a private house"[21] (*corruptius quam in priuata domo habiti*, 1.22.1). That Tacitus resents the political and social influence of slaves and freedmen is hardly a new observation,[22] but the oblique phrasing in significant here. *Corruptius quam* is comparative, underlining the implicit comparison between a private house and the imperial palace, where imperial freedmen have an extraordinary degree of leeway. Tacitus has primed his readers for an official/private contrast like the earlier one between *principi* and *priuato* (1.21.1). *Corruptius quam in priuata domo habiti* is the first place where the private/official contrast becomes outright humorous because the ideas overlap, and their overlap encapsulates the disruption of regular power dynamics. The phrase intensifies the contrast between what is appropriate for the emperor and what is appropriate for a private citizen. These behaviors overlap in Otho, and the combination suggests both that emperors are powerful enough to alter normal social dynamics and that they abdicate their nominal authority by allowing their freedmen to behave more freely than they would in a private home.

This incongruity restates Otho's central conflict in general terms. The passage is humorous because it overlays two opposed ideas in a succinct form that requires a twist in normal reasoning to make sense; emperors have a great deal of power, but they typically cede it to their freedmen. Tacitus' use of humor also allows him to continue elaborating on the tension between official and private without directly accusing the principate of hypocrisy, because he says that Otho's freedmen, not necessarily all imperial freedmen, were more corrupt than those who belonged to private houses. Tacitus implies that Otho's aspiration to the principate is the operative difference between him and private citizens, but he does not spell that out. The quip about Otho's slaves and freedmen reinforces the contrast that Tacitus has built. The official/private comparison encourages suspicion of imperial slaves and freedmen and hints that Otho's principate will relax the standards of integrity that would normally be required.

Finally, *corruptius . . . habiti* fits Cicero's and Quintilian's *subabsurda* (*De*

21. This translation is revised from Fyfe and Levene for a more negative translation of *corruptius*.
22. Damon (2003) gives a summary of Tacitus' contempt for freedmen in her note on 1.58.1.

Orat. 2.274; *Inst.* 6.3.99), an inane but cutting comment. Tacitus implies that the inappropriate behavior of Otho's freedmen was normal in the warped system of the principate. Tacitus' use of humor allows this passage simultaneously to shock and to make sense. Otho's behavior is wrong for what he is (a private citizen) but correct for what he aspires to be (the emperor). Although his freedmen have too much influence on Otho while he is a private citizen, their dynamic will be normal once he is emperor.[23] Otho's freedmen are corrupt and therefore inappropriate in a private house, but that same quality likens them to previous imperial households. They do not fit in a "private" context because they exercise too much influence, but nor do they fit an "imperial" context because Otho is not yet emperor.

Tacitus' use of humor in this passage encourages readers to judge Otho's household on private and imperial standards at the same time. *Corruptius quam in priuata domo habiti* only makes sense to a reader who accepts the warped reasoning that corrupt freedmen are more acceptable to an emperor than they would be to a private citizen. The irrational logic of this passage echoes the court of Nero (described at 1.13) and foreshadows the freedmen's arguments that Otho should become emperor. Tacitus arranges Otho's accession in such a way as to invite humorous interpretation because nonhumorous discourse would not express the contradiction as succinctly. The freedmen's arguments exemplify the inverted morality of the principate as they cite Otho's affinity with many faults of the previous regime to convince Otho to become emperor (1.22.1). The list of supposed rewards of empire (luxury, adultery, etc.) suggests that Otho will be another Nero and promotes the idea that frivolous and immoral desires are a requirement rather than a disqualification for the principate. The same thing is implied by the freedmen's comment that if Otho hesitated to do immoral things to attain power, that was not because of morality but laziness (1.22.1).

Tacitus also singles out Otho's astrologers as deleterious but inevitable influences: "people of this class always betray the powerful and deceive the ambitious; they will always be forbidden and always kept around"[24] (*genus hominum potentibus infidum, sperantibus fallax, quod in ciuitate nostra et uetabitur semper et retinebitur*, 1.22.1). The phrase *genus hominum potentibus infidum, sperantibus fallax* contains elegant parallelism, with a jingle between

23. Damon calls the passage a "wry appreciation" of imperial freedmen's influence (2003, 1.22.1).
24. Adapted from Fyfe and Levene to preserve the passive voice in the final clause.

potentibus and *sperantibus*. This clause alone would have sufficed for Tacitus to express his disapproval of astrologers. Instead, he expands the thought into a quotable *sententia* (*quod . . . retinebitur*).[25] The last part of the sentence has been recognized as humorous by Plass,[26] and it combines the force of a generalizing *sententia* and surprising *inconcinnitas*. Together, these typical figures of Tacitus' style produce a punchline. The final word changes the meaning because it disrupts the logic of the sentence (how can you forbid and keep something at the same time?) and reminds readers of the illogic of the principate (if something is forbidden, of course everyone would keep it).

Tacitus' jab at astrologers also brings together incompatible ideas in a way that promotes humor. *Vetabitur* and *retinebitur* are clear opposites. Because Tacitus joins these opposites with *et*, not *sed*, they collide with each other. The phrase also evokes the upside-down, irrational world of the principate that Tacitus has established as humorous. Here, Tacitus evokes a specific mechanism, identified in script theory as a "missing link," in which the logic is sound provided that the interpreter accepts an unstated false premise (Attardo, Hempelmann, and Di Maio 2002, 11). Here, if the reader accepts that forbidding something has the opposite effect, it makes sense that the prohibition against astrologers was never taken seriously. The astrologers are the primary target of the joke, while people who keep astrologers are a secondary, implicit target. The rhyming repetition of *uetabitur-retinebitur* appeals for its sound (a factor cited by both ancient and modern commentators as an enhancement to humor)[27] and echoes Cicero's contention that the best retorts hijack the original insult (*De Orat.* 2.277). Because Tacitus' narration is monologic there can be no initial insult, but after *uetabitur*, *retinebitur* has the force of a sarcastic reply. Tacitus wittily attacks a minor flaw of the principate without applying humor to its major flaws, in accordance with Cicero's and Quintilian's recommendations on good targets for humor (*De Orat.* 2.237; *Inst.* 6.3.28).[28]

25. The *sententia* exaggerates. Astrologers were repeatedly expelled from Rome, but astrology was not illegal (Damon 2003, *ad loc*). The exaggeration heightens the contrast between astrologers' real and ideal behavior. Astrologers are a target of similar humor elsewhere in Tacitus, including in the *Annals*, where Tacitus calls an attempt to banish them "frightening and ineffectual" (Woodman's translation, *atrox et irritum*, 12.52.3).

26. Plass calls this passage an example of *para prosdokian* that "reappears wherever political irrationality is to be found" (1988, 59).

27. Attardo, Hempelmann, and Di Maio call soundplay an "enhancing factor" in jokes (2002, 29). The Romans also used sound in humor. Cicero recommends punning (*De Orat.* 2.256–2.257). Quintilian thinks that the word "stomach" sounds funny for no discernable reason (*Inst.* 6.3.112). Alliteration is also frequent in Plautus' comedies.

28. Tacitus tends to disdain astrologers without suggesting that they were a major danger. Roman

Tacitus' joke on astrologers is not merely an amusing curiosity, but part of the larger point that Tacitus has been making about the principate. The joke about astrologers could not work without the background that Tacitus has built. In this joke, Tacitus quickly refers to that background, and the joke itself serves as both a reminder and development of that theme. The astrologer joke demonstrates the damage the principate has inflicted on the elite's ability to accurately perceive the world around them and reiterates a negative impression of the principate by prompting Tacitus' readers to reflect that "always forbidden, always kept around" makes sense only if one subscribes to the negative characterization of the principate that Tacitus has advanced.

In addition, the astrologer joke depends on the official/private contrast that Tacitus associates with Otho. Officially, astrologers are forbidden, but unofficially (privately), they are popular. Tacitus also links the official/private contrast to hypocritical imperial policy. After the remark about astrologers comes the example of Poppaea. Astrologers are privy to her private dealings, and she is called "an imperial marriage"[29] (*principalis matrimonii*, 1.22.2), a member of the private household of a public figure.[30] Poppaea's connection to astrologers properly characterizes only Nero's household, not Otho's, but because the information appears in a passage about Otho consulting an astrologer, and because Poppaea was once Otho's wife, the criticism extends to him as well. Tacitus' astrologer joke thus reinforces the similarity between Otho and Nero and confirms that Otho's dilemma between official and private was a persistent imperial problem.

After criticizing astrologers in general, Tacitus moves on to Otho's astrologer Ptolemaeus in particular. Although Otho has already come up with reasons to rebel, Tacitus claims that Ptolemaeus was an "instigator of crime"[31] (*sceleris instinctor*, 1.22.3) who persuaded Otho.[32] Otho accepts his astrologer's predictions, forming his ambitions into a concrete plan to make himself emperor. As I have noted, there is a discrepancy between the Otho of section 21, who tries to make up his own mind, and the Otho of section 22, who is persuaded by a

---

emperors did at times place restrictions on astrologers, but their elite clients were punished more regularly for soliciting subversive predictions (Rives 2011, 684–85). Therefore, astrologers were more likely a nuisance suitable for humor than a menace that required invective.

29. I have changed Fyfe and Levene's "royal" to "imperial."

30. At 1.13.3, when Poppaea was the "imperial whore" (*principale scortum*), she represented a problematic notion of "public," as a public figure with a public sexuality.

31. Adapted from Fyfe and Levene to be comprehensible outside the context of the original phrase.

32. Cramer theorizes that Tacitus disdained Ptolemaeus especially because he was of lower status even than an *eques*, not simply because he was an astrologer, as Tacitus is less disdainful of other astrologers (1954, 129–30).

group of unsuitable advisers. Otho's slaves, freedmen, and astrologers are portrayed as damaging yet fitting advisers for an imperial household. Previous emperors consulted their households on political matters, so it makes a perverse kind of sense that a successful rebellion begins with a future emperor turning to freedmen advisers.[33]

Tacitus' use of humor also associates Otho with Nero and demonstrates that Otho never managed to assert control during his principate. Tacitus continues to use the themes that he has set up with humor as he describes Otho's revolt. One of Otho's freedmen, Onomastus, plays a key role in the conspiracy (1.25.1),[34] and Otho's similarity to Nero works in his favor with Nero's former supporters (1.25.2).[35] The conspiracy narrative uses humor in the form of one of Tacitus' most famous epigrams: "so a couple of common soldiers took it upon them to hand over the Roman Empire—and they did it" (*suscepere duo manipulares imperium populi Romani transferendum et transtulerunt*, 1.25.1). Like the *sententia* on astrologers at 1.22.1, this passage becomes humorous in its last two words, which reveal that it is a compound sentence and that the second part contains a punchline.[36] The punchline conveys shock as much as humor, because the political influence of the two soldiers is unprecedented whereas that of astrologers was an open secret. Still, the use of humor is similar. Otho's coup is characterized by irrational logic and supported by a cast of supposedly insignificant people who in fact rule their rulers. Otho becomes emperor, but his freedmen and soldiers know that they facilitated his rise. As Otho becomes more powerful, Tacitus emphasizes the humorous element in the discrepancy between Otho's nominal and actual influence.

Otho and His Supporters

Tacitus presents Otho's relationship with his partisans as equally perverse but more complex. Tacitus' humorous characterization of Otho is already estab-

33. In contrast, both Vitellius' and Vespasian's imperial ambitions are encouraged by high-status men (1.52, 2.76). That Otho gets advice from his household is not in itself strange, but it is significant that Tacitus mentions no other councilors.

34. One of Onomastus' few other appearances is at 1.27, where he brings the news of the mutiny to Otho, who departs from a sacrifice to begin his coup. Fraser proposes that Onomastus' name is a joke because **Onoma**stus "names" Otho emperor (2007, 628). Tacitus does not draw attention to Onomastus' name at 1.25, but the later passage reflects the freedman's importance in Otho's coup. Fraser argues that 1.27 is influenced by Otho's contemptuous sense of humor, and that Tacitus subtly indicates Otho was mocking Rome even as he prepared to take control of it.

35. Later, Otho consciously exploited his similarity to Nero to win over the populace (1.78.2).

36. Plass discusses this *sententia* as an example of absurdity that reveals "conflict of intentions [that] affects fundamental moral and political norms" and has a punchline (1988, 35).

lished when Otho makes his first speech during the revolt against Galba. The speech expands upon established humorous motifs. In this speech, Otho acknowledges that he is divided between private and official concerns and attempts to turn this dilemma in his favor. According to Otho, the soldiers should remain loyal to him because their destinies are inextricably linked.[37] Before Otho speaks, Tacitus reiterates the tension in Otho's character: "Otho, for his part, was not slow to salute the crowd with outstretched hand and throw kisses to them. In every way he played the slave to gain a throne" (*nec deerat Otho protendens manus adorare uulgum, iacere oscula, et omnia seruiliter pro dominatione*, 1.36.3). The official/private contrast is present, even exaggerated. Behaving like a slave (*seruiliter*) would have been degrading for a Roman aristocrat, while *dominatio* connotes a stronger, more tyrannical power than *imperium*.[38] Again, Tacitus puts a punchline (*pro dominatione*) at the end, where it is both shocking and humorous in its contrast with Otho's behavior. *Seruiliter* is placed immediately before *pro dominatione*, where the contrast between the two emphasizes the incompatibility of Otho's slavish behavior and his desire to gain imperial authority. Tacitus uses this joke to criticize Otho, and to imply that he is not truly in control. The emperor is a slave to his supporters.[39]

Tacitus shows that Otho knows he is caught between public office and private life, between *imperium* and powerlessness. When he speaks to his troops, he introduces himself by these contrasts: "In what guise I come forward to address you, fellow soldiers, I cannot tell. Dubbed emperor by you, I dare not call myself a private citizen: yet 'emperor' I cannot say with another on the throne" (*quis ad uos processerim, commilitones, dicere non possum, quia nec priuatum me uocare sustineo princeps a uobis nominatus, nec principem alio imperante*, 1.37.1).[40] The contradictions are apparent. Even though Otho instigated

37. It is true that Otho's incumbency in the principate depends on the soldiers' favor, as Tacitus emphasizes the soldiers' importance to the principate especially in *Histories* 1 (Syme 1958, 153). The soldiers' destiny need not depend on Otho's, however, and many would presumably serve under the next emperor, too.

38. Tacitus criticizes Otho with serious invective here (Shochat 1981, 365). Syme describes Otho's attitude as "base and flattering" and his message as "hypocritical protestations" (1958, 153).

39. Pomeroy describes Otho's subservient behavior as winning him the principate but also preventing him from truly taking power and connects this behavior to the theatrical way that all imperial claimants behaved (2006, 183).

40. There is additional irony because Otho calls his soldiers *commilitones* before claiming that their true role is unknown. Otho's use of the term could be inappropriate, as Otho would have been a fellow soldier only in the loosest sense, if at all (Damon 2003, *ad loc*). Plass sees the first sentence as Otho's admission that he is a fraudulent or even treasonous emperor (1988, 121). Keitel considers the speech a sign that normalcy has been overturned, because the closest parallels in earlier historical writing have generals claiming that they do not know how to address a mutinous army

the rebellion and wants to be emperor, he avoids declaring his goal and instead makes his part in the coup sound passive. He claims to have become emperor at the soldiers' behest (*princeps a uobis nominatus*), concealing his agency by using a passive participle. Instead of claiming that he is emperor by his own power, Otho insists that he is emperor because his soldiers declared him emperor. Otho is lying (he instigated the revolt in which the troops declared him emperor), yet his servility toward his supporters reveals the accidental truth in this face-saving lie. Otho's soldiers control his coup.[41] Otho is lying, but his lie exposes the unstable power relation between him and his soldiers.

Otho's speech vividly demonstrates his weaknesses. The disconnect between what Otho tells his soldiers and what Tacitus' readers know to be the case demonstrates the discrepancy between what emperors say and what is true. Tacitus' readers can recognize the humorous tone in this passage, in part because of the dramatic irony of Otho saying that he cannot call himself emperor yet. As Otho says, he is both an emperor and a private citizen. Such a blatant contradiction is humorous because Otho seems to think people will believe his lie and because it points to the awkward truth. Neither interpretation should be discarded—as in O'Gorman's discussion of irony, both readings are significant (2000, 11–12). Otho is correct either way (he is a private citizen and will shortly become an emperor), but he is also certainly wrong (he is trying to become emperor but cannot control the people who made him emperor). The ambiguity of humor allows Otho's conflict between power and powerlessness to be discussed without being resolved.

Otho advertises his uncertainty about his role. His opening phrase, "In what guise I come forward to address you," (*quis ad uos processerim*, 1.37.1) conveys the instability of his position. Although the English translation suggests deception or difficulty interpreting the situation, the Latin phrase *quis ad uos processerim* does not suggest disguise as much as transformation, inside as well as out. Fyfe and Levene's translation is clearer, but I suggest that Otho's uncertainty is more pronounced: "[I don't know] who it is that I am as I address you." Otho is being deceptive, but Tacitus does not emphasize Otho's deception. Instead, the start of the speech suggests that Otho's position is genuinely fragile

---

as a way of shaming their troops into better behavior, while here Otho does not know how to identify himself to the army that he is riling up to mutiny (Keitel 1987, 74).

41. Bittarello suggests Otho's submission to his troops also implies sexual submissiveness (2011, 105). That element may indeed influence Tacitus' characterization of Otho, but Tacitus is too decorous to make the implication explicit.

and prone to crumble at the whim of his supporters.[42] Otho cannot maintain that he is a private citizen when his troops call him emperor, but nor can he be the emperor when somebody else is emperor.[43] Otho comes off as doubly helpless, able neither to reject nor accept power. The absurdity of Otho asking his partisans for permission to exercise power is humorous and also demonstrates their power over him.

Otho's first speech is a culmination of Tacitus' humorous portrayal of him so far and reinforces the humorous impression that was established earlier. Although emperors normally delegate responsibilities, Otho does more than that by obeying the wishes of his partisans even as he seeks greater nominal authority. The speech seems designed to flatter the troops, but while Otho at first seems to overstate the troops' importance, their real power gradually becomes clear.[44]

As he continues speaking, Otho introduces a historiographical *topos*, the breakdown of social roles and language during civil wars (Damon 2003, 1.37.1).[45] In describing Galba's cruelty, Otho contends that Galba gave virtuous names to his vicious policies. Slaughter is "correction," crimes are "remedies," punishments are "discipline," and so on.[46] Otho uses the trope of disordered communication in a straightforward way. His speech contains few signs of humor

42. Keitel sees the opening of Otho's speech as a reversal of anti-mutiny harangues in which generals express confusion about what to call their troops, a *topos* that emphasizes the chaos of civil war (1987, 74). This parallel heightens the irony, because Otho is encouraging a mutiny, not ending one.

43. The phrase *nec principem alio imperante* may also contain an etymological pun on *princeps*; there cannot be two emperors because two cannot be "first" at the same time. Thanks to Robert Babcock for this observation.

44. Tacitus drops hints that Otho understands that his supporters can dictate his choices. Later, Tacitus says that Otho understood the influence the soldiers had over him (1.83.1), but that is not yet clear in this passage.

45. This motif goes back at least to Thucydides, who articulated it in a famous passage on the chaos that enveloped Corcyra during the later stages of its disastrous civil war (3.82.3–4). O'Gorman explains that "Tacitus situates himself in a tradition of sceptical historiography" by his use of this motif, although she questions whether the meanings of words were ever truly stable (2000, 14–17). Keitel points out that *Histories* 1 engages with this motif often and may echo Sallust's treatment of similar themes (e.g., *Bellum Catilinae* 10.5), which gives it a specific referent in Roman civil war (2006, 223–24).

46. "What province is there in the empire, what military camp, that has not been polluted with massacre? He calls it 'salutary correction.' For his 'remedies' are what other people call crimes: his cruelty is disguised as 'strictness,' his avarice as 'economy,' while by 'discipline' he means punishing and insulting you" (*quae usquam prouincia, quae castra sunt nisi cruenta et maculata aut, ut ipse praedicat, emendata et correcta? nam quae alii scelera, hic remedia uocat, dum falsis nominibus seueritatem pro saeuitia, parsimoniam pro auaritia, supplicia et contumelias uestras disciplinam appellat*, 1.37.4). This passage is the first appearance in the *Histories* of the motif of breakdown of values in civil war and reflects as poorly on Otho as it does on Galba (Keitel 2006, 236).

besides irony, which is hard to avoid when assigning false names to things. Otho's irony is scathing rather than humorous as he attempts to persuade the soldiers. The sentence structure minimizes its humorous potential; some of the true names are given after the false ones, toward the ends of sentences, but other sentences reverse that order, and once the pattern is established, the corresponding quality is predictable.[47] Instead of combining opposites, Otho separates real and false virtues as clearly as possible. By clearly signaling his use of irony, Otho limits its ambiguity and also its humorous potential. From the start, he clarifies the correct interpretation of his speech for his audience. Before introducing the false names motif, he lists Galba's cruelties (*trucidauerit*, *decumari deditos iuberet*, the spate of murders from Obultronius Sabinus to Nymphidius, 1.37.2–3), so that when he employs irony, the soldiers already know that they should dislike Galba (and, given that they are committing mutiny against his regime, they probably already do). Otho notes the difference between the false and true terms by reminding his audience that Galba is responsible for the incongruity (*uocat*, *falsis nominibus*, *appellat*, 1.37.4) and blames Galba alone for the hypocrisy of the principate. When one man (Galba) uses positive terms to describe his own cruel behavior, nothing is wrong with reality as most people experience it. Instead, that man is probably just lying. Otho is therefore not engaged in Tacitus' larger pattern of humor but merely attempts to enlist a common rhetorical *topos* in his own defense.

Otho as Ineffectual Emperor

After Galba is killed and Otho becomes emperor, he struggles to exercise imperial power. As soon as Tacitus has related the deaths of Galba and his most prominent supporters, he depicts Otho's inability to control his own partisans (1.45). The senators and people scramble to switch to Otho's side in a passage replete with irony. While they flatter Otho, "the more false their gestures were, the more they did them" (*quantoque magis falsa erant quae fiebant, tanto plura*

47. *nisi cruenta . . . emendata et correcta* (1.37.4) is the sole example in which the false name follows the true name. When a false name comes before a true name, the true one is not a surprise: *seueritatem pro saeuitia, parsimoniam pro auaritia* (1.37.4) is a simple sequence of opposites, and both severity and greed have already been associated with Galba. The final pair, *supplicia et contumelias uestras disciplinam appellat* (1.37.4), is easy to guess because it refers to a typical characteristic of Galba.

facere, 1.45.1),[48] and "they were as much offended at [Marius Celsus'] efficiency and honesty as if these had been criminal qualities" (*industriae eius innocentiaeque quasi malis artibus infensi*, 1.45.2).[49] The irony illustrates the hypocrisy of the senators and people, showing that the emperor warps reality for everybody, not only for himself and his closest supporters. The senators' hypocrisy shifts the tone of the paragraph away from the somber one Tacitus used for the obituaries of Galba's partisans. The senators' frantic rush (described in a series of historical infinitives) confirms the deterioration of Rome's political structure under the principate. These are the survivors of much political strife, and they have survived because they are contemptible flatterers.

Even as the senators and people jockey for his favor, Otho's position is unstable: "Otho had as yet no influence to prevent crimes: he could only order them" (*Othoni nondum auctoritas inerat ad prohibendum scelus: iubere iam poterat*, 1.45.2). Tacitus demonstrates that Otho's power is fragile (Damon 2003, *ad loc*) by using another punchline. *Othoni nondum auctoritas inerat* conveys the main, nonhumorous point of the sentence, that Otho did not attain stable power after Galba's murder. *Ad prohibendum scelus* adds a salient, humor-generating detail by specifying which powers Otho could not yet exercise. (The crime is the murder of Marius Celsus, who was condemned because he did not renounce Galba until after Galba's death.) The crowd who demand his death refer to it as an execution (*supplicium*, 1.45.2). By calling it a crime (*scelus*), Tacitus changes the connotation significantly. Cicero says that calling a dishonorable thing by an honorable name is "very close to deception" or "very close to irony"[50] (*finitimum dissimulationi*, *De Orat.* 2.272). This irony (on the part of the historian) and deception (on the part of the characters) influences the tone of the passage toward humor. Add to that the irony of the emperor not yet having the authority to prevent anyone else from carrying out an execution, and *Othoni . . . scelus* takes on a darkly ironic tone. Tacitus escalates the irony with *iubere iam poterat*, an appendix to the sentence that is reminiscent of a punchline (Plass 1988, 13). The fact that Otho could

48. Fyfe and Levene translate this passage with the flatterers employing "extravagance in inverse proportion to their sincerity." I have opted for a more awkward translation that reflects the Latin word order because it demonstrates the punchline at the end. Damon (2003, *ad loc*) compares this epigram to one in the *Annals*: "the more illustrious each was, the more false and frantic," (trans. Woodman 2004, *quanto quis inlustrior, tanto magis falsi ac festinantes*, *Annales* 1.7.1). Syme quotes *falsi ac festinantes* among examples of "elevation [. . .] one of Tacitus' favourite devices for irony and for mockery" (1958, 349).

49. Plass cites the comment on false gestures as an example of "the special self-parody of people who in a way do believe what they know to be false" (1988, 5).

50. These are my translations.

command only crimes implies that his power is an illusion.[51] Otho can command crimes only because his supporters want to commit crimes, and Otho does not have the authority to go against them. By saying that Otho could order crimes, Tacitus wryly implies that Otho could not actually command anything but merely cultivated the impression that he had power by yielding to his supporters' demands in such a way that he appeared to have commanded whatever they were planning to do anyway.[52]

Elsewhere, Otho agrees with public opinion or manages to sway his partisans,[53] but here Tacitus implies that Otho is a hapless follower putting on a show of authority.[54] Humor is an apt tactic for communicating the paradox of Otho's authority because it can simultaneously convey that Otho was not taken seriously as an emperor and that he was still dangerous to Roman elites. While Otho's authority appears nonexistent, it also appears monstrous because Otho could legitimize his supporters' crimes. Because irony requires two simultaneous interpretations (O'Gorman 2000, 11–12), Otho can be both a puppet of the army and a bloodthirsty tyrant.[55] Irony without humor, however, might have revealed Otho as either the terrifying emperor or the in-too-deep private citizen, positing one as the truth and the other as an illusion. By using humor, Tacitus gives the impression that both the powerless and powerful aspects of Otho's character are essential, and that this union of opposites made Otho both an emperor and a powerless figurehead. I argue that Tacitus uses humor here, as evidenced by the joining of contrasts in Otho's character and the surprise of the punchline.

The Nighttime Mutiny

The contrast between Otho's power and powerlessness, as well as his humorous characterization, peaks when his supporters launch a minor mutiny. Otho

51. Damon makes this point and connects the passage to a mutiny of Otho's troops (2003, 1.45.2).
52. Despite their unwillingness to follow his orders, Otho's supporters seem to genuinely believe in his leadership. For example, at 2.39.2 they do not want to join battle without him.
53. Ash comments that Otho has "a talent for managing people" (1999, 90). For example, his first speech to the soldiers inspired them to rush off and defeat Galba (1.38.3).
54. Tacitus confirms this implication in the next paragraph, "the will of the soldiers was henceforward supreme" (*omnia deinde arbitrio militum acta*, 1.46.1).
55. Tacitus reinforces Otho's potential for tyranny with his gloating over Piso's head (1.44.1). Ash points out, however, that Tacitus reports the anecdote about the severed head as a rumor (1999, 89) and suggests that Tacitus characterizes Otho as a "decadent murderer and [. . .] a bewildered usurper who struggles to exert authority but finds himself powerless" (1999, 94). There need be no single, simple characterization of Otho.

never does attain much control over his supporters, and their bad behavior reinforces Tacitus' humorous characterization of Otho. While the civil war continues, "in the meantime a riot broke out in an unexpected quarter, and, though trivial at first, nearly ended in the destruction of Rome" (*paruo interim initio, unde nihil timebatur, orta seditio prope Vrbi excidio fuit*, 1.80.1). This phrase uses several devices that contribute to humor. It plays on the difference between expectation and reality, leaves its most shocking information for last, and includes soundplay (*initio, seditio, excidio*).[56] Because the main point of the sentence is that unrest came from an unexpected quarter, the immediate effect of the passage is more shock than humor, but the reminder of the influence that Otho's supporters had on him is also a reminder of the humor that Tacitus used earlier to characterize their relationship to the emperor.

According to Tacitus, some of the soldiers loyal to Otho believe that their officers are planning to betray him, so they kill them. The rioting soldiers proceed to the Palatine, although Tacitus does not say why.[57] Otho's dinner guests, senators and their wives, are at first afraid that Otho incited the riot, then more afraid that he is not responsible (1.81.1).[58] While they flee, the senators temporarily renounce their senatorial status: "officials threw away their insignia and avoided their massed entourages of attendants and slaves [. . .]. Few went home, most of them fled to friends, or sought an obscure refuge with the humblest of their clients" (*tum uero passim magistratus proiectis insignibus, uitata comitum et seruorum frequentia* [. . .] *rari domos, plurimi amicorum tecta et ut cuique humillimus cliens, incertas latebras petiuere*, 1.81.2). The senators remove their insignia because the power that those symbols usually communicate must be defunct if the army is rebelling. They shun their entourages and seek help from their clients to avoid displaying any signs of their status. In short, power relations have been reversed so that what indicated power now indicates vulnerability. The senators attempt to eliminate the signs of their weakness, while Otho attempts to salvage his nominal power by talking the soldiers down.

The fragility of official power reflects on Otho as well as on the senators. In

56. This pattern has a parallel at 2.68.1 (*orta seditio, ludicro initio*), where Vitellius' dinner is interrupted by soldiers demanding the execution of his ally Verginius (Damon 2003, 1.80.1).

57. In fact, Tacitus suggests that they had no good reason to do so. Damon compares Tacitus' version of the narrative to accounts in Suetonius and Plutarch and concludes that Tacitus "throughout insists on [the soldiers'] lack of control" (2003, 261). Tacitus has also expanded the significance of this episode and used it to illustrate the disorder of the times (Syme 1958, 153–55).

58. Plass sees the senators' fear of Otho's fear as a demonstration of Tacitus' penchant for antithesis and paradoxical themes (1988, 12, 40–41). Damon sees the repetition of verbs of fearing as paralleled at Plutarch, *Life of Otho* 3.5 (2003, *ad loc*).

Plutarch's and Suetonius' versions of the same events, the fate of the senators is barely remarked upon.[59] Tacitus emphasizes the senators' panic to show that the usual power dynamics were reversed. The senators have an expanded role in Tacitus compared to other accounts because their fear emphasizes the uselessness of official power in turbulent times. Otho used to rely on members of his household and now depends on the support of soldiers. The brief description of the senators' reactions reintroduces several elements that Tacitus has associated with a humorous characterization of Otho. These factors include the instability of authority, the influence of lowly people in times of crisis, and the correlation between power and deception.

Once the senators are out of the way, the soldiers break into Otho's dining room and make semi-coherent threats. Tacitus provides no explanation for their rampage but implies that Otho's partisans in the army were impatient with most authorities, from the Senate to their officers, with the exception of Otho himself (1.82).[60] On the way to Otho, the soldiers wound another pair of officers, inverting authority again.[61] In response to their demand that they be allowed to kill senators and other supposed traitors, Otho makes a desperate appeal: "At last Otho, contrary to imperial dignity, stood up on a couch and with great difficulty restrained them by means of prayers and tears. They returned to their camp unwillingly, and with a guilty conscience"[62] (*donec Otho contra decus imperii toro insistens precibus et lacrimis aegre cohibuit, redieruntque in castra inuiti neque innocentes*, 1.82.1). The scene plays on confusion about authority and adds an element of anticlimax because after the drama of an insurrection,[63] Otho halts the rebellion by making a fool of himself and simply begging the soldiers to stop.

Plutarch describes a similar scene, with Otho jumping onto a couch and crying (*Life of Otho* 3.7). The consistency between the accounts suggests that these details were part of a preexisting tradition, but that does not make Tacitus' treat-

59. Plutarch gives a similar account, including emotional details like the senators' fear first of Otho and then of whatever Otho fears (*Life of Otho* 3.5). Plutarch, however, does not describe the senators' escape beyond saying that they barely got away (3.6). Suetonius' truncated version does not mention that there were senators with Otho (*Otho* 8).

60. Later, Tacitus describes Otho's partisans as distrustful of all generals except Otho (2.33.3). The Othonians' distrust of their officers goes back to when they were Galbians (Ash 1999, 30–33).

61. Damon notes that it would be unusual for these two officers (one an officer of a legion and one of the praetorians) to be in the same place and that the disorganization within military units is a further demonstration of chaos in the army (2003, 1.82.1).

62. This translation is adapted to include a more adversative word for the Latin *contra*.

63. Initially, Tacitus says that the mutiny "nearly ended in the destruction of Rome" (*prope Vrbi excidio fuit*, 1.80.1).

ment of them less amusing. Plutarch leans heavily on a characterization of Otho as simply weak. He recounts the same details, but without the framing that Tacitus uses to establish that these details are humorous. Plutarch's Otho, therefore, is merely pathetic, while Tacitus' Otho plays to his contemptible strengths.

The contrast between power and powerlessness, as well as that between official and private, are familiar themes in Tacitus' characterization of Otho. The soldiers invade a private occasion attended by public officials (the emperor and senators) where they make a personal appeal to Otho, whom they trust despite their mistrust for all other authority figures. Otho's reaction confirms that he, too, is responsible for the confusion of private and official matters. Tacitus says that Otho acted "contrary to imperial dignity" (*contra decus imperii*, 1.82.1), an explicit subversion of the behavior expected of an emperor. Otho is forced to adopt this strategy, but Tacitus' phrasing suggests that Otho gave up the dignity of imperial power because he thought that sacrifice could help him stay alive and maintain a veneer of authority.

Part of the humor of this scene is its inappropriateness. Armed soldiers do not belong in the emperor's dining room. Tacitus emphasizes the details of the setting so that the comic elements become apparent. For example, the detail that Otho stood on a couch to persuade his troops combines a comic setting with a political speech. The couch is a reminder that the soldiers have broken into a dinner party and becomes a kind of substitute rostrum for Otho's inadequate speech. This puts a quintessentially public act (oratory) into a private context.[64] Otho begs and cries more than he persuades, and he barely (*aegre*) succeeds in calming the soldiers (1.82.1). The scene is a parody of public speaking in which tears substitute for persuasion.[65] Otho should be commanding an obedient army in public, but instead he is pleading with mutineers in his own dining room.

---

64. Tacitus sets some other political speeches in private contexts, but it is an unconventional choice that reflects the difference between the way power was exercised in the Republic and in the principate (Levene 2009, 214). Otho's dining room is also a luxurious setting, which may provide a further contrast. Phang suggests that this incident is a result of Otho's excessive generosity with the donative and indicates that he could not keep order among his troops (2008, 186).

65. Tacitus apparently considered the speech itself unworthy of report even in indirect discourse, yet Otho is not the only figure thought to have wept and pleaded with a mutinous army. Suetonius reports that Nero initially planned to weep before Galba's partisans and thereby change their minds in his favor, and he even announced this plan at the end of a dinner party (*Nero* 43). Nero never seems to have carried out this plan, however, and Suetonius uses the convivial setting to imply that the emperor was drunk when he formulated the idea, which would explain why it is so pathetic. Tacitus emphasizes Otho's connection to Nero and may have meant to introduce another parallel between them. If so, Otho's improbable success is doubly striking.

Otho's attempt to seem like an emperor is even more humorous because his speech succeeds, although badly, at placating the soldiers.[66] Everything turns out better than could reasonably be expected, were the warped logic of the principate not in operation. Although chaotic, the mutiny does not derail Otho's principate because the turbulent relationship between emperor and soldiers is already established. The soldiers seem ashamed of themselves (1.82.3), and two are punished (1.85.1), but they also receive a bribe (1.82.3) and continue to menace Roman elites (1.85.1). They do not get exactly what they want (to murder all officers and senators), but that is hardly a setback. Otho, for his part, seems frightened, making sure to bribe the soldiers before he addresses them in person (1.82.3). Nevertheless, he retains his nominal *imperium* and remains unharmed. (Although his soldiers never evince a desire to hurt Otho, his behavior shows his concern that they might.) The joke starts "soldiers rush palace; emperor stands on couch," but ends "emperor stands on couch; foils coup." Tacitus shifts the emphasis from the absurdity of the specific situation to the absurdity of the circumstances that made it possible. In addition, the absurdity of the episode is heightened because the events described are so far beyond the pale. The combination of fleeing senators, rebelling soldiers, and a powerless emperor is too much to accept as the product of a sane political system, and Tacitus' use of humor encourages the conclusion that the principate was in fact an insane system.

Otho After the Mutiny

The day after the mutiny, Otho makes a public speech to make sure it is over. Tacitus maintains the ironic contrast between Otho's nominal power and actual powerlessness and increases its absurdity. Before Otho's speech, Tacitus frames the soldiers as cynically aware of the political influence they exert: "The better sort wanted [Otho] to put a stop to the prevalent insubordination, but the great bulk of [the soldiers] liked insurrection and emperors who had to court their favor, and the prospect of rioting and plunder made it easier still to press them into civil war. He realized, also, that one who wins the throne by violence cannot keep it by suddenly trying to enforce the rigid discipline of earlier days"

66. To preserve their fragile quiescence, Otho appeals to them again a day later (1.82.3), a sign that they had not entirely abandoned their impulse to mutiny.

(*cum optimus quisque remedium praesentis licentiae posceret, uulgus et plures seditionibus et ambitioso imperio laeti per turbas et raptus facilius ad ciuile bellum impellerentur, simul reputans non posse principatum scelere quaesitum subita modestia et prisca grauitate retineri*, 1.83.1). Tacitus establishes that the soldiers understood the political ramifications of their actions. Their political manipulations are unsubtle, intentional attempts at gaining leverage.

Otho is determined to regain the authority he never had. He cultivates the soldiers' support by flattering and bribing them but does so out of strategy as much as desperation.[67] Tacitus presents Otho's second speech as cravenly self-serving rather than foolish. Even as Otho has become conscious of his contradictory position, Tacitus uses the speech to continue his humorous characterization of Otho by focusing on his hypocrisy. From its start, the speech is full of demonstrable falsehoods: "Fellow-soldiers, I have not come to fan the fire of your affection for me, or to instill courage into your hearts: in both these qualities you are more than rich. No, I have come to ask you to moderate your valor and to set some bounds to your devotion toward me" (*neque ut affectus uestros in amorem mei accenderem, commilitones, neque ut animum ad uirtutem cohortarer (utraque enim egregie supersunt), sed ueni postulaturus a uobis temperamentum uestrae fortitudinis et erga me modum caritatis*, 1.83.2). Contrary to what he claims, Otho is in fact nervous about the soldiers' loyalty to him. The "courage" and "virtue" that he praises are vices under flattering names—they actually refer to the soldiers' rashness during the mutiny (Plass 1988, 46). Because Otho's speech comes directly after Tacitus' description of the actual situation, there is an edge to Otho's hypocrisy. He, the soldiers, and Tacitus' audience all know the soldiers have been cynically forcing Otho's hand, but Otho maintains the fiction that they are just a little too enthusiastic. Among the ruins of his dinner party, Otho begged and wept, but in public, as emperor, he makes a face-saving speech in which he attempts to separate himself from his previous performance. In a private setting, where he can act like a private citizen, Otho implicitly admits he is powerless, but in a public setting, where he must be emperor, he acts as though he has power. Unfortunately for Otho, his strategy does not work on Tacitus' audience. Otho demonstrates the weakness of his faith in his troops by confidently addressing them as *commilitones*, which he did at another weak moment near the start of his revolt. Then, Otho called

67. Otho has learned from Galba's death (1.83.1). Bribery and flattery are not sustainable methods for controlling an army, but in the circumstances, they are the only realistic options.

his troops *commilitones* when he was not sure what to call himself (1.37.1), and he seems to use it dishonestly here, too.[68] Otho still has not secured his position, being neither emperor nor private citizen, so it is difficult to understand how the soldiers could take his assertions of authority seriously.

Otho emphasizes his good qualities as an individual rather than as an emperor. He frames the soldiers' frenzy as a side effect of affection for him (*amorem mei*) and asks them to curb their devotion. The soldiers' devotion to Otho speaks to his charisma, but an accidental cult of personality is not a secure basis for power. If it were, Otho would not need to keep flattering the soldiers. In fact, they have significant power over him.[69] Tacitus draws on his humorous characterization of Otho to show his helplessness before his supposed underlings. Tacitus also shows that Otho attempted unsuccessfully to conceal the fact that he could only plead with the soldiers, not command them. He draws attention to the powerful/powerless dynamic in Otho's characterization by connecting it to the official/private tension that has been a consistent theme in his character. Again, the warped logic of the principate joins Otho's power to his powerlessness because his submission to the will of his supporters propelled him to the principate.

Otho continues by investing the soldiers' bad qualities with good names (unruliness becomes *pietas*, self-interest becomes "honorable motives," (*honestas rerum causas*, 1.83.2). Thus, he inadvertently demonstrates the motif of language becoming contradictory in times of civil war—a phenomenon that Otho associated with his enemies in his first speech (1.37.4), but that Tacitus applies to Otho here. In the earlier speeches, Tacitus showed that Otho's use of this motif is hypocritical because all sides of the civil war use it with equal, unde-

---

68. Damon notes both occurrences of *commilito* (2003, 1.37.1). So far in the *Histories*, *commilito* has only appeared when the authority of the speaker was in question. Besides the opening of Otho's earlier speech, it appeared twice in Piso's speech to the mutinous soldiers (1.29.2, 1.30.2), once in reference to "comrades" slaughtered by Galba (1.31.2), once in Galba's reprimand to a soldier who claimed to have killed Otho (1.35.2), and finally here (1.83.2). Suetonius claims that Julius Caesar used the term to flatter his troops (*Caesar* 67), while Augustus stopped calling his soldiers *commilitones* after he won the civil wars because he found the term obsequious (*Augustus* 25). *Commilito* does not necessarily have a negative connotation, but its appearances so far in the *Histories* illustrate its ironic potential. Leaders call on their "fellow soldiers" when they fear their soldiers might be disloyal.

69. Flattery is prone to produce irony because a successful flatterer must stay close enough to reality to remain plausible, while irony needs to communicate that its speaker knows that the ostensible meaning is not the truth (Eisterhold et al. 2006, 1243). If the soldiers cannot tell that Otho's flattery is implausible, then this passage works as successful flattery. Most of them and all of Tacitus' readers, however, can see the contradictions, and therefore the irony, in this speech.

served confidence.[70] That hypocrisy is repeated here. Tacitus also draws attention to the absurd content of Otho's speech. Otho lectures the soldiers on the value of obedience (1.83–1.84). His arguments conflict with reality to such an extent that this speech, like his first speech, becomes inadvertently humorous. The contrast between the Otho who led the coup against Galba and the Otho who believes that soldiers should always obey orders and protect their emperor is ironic to the point of absurdity. That Otho's strategy succeeds is immaterial; it is ridiculous for a usurper to argue against his own methods. He gets away with contradicting himself because nobody in his audience acknowledges that he has done so.

In addition, Tacitus indicates that the soldiers understand the political implications of their situation and are probably not fooled by Otho's apparent change of heart. Perhaps "the better sort" (*optimus quisque*, 1.83.1) already think that mutiny is immoral, but the majority believe that further chaos will benefit them, and Otho does not change their minds. The troops do not challenge Otho, but Tacitus provides context to suggest that they are merely flattering him. They are not Otho's dupes, but they are in on the plot, and their complicity points out the incongruity of the situation by illustrating that the twisted logic of empire and civil war requires the participation of large numbers of people besides the most important leaders.

The end of the speech takes on an especially ridiculous tone as Otho praises the authority of the Senate. Because the senators were a major target of the troops' anger during the dinner party episode, the Senate is germane to the current crisis, but it is odd that an emperor whose support comes from an anti-Senate army should make a fervent appeal to the Senate.[71] Otho claims that "nor should any army ever hear those cries against the Senate. It is the fount of empire and glory of all the provinces which, by Hercules, those Germans—whom Vitellius greatly exhorts against us—would not dare to summon to punishment"[72] (*nec illas aduersus senatum uoces ullus usquam exercitus audiat. caput imperii et decora omnium prouinciarum ad poenam uocare non hercule*

70. In a speech delivered to his troops around the time that Otho addresses his own, Otho's rival Piso uses the same trope of meanings disordered by civil war to attack Otho. Piso attempts to undermine Otho by pointing out that "Extravagance deceives some people: they take it for liberality" (*falluntur quibus luxuria specie liberalitatis imponit*, 1.30.1). He even admits that Rome's Senate and people may have lost their authority and become "empty terms" (*uacua nomina*, 1.30.2).

71. Otho is "ironically forced to defend the things which his own usurpation threatened" (Keitel 1987, 76).

72. This translation is largely mine and attempts to preserve some of the tangled word order of Tacitus' Latin.

illi, quos cum maxime Vitellius in nos ciet, Germani audeant, 1.84.3). Otho's claim that even Germans hesitate to condemn the Senate is odd because even if it were true, it is irrelevant. In addition, Otho's characterization of the Senate is difficult to believe. Far from being the font of empire (*caput imperii*), the Senate has lost its former power.[73] The falsehood is obvious, and Tacitus creates humor out of Otho's obvious hypocrisy. His tone, indicated by the colloquial word *hercule*, may be either emphatic or flippant.[74] Otho makes himself less credible because he founds his argument on the unbelievable premise that the Senate has power in Rome.

For Tacitus' readers, the humor is enhanced by the impression that the troops appear to take Otho's speech seriously.[75] Otho expresses a ridiculous opinion that his troops nevertheless treat as serious. The discrepancy between the content of Otho's speech and the soldiers' reaction to it creates humor and illustrates the fact that an emperor's lies are treated as true even when his authority is a fiction. Although he has no power to command his troops to do anything that they do not already want to do, Otho leverages the fiction of his power to make the soldiers more orderly. The humor reaches a climax when Otho claims that they need not fear Vitellius because "the Senate is with us" (*senatus nobiscum est*, 1.84.3).[76] The senate did not help Otho during his coup, nor have they done much for him since. Otho builds up to *senatus nobiscum est*

73. In addition, *decus* appeared at the end of the banquet scene as a facet of imperial dignity, when Otho acted *contra decus imperii*. Otho's mention of dignity here (*decora omnium*) is therefore a reminder of his earlier pleas on behalf of the senators. Haynes argues that for Otho to act "against the imperial dignity" and remain emperor is so contradictory that it suggests the imperial dignity was a sham all along (2003, 65). The reappearance of *decus* suggests that this speech is an unconvincing attempt to restore a shattered façade.

74. *Hercule* and its variations (often *hercle*) are frequent in comedy. Nicolson estimated that it appears once every fifteen lines in Plautus (1893, 99). Tacitus uses *hercule* almost exclusively in speech—it is most frequent in the *Dialogus*, and in at least one instance (*An.* 12.43.2) it appears outside direct quotation but in a passage that implies speech (*Lexicon Taciteum*). *Hercule* is therefore not entirely inappropriate in Otho's speech, but it lays a greater emphasis on Otho's point about the Senate and therefore focuses attention on one of the worse parts of his argument.

75. The troops' reaction is reported at 1.85.1, where they appear willing to accept what Otho has said, although they probably do not believe it.

76. Keitel suggests that Otho's praise of the Senate is influenced by Lucan's *Pharsalia* 2.531–533, where Pompey declares that the blessing of the Senate validates his side of the civil war (1987, 76). I find it suggestive that Pompey refers to his partisans as "those to whom the Senate gave nonprivate arms" (my inelegant translation, *quibus arma senatus / non privata dedit*), which recalls the distinction between public and private that Otho has been attempting to negotiate throughout. Elsewhere, Keitel calls Otho's praise of the Senate "both bitterly funny and apt" (1991, 2782). Celotto (2021) expands upon the parallels between *Pharsalia* and the civil war between Otho and Vitellius, in which Otho refigures first Caesar (active, ambitious) then Pompey (unsuccessful and concerned for the fate of his troops).

as if it were an unanswerable argument, but Tacitus' readers know that the Senate would have supported any victor.[77]

Otho describes the Senate as if it were the most consistent thing in Rome (1.84.4):

> The eternity of our empire, the peace of the world, your welfare and mine, all depend upon the safety of the Senate. Instituted with solemn ceremony by the father and founder of Rome, the Senate has come down in undying continuity from the kings to the emperors: and as we have received it from our ancestors, so let us hand it on to our posterity. From your ranks come the senators, and from the Senate come the emperors of Rome.
>
> *aeternitas rerum et pax gentium et mea cum uestra salus incolumitate senatus firmatur. hunc auspicato a parente et conditore Vrbis nostrae institutum et a regibus usque ad principes continuum et immortalem, sicut a maioribus accepimus, sic posteris tradamus; nam ut ex uobis senatores, ita ex senatoribus principes nascuntur.*

Otho's defense of the Senate repeats the motif of hypocrisy as part of the normal workings of the principate. The Senate is given credit for (nonexistent) world peace (*pax gentium*) and the safety of the emperor and the soldiers, despite being proven incapable of guaranteeing even their own safety.[78] The current civil war has little to do with the Senate.

Invoking Romulus' authority, Otho claims that the Senate has "come down in undying continuity from the kings to the emperors" (*a regibus usque ad principes continuum et immortalem*, 1.84.4). This statement emphasizes the Senate's existence and avoids the question of its influence. Between the kings and the emperors, the Senate wielded power during the Republic, but Otho mentions only kings and emperors. His contention that the Senate has not changed is almost plausible if we compare the role of the Senate during the monarchy with

---

77. One of Tacitus' most expert modern readers, Ronald Syme, considered that Otho here "speaks as a military emperor should speak" (1958, 155). I cannot point out any feature in the text that would make Otho's speech definitively inappropriate for a military emperor, but I suggest that most of Otho's points in this speech are patently dishonest.
78. In Domitianic documents, peace depends on the safety of the emperor rather than that of the Senate, and *pax gentium* resembles one of Otho's coin slogans, *pax orbis terrarum* (Damon 2003, *ad loc*). During Otho's rule, however, neither the Senate nor the emperor can guarantee anyone's safety, including their own.

its role under the principate. From the perspective of an emperor, the Senate has not changed much from what it was under the rule of the kings. The implicit comparison between a powerful Senate and a Senate controlled by a monarch is humorous in context because it points out the similarities between emperors and kings in an emperor's own words.

Finally, Otho obliquely admits that he needs the soldiers' support to stay in power: "From your ranks come the senators, and from the Senate come the emperors of Rome" (*nam ut ex uobis senatores, ita ex senatoribus principes nascuntur*, 1.84.4). Otho presents this statement as if it were clear; soldiers become senators, from whom emperors come, so therefore soldiers, senators, and emperors are all on the same continuum.[79] Otho's politically astute partisans understand that he is drawing a direct connection between their support and his authority. Still, Otho's argument is demonstrably false. His sudden interest in protecting the Senate indicates that he understands how he came to power but still cannot control his supporters. Although he aligns himself with the Senate, he also shows how irrelevant the Senate has become. In contrast to the impressive specter that Otho attempts to conjure, the Senate is an empty tradition that needs protection from the Roman army. In an attempt to make himself appear to be Rome's true ruler, Otho claims that his authority belongs ultimately to the Senate but in the process, he shows that the army commands him. The contrast between Otho's nominal authority and actual powerlessness is especially strong here, and Tacitus combines it with a reminder that the Senate occupies a similar position. In this way, the most humorous parts of Otho's speech are also instrumental in showing how authority is constructed under the principate.

The End of Humor in Otho's Characterization

Otho's speech after the nighttime mutiny is the last instance in which Tacitus uses humor to characterize Otho. Otho's security wanes further as he is forced to fight a civil war. After Book 1, Tacitus shifts his focus to Vitellius and Vespa-

79. The first half of this sentence is baffling: most emperors had been senators, but few soldiers became senators. Syme excuses the comment as referring "only to the officers" yet still finds it improbable (1958, 183). Damon explains that Otho "exaggerates the upward mobility possible" for a soldier to pander to his audience and that soldiers becoming emperors might have made some sense in the era of Nerva and Trajan (2003, *ad loc*).

sian, returning to Otho only when he is on the point of defeat. In Book 2, Tacitus begins to characterize Otho as simply powerless, rather than as trapped between power and powerlessness. Otho still cannot reliably command his own troops, despite their affection for him, and Tacitus has repeated this fact enough that it loses its implied contradiction and seems normal. Tacitus has also drawn enough parallels between Otho and other emperors (frequently Nero) that Otho's contradictions have begun to seem less like a humorous anomaly and more like typical imperial behavior.

At the end of Book 1, as Otho departs from Rome to oppose Vitellius, Tacitus uses themes that he has previously treated with humor but strips them of the context that made them humorous before. Book 1 ends with Tacitus reflecting on the similarities between flattery of the emperor and flattery in private houses: "Their motive was neither fear nor affection, but a sheer passion for servility. One can see the same in households of slaves, where each obeys his own interest: public dignity counts for nothing" (*nec metu aut amore, sed ex libidine seruitii, ut in familiis, priuata cuique stimulatio, et uile iam decus publicum*, 1.90.3).[80] This passage rounds out several of the motifs discussed above; love for acting servile, the influence of enslaved people in prominent households, and disregard for decorum have all been typical of Otho's principate. Here, however, Tacitus does not emphasize the potential for humor. The word order no longer implies one meaning before confirming another. There are contrasting scripts, but they do not overlap: *nec metu aut amore, sed ex libidine seruitii* preserves the sense of wrongness that pervades many of the earlier, humorous passages, but the addition of a clear adversative conjunction (*sed*) distinguishes Tacitus' tone here from the humorous one he used with *uetabitur et retinebitur*. Instead of linking fear and love with the desire to be a slave, Tacitus separates them.[81] Similarly, the comparison between a private household and the state is clearly a *comparison*. Tacitus separates the private and official elements with *ut*, and *familiis*, *priuata*, and *cuique* reinforce the idea of privacy without drawing out similarities between private and imperial households. Repetition without variation is emphatic, not humorous.

Unlike Otho's previous speeches, this speech is reported in indirect dis-

80. I follow Damon (2003, *ad loc*) in reading *stimulatio* instead of *simulatio*. Wellesley's text reads *simulatio* on the basis of a stronger manuscript tradition, while Damon argues for *stimulatio* on the basis of sense.

81. Tacitus even separates pairs that could go together logically: fear (*metu*) could be congruent with "a passion for servility" (*libidine seruitii*), but Tacitus opts to keep them separate.

course. Otho might have considered his speech persuasive, but Tacitus does not (Haynes 2003, 4–6). Indirect discourse eliminates the opportunity for Tacitus to present a contrast between what was plausible in Otho's speech and what was believed, and therefore curtails the potential for humor. Finally, *uile iam decus publicum* presents a problem, but a simple one. *Iam* suggests that *decus publicum* was valued at one time, and that it had become devalued.[82] Tacitus no longer refers to an ideal from which the principate has departed, and therefore does not point out what ought to have been; the degraded state of Rome has ceased to be a productive tension and become a mere fact. The humorous passages helped to establish and complicate the operations of the principate, but by the end of Otho's reign the violations are no longer humorous.

In his description of Otho's suicide at Bedriacum, Tacitus resolves the major contradictions in Otho's character. Although family members and freedmen are present at his death (his nephew is upset with his decision; freedmen help confirm his death, 2.48–49), they do not influence his decision to die, which he makes independently and apparently out of concern for the fate of his partisans. He takes responsibility for the deaths of his soldiers and wants to prevent further deaths (2.47.1). Perhaps Otho still could not control his supporters—some kill themselves at his funeral, out of devotion (2.49.4)—but he finally acts as a leader and even displays courage.[83]

---

82. *Decus publicum* parallels the *decus imperii* that Otho flouted at 1.82.1, where Tacitus provided a reason to expect the deterioration of *decus*.

83. Tacitus' version of Otho's death has received considerable scholarly attention as a departure from Tacitus' contemptuous treatment of Otho's life. Harris suggests that Otho's suicide made up for his failures as an emperor (1962, 73). Späth claims that Otho displays "an exemplary masculinity" at his death (2012, 432). Scott points out that Otho's suicide bears some resemblance to a ritual *devotio*, and that Cassius Dio (epitome 63.13.2, by the Leunclavian book division) quotes Otho comparing himself to self-sacrificing Roman heroes, including Decius (1968, 89). Griffin points out that Martial 6.32 compares Otho's death favorably to Cato's, which was considered an exemplary suicide (1986b, 194). Edwards cites the Martial epigram as proof that Otho's suicide was "wholly admirable," although Tacitus has perhaps treated Otho more harshly than other historians did (2007, 38–39). Otho's death may, however, also parallel Catiline's, an equally dramatic but less positive example (Scott 1968, 90). Ash agrees that Otho's suicide is foreshadowed by established elements of his character, but that it is still a surprise (1999, 83–85, 90). Keitel focuses on Otho's rhetoric, calling Otho consistent because his characteristic "boldness" is on display both when he takes power and when he abdicates it. She also sees a parallel with Catiline (1987, 79). Martin sees Otho as a hapless emperor who did finally manage to spare Rome from civil war, to Tacitus' approval (1981, 84); Perkins understands Tacitus as approving of Otho's suicide (1993, 848n4); and Bittarello sees some of his behavior at his death as a reversal of his earlier characterization (2011, 107), while Scott and Plass consider his change of heart too little, too late in a hopelessly degraded era (Scott 1968, 91; Plass 1995, 82).

Conclusion

Tacitus used humor in his characterization of Otho to establish an ongoing tension between power and powerlessness. The pair of opposites are not in themselves amusing, but humor allows Tacitus to present contradictory elements in Otho's character as part of a paradoxically coherent whole. In addition, Tacitus connects the contradictions in Otho's character to those in the principate generally. Although the *Histories* picks up at a point of transition, Tacitus emphasizes the continuity between one set of emperors and the next by emphasizing Otho's connections to Nero, then by drawing out the contradictory expectations that continue to haunt the principate. Tacitus makes use of humor to communicate these ideas, but he decreases the prominence of humor after the point has been made.

TWO

Humor as Precedent

The Trial of Libo Drusus

In this chapter, I examine Tacitus' use of humor in the trial of Libo Drusus, an event rather than a diachronic pattern of characterization. In this episode, which Tacitus describes as a precedent for later treason trials, Libo Drusus is accused of treason and eventually kills himself.[1] Although much of Tacitus' humor is dark, this episode is especially horrific. Some of Tacitus' most pointedly humorous comments serve to highlight the injustice of Libo's treatment and the futility of his suicide, and Libo himself is the target of much of the humor, although he is too pitiable to deserve it by either ancient or modern standards.[2] At best an underachiever in treason, Libo does not fit the script of energetic traitor which the prosecutors attempt to ascribe to him, nor does he live up to the role of historical martyr. Elsewhere in Tacitus, the victims of tyranny come to dignified, exemplary ends,[3] but Libo manages to seem only pathetic, not admirable. "Traitor" and "innocent martyr" are incompatible scripts, and Libo follows patterns typical of each, often at the same time. This creates an ominous form of humor.

The main target of humor in this episode is Tiberius' treason trials, for which Tacitus expresses strong disapproval. Tacitus portrays Libo as too harm-

1. The more common form of the defendant's name was Marcus Scribonius Drusus Libo. Tacitus reverses the order of the last two names. Pettinger summarizes the relevant concerns (2012, 219–20) and credits Weinrib (1968, 262–64) with producing evidence for "Drusus Libo" being the more typical form. Sumner notes that "Libo Drusus" occurs only in Tacitus, while "Drusus Libo" appears elsewhere (1970, 275n113). Because Tacitus reverses the order of the names, and because scholarship on Tacitus usually follows that pattern, I use the name that appears in Tacitus.
2. Cicero (*De Orat.* 2.237) and Quintilian (*Inst.* 6.3.31) advise not to mock the pitiable.
3. Seneca's death is a paradigmatic example (*An.* 15.60–64).

less to prosecute, and thereby suggests that the charges leveled against him were absurd and the legal system inconsistent.[4] Because Libo himself cannot live up to the role of judicial martyr, however, Tacitus' use of humor is double-edged, and Libo becomes a target of humor as well as legal prosecution. Although Tacitus presents Libo as a victim of injustice, he also sees him as an inadequate person worthy of contempt. Libo could not have posed a danger to Tiberius because he was too pathetically incompetent, not because he was remarkably virtuous. The humor in this episode can therefore be especially dark, as Tacitus mocks both imperial politics and the failings of a miserable individual. Nevertheless, this episode uses humor. Like Otho, Libo attempts to fill multiple roles and is consistently inadequate in them. His deficiencies might create humor in themselves as real and ideal scripts overlap in his character, but even more significant is the contrast between his pathetic behavior and the zeal of the Tiberian prosecutors. They portray Libo as a dangerous traitor, a script that bears little resemblance to his conduct, as Tacitus makes clear. Yet even when Libo's pitifulness is revealed, he is prosecuted and punished as if he is a real threat.

Tacitus begins the Libo Drusus episode immediately after a description of Tiberius' conflict with Germanicus, who was at the time conducting a military campaign in Germany. Tiberius sends messages to Germanicus urging him not to overextend his forces by continuing the campaign, then commands him to leave Germany (2.26.2–4). Tacitus concludes that section by saying that Germanicus understood that he was being recalled because of Tiberius' envy (*per inuidiam*, 2.26.5). Tacitus does not explicitly endorse Germanicus' theory, but nor does he deny it, and its presence promotes a sense that Tiberius was jealous of and frustrated with other aristocrats and sought control over other members of the imperial family.[5] Into this paranoid context, Tacitus sets the prosecution of Libo Drusus.

In contrast to Germanicus, Libo Drusus does not seem to have done much of note. He was, however, another scion of Augustus' family and roughly the same age as Germanicus (Pettinger 2012, 232). Specifically, Libo was the grandnephew of Augustus' first wife, Scribonia (2.27.1–2). He has already been accused of treason when he first appears in Tacitus, and it seems that if Tacitus

4. Indeed, Tacitus frequently notes the absurdity of the imperial legal system (Plass 1988, 65–67). Libo's trial introduces ideas central to Tacitus' criticisms.

5. Goodyear suggests that Tiberius' true motivation in recalling Germanicus was to derail his impractical plan to conquer Germany (1981, 2.26.2–5). Although this is a plausible explanation for Tiberius' reprimand, I do not think Tacitus makes it necessary, and indeed Goodyear draws from Suetonius to construct the theory.

had meant to imply that Libo had committed treason, he might have provided the pertinent details of that treason rather than of the accusation.[6] Instead, Tacitus interrupts his introduction of Libo Drusus to explain the proceedings against him: "The beginning, course, and end of the proceedings I shall discuss with particular care, because then were first discovered the elements which during so many years gnawed away at the state" (*eius negotii initium ordinem finem curatius disseram, quia tum primum reperta sunt, quae per tot annos rem publicam exedere*, 2.27.1).[7] Tacitus frames the episode as significant for its future implications, not because Libo is significant in himself. Tacitus emphasizes this case's impact on future treason trials, not the potential impact of treason on Rome.[8] The episode is therefore framed from the start as programmatic rather than specific, and Libo's treason (if there was any—other evidence suggests that there probably was) is less damaging than his trial was.[9] Libo Drusus is not significant for his accomplishments, but because of the precedent set by his trial.[10] He is the center of events but has little personal agency, nor is his char-

6. Tacitus was capable of writing a less ambiguous narrative of rebellion. For example, his summary of the life of Aelius Sejanus at the start of Book 4 flatly declares that he had designs on imperial power (4.1.1–3). There follow several pages of details. Sejanus is a more significant historical figure than Libo, yet the level of clarity that Tacitus provides about him shows that the historian was not automatically cagey about the guilt or innocence of prospective usurpers. In another example, Tacitus treats the Pisonian conspiracy against Nero as a fact, although its origins are obscure (15.49.1). Even in smaller episodes, Tacitus can make his opinion clear. He says that Plautius Silvanus certainly threw his wife from a height for no clear reason, that the most convincing evidence of this narrative was confirmed by Tiberius (!), and that his previous wife was found not guilty of bewitching him (4.22.1–2). Tacitus could have presented Libo's case damningly, but he chose instead to keep the facts vague.
7. Unless otherwise noted, I use Woodman's 2004 translation of the *Annals*.
8. Tacitus makes the *maiestas* trials a major event. Martin finds them foreshadowed also at the end of Book 1 (1981, 118–19).
9. Tacitus is also more interested in this episode than Suetonius and Cassius Dio are and devotes an unusual amount of space to its implications for the Senate (Baar 1990, 97).
10. Libo's historical innocence or guilt is unclear. Tacitus rarely lists any of the major charges brought during *maiestas* trials, nor does he provide much evidence, and in Libo's case he minimizes the seriousness of the charges (Rogers 1952, 281–82, 310–11, 285). Walker argues that Libo's case would not have been taken so seriously if the charges against him were not grave, but that Tacitus allows his readers to forget about the charges (1952, 93). Shotter considers the possibility that Tacitus concealed Libo's guilt on purpose (1972, 88). Rutledge notes that Catus and Fulcinius Trio were able to gather incriminating evidence independently of each other, making Libo's guilt more likely (2001, 160). Pettinger argues that Tacitus' portrayal of Libo as a hapless innocent is false and that in fact Libo probably did support a revolt against Tiberius (2012, 1). Levick says that Libo "certainly" wanted to overthrow Tiberius and that the charge against him would not properly have been *maiestas* but revolution (2013, 45–46). Márványos considers a variety of ancient and modern sources to conclude that Libo's trial involved new precedents meant to intimidate Tiberius' enemies (2015, 163–76). Among the ancients, Suetonius briefly but unambiguously incriminates Libo (*Tiberius* 25), and Velleius Paterculus says that Libo conspired against the emperor and that Tiberius dealt with him justly (2.129.2, 2.130.3). There is reason to believe that

acter essentially interesting to Tacitus. From the start, Tacitus presents Libo as an insignificant cipher at the center of one of the first Tiberian treason trials, and it is the treason trials, as much as their first defendant, that are criticized with humor in this episode.

After Libo's introduction, Tacitus lays out the mildly subversive pursuits in which Libo was induced to engage by his friend Firmius Catus (2.27.2):

> Firmius Catus, a senator, from Libo's closest circle of friends, impelled the young man—misguided as he was, and susceptible to illusions—to resort to the promises of the Chaldaeans, the rites of magicians, and even the interpreters of dreams, while at the same time he kept pointing to his great-grandfather Pompeius, his great-aunt Scribonia (who had once been Augustus' spouse), his cousins the Caesars, and his house full of images; and he encouraged him into luxuriousness and debt, acting as the partner of his lusts and obligations in order to entrap him by additional evidence.
>
> *Firmius Catus senator, ex intima Libonis amicitia, iuuenem improuidum et facilem inanibus ad Chaldaeorum promissa, magorum sacra, somniorum etiam interpretes impulit, dum proauum Pompeium, amitam Scriboniam, quae quondam Augusti coniunx fuerat, consobrinos Caesares, plenam imaginibus domum ostentat hortaturque ad luxum et aes alienum, socius libidinum et necessitatum, quo pluribus indiciis inligaret.*

This complex sentence deserves close attention. Instead of focusing on Libo, it shifts attention to the character and activities of Firmius Catus, the subject of the sentence to Libo's object. The syntax is significant because it reflects Catus' blatant manipulation of Libo. Catus acts; Libo reacts. Although Libo cannot perceive Catus' sinister intentions, Tacitus' readers can. Catus encourages Libo's three most incriminating traits: his consultation of fortune-tellers, his connections to the imperial family, and his unsustainable lifestyle. Tacitus affirms that these practices were fact but presents them as innocent until Catus cast them in a malicious light. Tacitus lays responsibility for the substance of the treason

Libo planned a revolt against Tiberius. My discussion, however, focuses on the impression of Libo that Tacitus creates regardless of the historical truth of Libo's guilt or innocence, and Martin has summarized that impression beautifully: "it is wholly unlikely that Libo Drusus had the competence to plot effectively against the emperor, though that does not mean that he did not toy with half-baked schemes that could be construed as treasonable" (1981, 121).

allegations on Catus, whom he calls not only Libo's friend but "from Libo's closest circle of friends." The impression of Catus is highly negative.[11]

Libo, in contrast, seems less malicious than duped.[12] Tacitus calls him *improuidus* and *facilis inanibus*, both of which confirm his poor judgment.[13] *Inanibus* is also interesting because although its meaning is tied to *facilis*, it immediately precedes the three types of divination in which Libo engages (*inanibus ad Chaldaeorum*, etc.). Tacitus does not draw a direct equivalence between "illusions" (*inanibus*) and the occupations of astrologers, *magi*, and dream interpreters, but he implies a connection through the proximity of the words. If the three methods of divination are *inania*, they are implicitly not worthy of serious concern.[14] Divination was sometimes considered treasonous in ancient Rome, and Tiberius was an astrology enthusiast,[15] but Tacitus implies that all these forms of divination are nonsense.[16] Although Tacitus presents divination as trivial, its ineffectiveness does not diminish the seriousness of Catus' exploitation of his friend Libo. In addition, Catus seems to have gone to some effort to overdetermine Libo's guilt by asking him to consult several types of diviner. If Libo had asked treasonous questions, he could presumably have been condemned for doing that once as easily as for doing so four times. In fact, Tacitus does not say what Catus alleged that Libo asked these diviners, making it possible that Libo asked innocent or merely stupid questions. Tacitus establishes a stark contrast between Libo's behavior and the image of him conjured by his accusers.

Tacitus similarly undercuts Catus' insinuation that Libo's distinguished

---

11. Catus was expelled from the Senate for making a false *maiestas* charge, a fact that Tacitus mentions later (4.31.4) and which Koestermann understands as central to Tacitus' construction of his character (1963, 2.27.2).
12. Libo may also be outright dim (Gärtner 2010, 414).
13. *Inania* is difficult to translate precisely. Furneaux translates it as "empty projects" (1896, *ad loc*). Goodyear uses "idle illusions" (1981, *ad loc*). Michael Grant translates it as "absurdities" (1996, 90). Tacitus also uses *inania* to describe the false charges brought by Nero against Lucius Silanus (*inania simul et falsa*, *An.* 16.8.1).
14. The Roman legal system could treat magic as a serious crime (Rutledge 2001, 88–89). Nevertheless, Tacitus seems to disdain the charge of magic against Libo.
15. Later, Lollia Paulina would be charged with seeking prophecy from "Chaldeans" and "magicians" at the behest of Agrippina the Younger (12.22.1). Lollia's questions were apparently about her chance of marrying rather than becoming emperor, but nevertheless the accusations led to her death (12.22.3). Tiberius' interest in and association with astrology is documented in multiple ancient sources. Tacitus mentions that Tiberius practiced astrology personally (*An.* 6.20.2).
16. Tacitus' contempt for divination may be influenced by its perceived foreignness; all these methods were associated with the Near East (Furneaux 1896, 2.27.2). Disdain for foreigners could compound Tacitus' contempt or simply reflect the common perception that astrologers were foreign (Ripat 2011, 128).

ancestry would lead him to think of usurpation. The gist of the accusation is unsurprising. Male members of the imperial family who might aspire to the principate were often considered threats by Julio-Claudian emperors.[17] Libo's named ancestors, however, are not stellar connections to the imperial family. Libo was descended from Pompeius Magnus through Sextus Pompeius.[18] Although both were powerful generals, they were also defeated enemies of Julius Caesar and Augustus. These ancestors do not support the idea that Libo was an important member of the imperial bloodline, and although they might support an accusation that he was likely to rebel against the emperor, that is not the narrative that Catus foregrounds. Instead, he plays up Libo's relation to Augustus' second wife, Scribonia. Even as Tacitus focalizes this detail through Catus, he makes it sound tendentious by calling her "Scribonia (who had once been Augustus' spouse)" (*Scriboniam, quae quondam Augusti coniunx fuerat*, 2.27.2). Scribonia was the mother of Augustus' sole surviving biological child, Julia, and therefore the ancestor of all his natural descendants, but she was also the woman Augustus summarily divorced in favor of Livia.[19] It was Livia, not Scribonia, who became empress, whose image was reproduced in imperial portraiture, who was awarded the title Augusta at Augustus' death, whose son succeeded Augustus, and who was later deified.[20] (Livia was alive and influential at the time of Libo's trial.) Libo's connection to the imperial family through Scribonia would have had little relevance compared to Tiberius' much stronger claim as the son of Augustus and Livia. Tacitus introduces Libo as one of the

17. There are several instances of this phenomenon in the *Annals*. Britannicus is a prominent example as Claudius' son and a major political rival to Nero (13.14–13.15), but others, such as Torquatus Silanus (16.7–16.8), are perceived as threats despite more distant relationships to the imperial family.

18. Rutledge doubts that Libo's lineage was distinguished enough to present a threat to Tiberius when Germanicus was still alive (2001, 160). Pettinger provides two appendices on Libo's family (2012, 219–34). He argues that the family was distinguished on both sides and that evidence of Scribonia's closeness with her daughter and granddaughter suggests that Libo's branch of the family would have frequently interacted with their imperial cousins (2012, 225, 230). Although Pettinger's analysis is compelling, it is derived from scholarship and multiple primary sources, not exclusively from Tacitus. Tacitus puts no glorious cast on Libo's ancestry and may even have minimized the importance of his lineage on purpose.

19. Augustus and Scribonia married in 40 BCE and divorced in 39, when Augustus immediately married Livia (*Oxford Classical Dictionary*, "Scribonia"). Cassius Dio specifies that Augustus divorced Scribonia the day their daughter was born (48.34.3), that is, as soon as possible.

20. There is ample evidence of Livia's extremely high status. Corbier comments that although Tiberius was displeased by the Senate's offer to add "Julia's [i.e., Livia's] son" to his imperial titles, the proposal itself suggests that his familial relationship with Livia helped legitimate his principate (1995, 186). Coinage in the Roman East adopted Livia's image in parallel with that of Augustus (Severy 2003, 114–15). Harvey contends that coin portraits reinforced Livia's image as an imperial wife and mother and later as a goddess (2020, 6).

powerful Scribonii (Pettinger 2012, 224–25), but many belonged to that *gens*. Ultimately, Libo remains an undistinguished character who could pose little threat to Tiberius.

Catus insists on the prominence of Libo's family to Libo himself, presumably because Catus wanted to goad Libo into doing something treasonous. By focalizing these arguments through Catus, Tacitus foreshadows the prosecutors' argument that Libo presents a risk of treason; Libo is from a distinguished family adjacent to the emperor's, he spends more money than he can afford to, and he consults fortune-tellers. These characteristics are liable to indicate treason in Tacitus' *Histories*, where Otho spends too much and consults astrologers immediately before deciding to become emperor (*Hist.* 1.21–1.22). Simultaneously, however, Tacitus sows another possible interpretation, in which all these qualities are simply frivolous, or even comical. Consulting fortune-tellers is a mere "illusion," Libo's aristocratic ancestry is less politically useful than Catus makes it out to be, and spending too much money is as characteristic of comedy's *adulescens* as it is of a future emperor. The contrast between treason and innocuous frivolity creates absurdity in Tacitus' portrait of Libo and sets up expectations that carry into future *maiestas* trials. The flimsy basis of the charges against Libo will be repeated later.[21]

Finally, this paragraph removes Libo's agency, making Catus the impetus for his quasi-treasonable behavior. Catus is the subject of the sentence and, as the final clause reveals, he is responsible for guiding Libo in a perilous direction for the purpose of denouncing him later. Tacitus makes Catus out to be an untrustworthy figure, and in addition he suggests that Catus' behavior was more dishonest than Libo's. Although Catus did not aspire to the principate, he encouraged Libo's ambition, which he would later frame as subversive.[22] By this

21. *Maiestas* was not a new charge, but Tacitus represents the increased prominence of *delatores* as an innovation of Tiberius' regime (Walker 1952, 84–92). *Delatores* already existed, but their influence probably did increase during the early principate (Robinson 2007, 207, 214–15). It is also possible that Libo was not prosecuted under the *maiestas* law but instead as a magician or conspirator, under a different statute but for the same behavior (Rutledge 2001, 159).

22. Tacitus attributes great importance to the councilors of would-be emperors in the *Histories*. Conflicts between Titus Vinius and Cornelius Laco determined many of Galba's policies (1.6, 1.13, 1.33–34), and without Valens and Caecina, Tacitus implies, Vitellius would never have stirred to become emperor (1.52). Also notable are several advisers to Vespasian, including Mucianus, the governor of Syria to whom Tacitus attributes the power to select an emperor (1.10) and who later helps persuade Vespasian into taking action (2.77–78). There is no direct parallel in the *Annals*, but Nero's accession is engineered by Agrippina with the complicity of her domestic staff (12.66–67). Tacitus therefore lays much blame on the supporters of aspiring emperors, rather than on the emperors themselves.

measure, Catus did more to subvert the principate than Libo did. Worse in Tacitus' view is Catus' intention to betray Libo's friendship. As the plot unfolds, Libo becomes a hapless dupe in Catus' scheme. Although Tacitus treats Libo's allegedly treasonous activity as frivolous and nonthreatening, he suggests that Catus' scheming was a real threat to elite friendship. Whether Libo's behavior is treasonous or innocuous, Catus presents a danger to Roman traditions. Catus' insistence that Libo is a threat clashes with Tacitus' implication that Libo was merely gullible. That contrast may not quite rise to the level of humor, but it establishes Libo's essential character (weak, suggestible) and the character that prosecutors will impute to him (ruthless, ambitious). These two scripts are incompatible and will develop into a humorous contrast during Libo's trial.

By presenting two incompatible characterizations of Libo, Tacitus illustrates the incongruities that underpin the *maiestas* trials. Much of the evidence put forward by Catus as incriminating is treated as insignificant by Tacitus. The trials are cruel because they provide a monetary incentive to betray friends and partake in a circular logic by which accusers are so eager to detect treason that they fabricate it. Libo's trial is the first of the treason trials, but Tacitus uses a similar framework when he discusses later trials. The humorous contradictions here foreshadow Tacitus' scathing portrayal of later trials. Without detailing why accusations of *maiestas* could get out of control, Tacitus economically shows the frivolity of the accusations against Libo. Humor and irony play a significant part in establishing the irrationality of the later treason trials.

Tiberius' initial reaction to Catus' accusations reinforces the sense that Libo was not a serious threat. Catus introduces his evidence carefully. He gathers witnesses, including slaves, who will confirm his accusations and enlists Flaccus Vescularius as an intermediary to the emperor (2.28.1). Tiberius' response, however, is characteristically inscrutable. Instead of openly accusing Libo of the crimes which Catus suggests he committed, Tiberius treats Libo with a measure of favor, either because he needed time to consider the charges or because he wanted to draw Libo out: "Caesar, while not spurning the evidence, declined a meeting [with Catus]" (*Caesar indicium haud aspernatus congressus abnuit*, 2.28.2). *Haud aspernatus* is a wonderfully ambiguous description of Tiberius' reaction in that it could indicate either a plain fact or that Tiberius was interested in the case despite declining to address it directly. On the one hand, Tiberius might have considered the matter beneath his attention. On the other, he could have taken it seriously and devised a complex plot against Libo's machinations.[23] Whatever his intentions, Tiberius' reaction is less than transparent. He makes Libo a praetor, which seems to aid neither plan—if Libo was plotting treason, advancement to a praetorship seems unlikely to change that, and if he was not, Tiberius had no reason to pay special attention to him.[24] Tacitus implies that Tiberius encouraged Libo to be confident of imperial favor and therefore careless about committing treason, but he does not clarify why Tiberius would have wanted that. It is further baffling that after deciding not to personally question Libo about the accusations, Tiberius instead "invited him to parties, and was neither estranged from him in looks nor more volatile in language (he had so buried his anger)" (*conuictibus adhibet, non uultu alienatus, non uerbis commotior (adeo iram condiderat)*, 2.28.2). Here Tacitus illustrates Tiberius' anger at Libo but still portrays him as doing the opposite of what Catus might have expected him to do. He socializes with Libo instead of having him prosecuted or acting aggressively toward him.[25] Much of this behavior could be attributed to Tiberius' scheming, but Tacitus does not indicate that Tiberius ever pushed for Libo to be tried for treason.[26] Catus and the prosecutors who joined him later are framed as most responsible.

Tiberius' reaction to this initial accusation of treason, then, was to favor the accused and ignore the problem. Whether or not Tiberius believed Libo was plotting treason, he did not treat him as an imminent threat. Rather, Tiberius appeared more interested in allowing the conspiracy to play out than in preventing it. The emperor's indifference might even imply that Libo was innocent (Gärtner 2010, 415). If Tiberius saw Libo as an immediate problem, this is an

23. Either interpretation would be compatible with Tacitus' narrative. As often, Tiberius' motivations are difficult to determine and possibly concealed on purpose by either Tiberius or Tacitus (or both). Here, Tacitus provides little evidence that Tiberius took any action, and the main cause for suspicion against him is his characterization elsewhere in the *Annals* (Walker 1952, 94, 98–99). Baar suggests that Tacitus takes advantage of the *maiestas* trials to portray Tiberius as cruel and out of step with the aristocracy (1990, 90), which is consistent with his characterization here.
24. Libo was already assigned a praetorship by Augustus (Levick 2013, 48–49), but Tacitus does not record this detail.
25. Goodyear interprets Tiberius' hesitation as normal: "If Libo wanted to hang himself, was Tiberius to refuse him enough rope?" (1981, 2.28.2). Goodyear is correct that Libo might have incriminated himself had he been allowed more time, but I do not see why Tiberius would have waited for further evidence if he was already convinced of Libo's treason, nor does Tacitus' Tiberius later hesitate to support unfair prosecutions. Tiberius' reaction indicates a lack of urgency about an ostensibly serious matter.
26. Although Tacitus has a reputation for criticism of Tiberius, other sources do suggest that Tiberius encouraged the trial (Gärtner 2010, 416). Perhaps Tacitus expects that his audience will understand Tiberius to be guilty, but even if Tiberius wishes death on Libo, the signs he gives are unclear (O'Gorman 2000, 84).

incomprehensible reaction, especially if we understand Tiberius as the paranoid instigator of the *maiestas* trials. Tacitus could also have provided a compelling reason for Tiberius' hesitation, as Suetonius did. He reports that Tiberius was not sufficiently entrenched as *princeps* to challenge Libo at this time (*Tiberius* 25). Tacitus declines to provide any such explanation. Instead, I argue, Tacitus describes Tiberius' reaction so that it seems he either did not believe Libo was organizing a conspiracy or he believed that Libo's conspiracy was not a serious threat.[27] If even Tiberius did not believe Libo was dangerous, the reaction of the prosecutors is even more ludicrously exaggerated.

Despite Tiberius' indifference, Libo attracts trouble when one of his fortune-tellers, "a certain Junius" (*Iunius quidam*), reports that Libo asked him to consult the spirits of the dead. Junius denounces Libo to Fulcinius Trio, an infamous *delator* (2.28.2–3). Tacitus makes no connection between Tiberius and the fortune-teller. "A certain Junius" is an unusually vague introduction even for a minor figure,[28] and Fulcinius Trio, although connected to Tiberius, is not apparently acting on Tiberius' orders. Tacitus never specifically denies that Tiberius conspired with a *delator* and "some Junius" to bring a case against Libo, but that possibility seems unnecessarily complicated.[29] In addition, Tacitus does not report Libo's questions for the dead, although the content of the questions could have been material to a treason charge (Pettinger 2012, 26–27).

Even though Tiberius appears not to have immediately reacted against Libo, the timing makes little difference to the outcome of the trial. The informers already have their business down to a science. The *delatores* are so intent on the prosecution that Firmius Catus, the original plotter, competes with several others, including Trio, for the right to prosecute Libo (2.30.1). There is subtle

---

27. The alleged crime was serious, but Tiberius seems not to have believed in it. Libo may not have been guilty (Gärtner 2010, 415). Tiberius' early indifference to the accusation stands in contrast to his stance during the trial.

28. Minor characters are often introduced with a quick note on their usefulness. Locusta, mentioned at 13.15.3, is a convicted poisoner; Otho's counselor Ptolemaeus is an astrologer who accompanied Otho to Spain (*Histories* 1.22.2); and Onomastus is contextualized as Otho's freedman (*Histories* 1.27.1). Other minor characters are described in a word or two: Eucaerus is an Alexandrian *tibicen* (14.60.2); the false Postumus Agrippa is a slave called Clemens (2.39.1). Junius has no characteristics ascribed to him. Tacitus does not even confirm that calling up ghosts was his profession.

29. Presumably Trio would not have prosecuted Libo had he not believed that Tiberius would accept the prosecution, but nor would he have required an imperial command to bring the case. Tacitus suggests that Trio brought his accusation directly to the Senate without consulting Tiberius. Because Tacitus rarely spares Tiberius from suspicion, it is unlikely that he wants his readers to find a conspiracy here.

humor in the rivalry between prosecutors. Catus' carefully collected evidence is suddenly nearly stolen by another accuser on the hunt for a windfall of incriminating information. Tacitus gradually increases the number of people poised to profit from alleged treason. The effect is at once ominous, as if the prosecutors were vultures circling above a dying animal, and ridiculous, because Libo attracts so much attention despite his insignificance. Again, Tacitus emphasizes the contrast between the reality of Libo's ineffectiveness and the fantastical narrative constructed by the prosecutors. The legal system appears susceptible to manipulation by the worst people and prone to focus on low-hanging fruit rather than on credible accusations.

Libo, meanwhile, panics. According to Tacitus, Libo took steps to make himself pitiable, but Tacitus makes his dramatized misery ridiculous: "Libo meanwhile, having changed his clothing, made a round of the houses with leading ladies, besought his in-laws and demanded a voice to protect him against danger—only to be met with universal refusal and, despite the different pretexts, identical alarm" (*Libo interim ueste mutata cum primoribus feminis circumire domos, orare adfines, uocem aduersum pericula poscere, abnuentibus cunctis, cum diuersa praetenderent, eadem formidine*, 2.29.1). Without denying the potential pathos of Libo's situation, Tacitus accumulates details about Libo's conduct that conflict with the informers' characterization of him as a dangerous traitor. Rather than dangerous, Tacitus' Libo is overwhelmingly pathetic. Appealing to relatives for pity is the resort of someone without resources.[30] If Libo's relatives fear to support him in court, it seems unlikely that they would have supported a coup on his behalf.[31]

Tacitus implies that Libo put on a pitiable façade to manipulate people into supporting him, which in another character might suggest that he was a canny criminal, not least because his behavior includes ancient tropes associated with evoking pity in a problematic legal case (Woodman 2004, 53n32). Contrary to that possibility, Tacitus uses this incident to demonstrate Libo's ineffectiveness. Appealing to relatives for pity is the resort of someone without his own resources, and Libo cannot generate sympathy even among his own relatives. Tacitus takes advantage of the contrast between Libo, the conniving conspirator

30. Santoro L'Hoir also identifies a theatrical motif in Libo's change of costume (2006, 221), which may relate to the parallels between performance and deception that occur elsewhere in the *Annals*.

31. The verb *circumire* also has a connotation related to canvassing for political office (*OLD circumeo* def. 6c). Libo is engaged in political activity here, but he is unsuccessful.

(advanced by the prosecutors) and Libo, the disorganized fool (advanced by the substance of Tacitus' narrative). Had Libo desired to commit treason (and Tacitus has already cast doubt on that premise), he would certainly have been incapable of gathering support for a successful conspiracy. Tacitus refuses to clearly exculpate Libo, but he also makes it impossible to understand Libo as a true villain. Whatever Libo's faults (and there are plenty), he is not a serious threat to the principate, and the prosecutors' reaction is again revealed to be extreme.

Instead of exploring the facts of the case, Tacitus repeatedly emphasizes Libo's helplessness. That he asks multiple relatives for their help is only the earliest sign that Libo cannot muster a serious defense. Tacitus adds that Libo was either sick or feigned sickness at an initial hearing before the Senate (2.29.2). Libo's sickness, real or feigned, introduces another element of potential deception.[32] Humor and deception often go together in Tacitus, and deception is especially prominent in Tacitus' treatment of Tiberius.[33] Tiberius' obvious dishonesty trumps Libo's possible malingering. When Libo pleads for his life, Tiberius betrays no facial expression and "recited the documents and authorities, controlling himself in this way so that he would seem neither to soften nor to sharpen the charges"[34] (*libellos et auctores recitat* [. . .] *ita moderans, ne lenire neue asperare crimina uideretur*, 2.29.2). Tiberius remains unmoved in the face of Libo's dramatics. Tacitus does not give a reason that Tiberius would have concealed his opinions on Libo, but that makes his apparent deception even more difficult to understand and plays up the contrast between their characters.

Libo's distress is the antithesis of Tiberius' calm (Shotter 1972, 90–91), but Tiberius' calm, too, is deceptive. Earlier in the episode, Tacitus described

32. The possibility that Libo was dishonest also decreases any pity that Tacitus might have sown earlier (Shotter 1972, 90). Or perhaps Libo's dishonesty is grounds for pity in itself (Goodyear 1981, 2.29.2).

33. Especially relevant is a chapter in O'Gorman's *Irony and Misreading in the "Annals" of Tacitus* in which she describes Tiberius as the object of constant reading and misreading by other characters. Tiberius is difficult to understand in part because the momentary revelations of his true opinions are so destabilizing that complete ignorance of his wishes would be preferable (2000, 78–105). On the other hand, Woodman cautions against assuming that Tiberius always lies (1998, 42–43, 63). Although Woodman brings up important caveats, the Libo Drusus episode explicitly looks ahead to future trials and therefore can be fairly compared to later characterizations of Tiberius.

34. I have altered Woodman's translation to indicate that Tacitus implies a bit more conscious intention on Tiberius' part in the purpose clause. I am aware of Goodyear's comment that *moderans* should be translated as "directing himself" or "following a (middle) course" and that a translation like "controlling" is too strong (1981, 2.29.2), but I think the stronger translation is warranted.

Tiberius as outwardly calm but secretly fuming (2.28.2). Here, Tiberius is possibly still furious at Libo for the same crime. Despite his grudge against Libo, Tiberius behaves indifferently, neither changing his expression nor appearing to influence the trial (2.29.2). Tiberius' hypocrisy has a notable position in this programmatic episode. First, Tacitus demonstrates the contradiction with unusual clarity. He assesses Tiberius' feelings before the trial and at the trial, without his usual ambiguity. Tiberius has a strong opinion, so therefore his apparent indifference is a façade. His fabricated reaction promulgates a persona of self-control and fairness, but Tacitus has already undermined this persona.

Crucially, the Senate recognizes that Tiberius' indifference is a fraud. The senators are Tiberius' primary audience for his façade of justice, but also for his hidden message that Libo should be dealt with harshly. The senators apparently understand both the explicit and implicit parts of Tiberius' message. They must understand that Tiberius meant for Libo to be condemned because they condemn him hyperbolically at his death. They also pretend, however, that Libo's trial exemplifies impartial justice.[35] Tacitus will criticize the Senate for flattering the emperor, but in this passage the emperor's and the senators' behavior reinforce each other. Tiberius is not directly responsible for the posthumous verdict of the Senate, nor is the Senate responsible for Tiberius' encouragement of unfair prosecutions, but their combined behavior demonstrates a type of non-explicit, ironic communication much like the one Nero will later use with his underlings. It also sets the stage for later *maiestas* trials.[36] The façade of justice has been revealed to be a façade. Tacitus constructs a sharp contrast between Tiberius' bias, which is obvious to a reader, and his dissembling, which suffices to communicate both his true intentions and his desired excuse to the Senate. In this passage, the ironic element does not necessarily constitute humor, but the mechanisms of the trial provide a contradictory background that explains how a false impression of Libo could have been accepted.

---

35. Bhatt argues that Tacitus frames Tiberius' tyranny as a system in which laws encourage corruption and the corruption of senators in turn reinforces Tiberius' power (2017, 311). The Senate's flaws and Tiberius' faults are, therefore, difficult to distinguish, and both parties can deny responsibility.

36. Although both Senate and emperor are involved, Tacitus lays greater blame on Tiberius than on the Senate. Individual senators, including Catus, acted as informers and prosecutors, but the Senate as a body does not appear in the narrative until the trial, and then Tacitus suggests that they would not go against Tiberius' wishes, even when those wishes were deliberately obfuscated. Tacitus disapproves of the Senate's obsequious behavior toward Tiberius but emphasizes it only later, when the Senate reinforces the verdict against Libo by decreeing celebrations (2.32.1–2). Tacitus assigns less responsibility to the Senate but still blames them for abdicating responsibility.

The political illogic of Libo's trial should tear the proceeding apart, but the prosecution remains strong in contrast to its victim's weakness. Libo seems defeated from the inception of the charges against him, as evidenced by Catus' meticulous plotting, but several other prosecutors join the case even though securing a conviction will not be difficult. The multi-prosecutor pile-up was foreshadowed in chapter 28, when Trio became involved in the case, and at Libo's trial the many prosecutors are just as unnecessary as they seemed then. Catus had managed to be included in the prosecution at the trial, as had Fonteius Agrippa and Caius Vibius. (Tacitus does not explain how the last two joined the case.)[37] They argue over the right to speak the main oration because that speaker has the most to gain from the case: "they started competing for the prerogative of declaiming against the defendant, until finally Vibius, on the grounds that they would not yield to one another and that Libo had entered without an advocate, pronounced that he would lay down the charges individually" (*certabantque cui ius perorandi in reum daretur, donec Vibius, quia nec ipsi inter se concederent et Libo sine patrono introisset, singillatim se crimina obiecturum professus*, 2.30.1). Their argument highlights the imbalance of power between the prosecution and the defendant. While the prosecutors argue about the right to read the charges, Libo, who is too powerless to find allies and too sick to walk, has no legal backup (*sine patrono*, 2.30.1). Again, Tacitus emphasizes the incongruity between the charges brought by the prosecutors and Libo's actual behavior. In contrast to the prosecutors who insist on the seriousness of their case, Libo is at best a soft target and perhaps even innocent. Libo is more incompetent than pitiable, but there is a strong contrast between the threat he is reputed to be and his behavior as reported by Tacitus. Without making a joke per se, Tacitus

37. Tacitus follows up on the careers of the last two prosecutors. Fonteius Agrippa stayed in Tiberius' favor long enough for Tiberius to provide his daughter with a dowry after she was passed over to become a Vestal Virgin (2.86.1–2). Vibius Serenus was exiled for inflicting corporal punishment on a Roman citizen without due process (4.13.2; Furneaux 1896, *ad loc*). Later, he was recalled so that he could be prosecuted by his own son on charges that included a conspiracy to murder the emperor and incite a revolution (4.28.1–3). Serenus defended himself by challenging his son to produce co-conspirators. When the son named two of Tiberius' close friends, Tiberius became uncomfortable, and the son attempted to abandon the trial after being unable to continue it based on the evidence of slaves (4.29.1). The trial was continued after the son was "dragged back from Ravenna" (*retractus Rauenna*), apparently because Tiberius openly hated Serenus (4.29.2–3). In the end, Serenus was condemned to return to exile (4.30.1), yet his trial constitutes an interesting callback to Libo's because both involve the testimony of slaves, the possible fabrication of a conspiracy, and Tiberius as the guiding will behind a legal process. Tacitus' later comments on Vibius Serenus illustrate the afterlife of Libo's trial and cultivate a sense that prosecutors might suffer dramatically for their part in these trials, but even that would not constitute justice.

suggests that the situation is so rife with contradictions as to be humorous—the prosecution is patently overzealous, and the defendant is not only less dangerous than their reaction suggests, but perhaps not dangerous at all.

Much of the evidence presented against Libo is similarly laughable. Tacitus says that Serenus, who read the charges, "produced documents of such derangement as to indicate that Libo had consulted whether he would have the wealth to cover over the Appian Way right to Brundisium with money. The other contents too were of this type—empty, stupid, and, if you interpreted more leniently, pitiable" (*protulit libellos uecordes adeo, ut consultauerit Libo, an habiturus foret opes, quis uiam Appiam Brundisium usque pecunia operiret. inerant et alia huiusce modi stolida uana, si mollius acciperes, miseranda*, 2.30.1–2). Tacitus presents this accusation as absurd.[38] Even if Libo did ask a fortune-teller this question, it barely resembles the inquiry of a competent adult. The prosecutors seem to be implying that Libo asked whether he would gain great wealth as a veiled way to uncover a possible imperial destiny, but the phrasing of the question does not support the idea that Libo meant to conceal his malice. Instead, it makes his ambitions sound unrealistic and incoherent. Enough money to cover a long road is a fanciful rather than practical wish that cannot be connected to the principate without a significant leap of logic. A person who expresses such a wish is probably not thinking strategically about how to become emperor. By reporting the charge in these terms, Tacitus again makes the charges against Libo seem humorous.[39]

Tacitus spells out the absurdity of other charges against Libo as well. Some of the evidence is in "deranged" documents (*uecordes*). *Vecors* is a strong word. The evidence is not simply false but so false that it seems incompatible with reality.[40] Similarly *alia* [. . .] *stolida uana* is more than a statement that the accusations were false.[41] *Stolida* is another unusually strong term. The evidence

38. "This accusation arguably supports, rather than refutes, Libo's innocence, due to its absurdity" (Márványos 2015, 165). Seager calls this evidence "utterly absurd" (2005, 75), Syme calls it "poor stuff, and childish" (1958, 399), and Goodyear calls it "particularly absurd" (1981, 2.30.2).

39. Presumably, Tacitus elided charges related to predicting the future of the emperor or the empire (Maiuri 2012, 91).

40. *Vecordes* could also be a transferred epithet for Libo's derangement (*Lexicon Taciteum*, *vecors*), which is certainly how the prosecutors want the evidence to be perceived, but the adjective more directly applies to the improbability of the evidence (Bhatt 2017, 316).

41. The *Lexicon Taciteum* categorizes *uana* here as belonging to a special sense that specifically means "stupidly ambitious" (*stulte ambitiosus*). Although this is the impression that Libo's accusers wish to cultivate, I prefer the possibility that *uana* here means "groundless" (*OLD vanus* definition 3, which includes an example from *An.* 4.59.1, where it is applied to rumors). My interpretation is supported by its use in close context with *stolida*, which does not appear to mean "stupidly

against Libo, in Tacitus' view, actually strains credulity. Tacitus' tone is polemical rather than humorous, insofar as he presents the evidence as a sham. He ends the sentence, however, by adding that Libo's alleged actions were "pitiable" (*miseranda*), if considered more tolerantly. *Miseranda*, the last word in the sentence, might not quite be a punchline, yet it is a final, surprising reminder of the interpretation of Libo that Tacitus has constructed in opposition to the one conjured by the prosecutors. Again, Tacitus draws a contrast between Libo the purported traitor and Libo the hapless young man.[42] The accusations against Libo range from totally implausible to pitiable, but none are convincing. Tacitus provides several reasons that Libo's predicament might outrage the reader, but he also suggests that it might provoke humor. Tacitus' indignant tone emphasizes that Libo's death was an injustice and a precedent for further injustices, but that does not eliminate humor, because the trial was not only unjust, but it was obviously so.[43] Libo's trial is not merely an act of imperial tyranny but the result of the Senate's acceptance of tyrannical rule. The humorous contrast that Tacitus has built between Libo-as-traitor and Libo-as-hapless underscores the injustice committed against him. Without the humorous contrast, however, it might not be clear that Libo was harmless, nor that the Senate's condemnation of him was based on evidence that should have been disregarded.

Tacitus includes a final humorous condemnation of injustice in his description of the evidence that sealed Libo's conviction. Mysterious marks in Libo's handwriting were found on a single document (2.30.2). Tacitus does not seem convinced that the marks were necessarily sinister (Furneaux 1896, *ad loc*), but the Senate takes the marks as conclusive.[44] Because Libo denied

---

ambitious" either in Tacitus or in Latin generally. Koestermann suggests that *stolida uana* refers to Libo's deficient judgment, citing a parallel use of *stolidus* in Seneca's *Epist.* 70.10 (1963, *ad loc*), while Goodyear understands the phrase as emphasizing Libo's "stupidity" (1981, 2.30.2). I agree that stupidity is consistent with Tacitus' characterization of Libo, and that the phrase could suggest incompetence, but not that either adjective necessarily confirms that Libo was overambitious. Gärtner understands *stoliditas* as a quality that could encourage treason (through a lack of good judgment) and inspire pity, as *miseranda* suggests (2010, 416). Finally, the phrase is vague enough to allow *uana* to mean both "stupidly ambitious" and "groundless."

42. Suetonius does incriminate Libo, but that only makes Tacitus' refusal to do so more striking. Suetonius locates Libo's trial among political upheavals (although he does not describe the trial) and introduces Libo by saying he was fomenting revolution (*Tiberius* 25).

43. Although I argue that Tacitus implies Libo was too incompetent to be a genuine threat, his trial might have been unjust even if he had committed treason. Gärtner argues that Seneca's letter 70, which discusses Libo's suicide, also implies that the outcome of the trial was decided before it began (2010, 413).

44. Shotter argues that Tacitus presents the marks as serious evidence; *tamen* separates them from the useless evidence (1972, 92). *Tamen* could, however, emphasize the unlikeliness of the evidence, presenting a contrast between the poor evidence and the relentlessness of the prosecution.

making the marks, it was decided that his slaves should confirm under torture that the writing was his (2.30.2–3). Tacitus says that this presented a legal problem "because by an old senate's decision any investigation bearing on the life of a master was prohibited" (*quia uetere senatus consulto quaestio in caput domini prohibebatur*, 2.30.3). Tacitus' formulation suggests respect for this law insofar as it was precedent. Tiberius finds an ingenious, unprincipled way to circumvent the rule; the slaves are sold to an official so that they are no longer Libo's (2.30.3).[45] Tacitus emphasizes the underhandedness of this tactic by calling Tiberius "astute to devise a new legality" (*callidus et noui iuris repertor*, 2.30.3), stressing his calculation and willingness to change custom, a tendency that is more sinister because of the ominous sense of the Latin word *nouus*.[46] This is another sign that Libo's trial was unfair, and that Tiberius helped to skew it.

Tiberius' solution to the prosecutors' problem belies his façade of impartiality. Despite Tiberius' claim that he would not support either side, the legal question about slave testimony reveals Tiberius' prejudice so clearly that even Libo notices (Gärtner 2010, 414). Libo finally realizes that Tiberius has decided his guilt, but this realization neither helps Libo nor convinces Tiberius to drop the charade. Libo makes "final pleas" to Tiberius, who tells him that the Senate is in charge (2.30.4–2.31.1). By reminding readers of the hypocrisy of Tiberius' position, Tacitus illustrates the perversion of justice in Libo's trial. Because no one but Libo is willing to acknowledge this injustice, there is a strain of dramatic irony in this passage. Tacitus also delays Tiberius' disingenuous advice that Libo should direct his pleas to the Senate. Because readers know that Tiberius has been lying and refuses to drop the façade, there is ironic humor in his ultimate insistence that Libo must continue to hold the Senate responsible for his trial and conviction. Tiberius insists on the Senate's authority in the moment when Libo has finally realized that Tiberius was in fact responsible for his misfortunes. By highlighting both Libo's foolishness and Tiberius' hypocrisy, Taci-

45. The legal situation was more complicated than Tacitus implies. Although this law was venerable enough that Cicero referred to it as *mos maiorum* (*Pro Rege Deiotaro*, 1.3), it also seems to have been waived in cases of *maiestas* (Furneaux 1896, *ad loc*). Koestermann and Goodyear cite Cassius Dio 55.5.4 for the same law being circumvented by Augustus (1963, *ad loc*; 1981, *ad loc*). The prohibition on slaves being tortured for evidence against slaveholders seems to have been so permeable that Rutledge thinks Tacitus was simply mistaken to characterize it as unprecedented (2001, 159).

46. *Callidus* also has a negative connotation in Tacitus. The *Lexicon Taciteum* records only one use of the word with a positive connotation and more than twelve (including this passage) in which Tacitus uses *callidus* in a negative sense (Baar 1990, 53). Gärtner (2010, 414) also supports a sinister connotation of *callidus* here.

tus draws a humorous contrast between them and portrays the Senate as cravenly indifferent.

At this point in the trial, everyone, even Libo, has concluded that Libo will be condemned. Tacitus focuses less on Libo's haplessness once the prosecutors have finished their case for his villainy. Now, the second contrasting script appears: that of the political martyr. Libo remains hapless and possibly innocent, but his haplessness is contrasted not with sophisticated villainy but with the dignified political suicide for which a nobler figure might opt. Tacitus composed several narratives of aristocratic suicide, including Seneca's in *Annals* 15, Otho's in *Histories* 2, and Calpurnius Piso's in *Annals* 3. These suicides share honorable qualities that are notably lacking in Libo's. Seneca, Otho, and Piso all retain a steely calm as they approach their deaths, whereas Libo panics. The other suicides are sometimes attended by freedmen and family members, but Libo is the only one who calls on his attendants to help kill him.[47]

Libo's suicide reads like an inversion of an admirable political suicide. Tacitus remarks on the presence of two groups of people: the soldiers who surrounded Libo's house and the slaves to whom Libo appealed for an executioner (2.31.1).[48] Tacitus says that the soldiers were both audible and visible, which makes them an immediate, threatening presence.

Libo's slaves witness his suicide in part because Libo had been wallowing in a final banquet, which must have been prepared and served by someone.[49]

47. In other historians' accounts, Nero also asked his attendants to help kill him (Suetonius, *Nero* 49). The books in which Tacitus would have presumably dealt with Nero's death are unfortunately lost, however, so direct comparison is impossible.

48. The presence of soldiers is unusual because it implies that Libo was being kept in Rome rather than being allowed to go into exile, which might otherwise have been allowed for a man of his status (Pettinger 2012, 35–36). Melounová (2014, 409) describes exile as a punishment for *maiestas* and suggests that it may have been the typical punishment for aristocrats found guilty of the crime.

49. That Libo kills himself at a final revel is another departure from most political suicides described by Tacitus. It is not, however, incompatible with the serious spirit in which most of these suicides are described. Seneca, for example, also kills himself at a final dinner, although in his case Tacitus presents the circumstances as an accident based on the news of Nero's disfavor reaching him at dinner (15.60.4) and the presence of his friends frames Seneca's death as exemplary rather than poorly managed (15.62.1–15.63.2). In another parallel, Tacitus' Petronius throws a final party to stage an elaborate, sarcastic suicide. Tacitus portrays Petronius as calm and defiant in the face of death (16.19.1–3), not solemn but still impeccably brave (Griffin 1986b, 199). Griffin names witnesses and calm on the part of the victim as two exemplary qualities of idealized Roman suicide (1986a, 66). Pearce sees suicide at *convivia* as "honorable and redeeming," especially because it is often a mark of defiance against a tyrannical emperor (2010, 65). The setting of Libo's suicide is therefore not incompatible with the essential elements of idealized political suicide, but other elements are out of place. In particular, Libo does not appear to be motivated by defiance of tyranny, or if he is he does not communicate it.

Libo's appeal to his slaves, however, is inappropriate, because he wants them to kill him so he can avoid killing himself (2.31.1).[50] This is not a typical political suicide. It impugns Libo's bravery (because he cannot bring himself to do the deed) and expands on the complex tension between Libo and his slaves. Libo's cowardice makes him seem even more pathetic and therefore even less likely to have been a serious threat to Tiberius.[51] At trial, the slaves' evidence was a deciding factor, and at Libo's suicide, they remain crucial. Although the slaves themselves are without historical agency, the prosecutors attempted to use them as a means to convict Libo, and now he wants to use them to end his life. The irony of their role is compounded by the fact that, as slaves, they cannot kill Libo without being subject to execution themselves. Libo seems to disregard this consideration, but it must have occurred to the slaves. Their presence at his suicide is therefore dissonant with the ideal role of both the disgraced aristocrat and his slaves.

The manner in which Libo attempts to persuade his slaves to kill him is significantly humorous even as it is pathetic and perhaps pitiable. Libo entreats, grabs hands, and attempts to give the sword to one of his slaves (2.31.1). This is about as practical a plan as measuring one's own wealth in comparison to the surface area of the Appian Way, especially because Libo's slaves are understandably leery of committing a capital crime. Libo's plan for his suicide conflicts with Roman philosophical ideas about suicide not only because he does not live up to Roman ideals, but also because he underestimates the gravity of the situation. Libo's slaves are unsettled by his behavior and beat a sloppy retreat: "And, as they, while they feared, while they fled, overturned the light placed on the nearby table, in darkness now fatal to himself he directed two blows into his vital organs"[52] (*atque illis, dum trepidant, dum refugiunt, euertentibus adpositum mensae lumen, feralibus iam sibi tenebris duos ictus in uiscera derexit*, 2.31.2). Unlike the exemplary suicides of admirable figures, Libo's death is abrupt and teaches no lessons. Because the lamp is extinguished, the suicide goes literally unwitnessed, and even if it had been visible, Libo's internal audience (his slaves) appears to have been focused on avoiding culpability for his death.

---

50. The construction in which Libo asks his slaves to kill him is notably vivid and dramatic for its asyndeton and alliteration (Koestermann 1963, *ad loc*). Tacitus has placed much emphasis on this detail.
51. Shotter calls this passage evidence of "Libo's obviously impressionable mind" (1972, 96).
52. I have altered Woodman's translation of *dum trepidant, dum refugiunt* so that the English is more awkward and has finite verbs in it. The Latin is sufficiently awkward at this point that I believe this change is merited to reflect the hesitancy of the slaves' retreat.

The trivial detail of the overturned lamp becomes a symbolic trigger of Libo's death. He dies after the lamp is upset, as the room is plunged into darkness. In contrast to the calm deliberation of other scenes of suicide, Libo's happens almost at random, as if a minor accident was required to touch off the process. Although the information about the lamp is relegated to an ablative absolute and Libo is technically the subject of the sentence, he is neither named nor emphasized. His role is clear from context, but the only words that refer to him are *sibi* and *derexit*. He expresses no final words or intentions, nor any reason for his suicide. Tacitus spends more time describing the sudden darkness than Libo's death. Tacitus also says that Libo used two blows to kill himself, and his clumsiness contrasts with the ideal political suicide.[53] Instead of imprinting Libo's personality onto his death, as Tacitus does even with figures he dislikes,[54] Tacitus has Libo disappear into a sudden darkness. Santoro L'Hoir has interpreted the entire scene as theatrical and similar to Agrippina's death (2006, 221),[55] but Tacitus has replaced tragedy with absurdity in his characterization of Libo.

Libo's final moment continues a theme that Tacitus has already established as humorous. Libo is too pathetic to be a threat to Tiberius or to Rome.[56] Where a Seneca or a Cato might present an example of resistance to tyranny, Libo does not even do that because he never intended to resist tyranny. Instead, Libo's suicide is the culmination of his foolish character. We have already seen that he was too foolish to be a dangerous conspirator. Here, we see that Libo is so radically unsuited to the role of traitor that he cannot even pull off the role of political martyr, because his suicide, like his life, ignores serious political concerns. Tacitus invites scornful laughter at Libo, but the very fact that he is worthy to be

53. Suicide by stabbing ideally required only a single blow. By Tacitus' time, suicide had become highly codified among elite Romans and methods involving edged weapons were considered the norm (van Hooff 2002 [1990], 47, 50–54).

54. For example, as he does in his contemptuous obituary of Ofonius Tigellinus at *Histories* 1.72.1–3. Tacitus emphasizes the sordid circumstances of Tigellinus' death and connects the shame of Tigellinus' life to the shame of his death, tailoring his suicide to his character. The only quality that Tacitus emphasizes in Libo's death is his lack of clear direction.

55. Libo's disappearance into darkness has a modern parallel in the ending of Tom Stoppard's play *Rosencrantz and Guildenstern Are Dead* (1967), in which the hapless title characters' sudden disappearance eschews a staged death scene and emphasizes their insignificance. On the other hand, Plass understands Libo's suicide as "nightmarish" and "Hades on earth," a more solemn reading (1995, 94). I suggest that without ignoring the horrific elements of this episode, we can understand its "nightmarish" qualities as both harrowing and absurd.

56. Walker calls Libo "an innocent and even silly victim" (1952, 95).

laughed at proves him innocent. This rhetorical strategy is perhaps cruel, but Tacitus has little interest in rehabilitating Libo, and in fact Libo's complete failure may also reflect poorly on the Roman aristocracy, whom Tacitus criticizes for allowing emperors to behave as they do.

Tiberius' reaction to the news of Libo's death is also notable for its irony. The Senate concludes the case against Libo, finding him guilty. Tiberius repeats his assertion of impartiality in the case: "and Tiberius swore that he would have asked for the man's life, despite his guilt, if he had not hastened his voluntary death" (*iurauitque Tiberius petiturum se uitam quamuis nocenti, nisi uoluntariam mortem properauisset*, 2.31.3). In this coda to Libo's life, Tiberius' comment is hypocritical to the point of absurdity.[57] Tiberius takes credit for his own hypothetical *clementia* after Libo has already killed himself. *Clementia* was a signal virtue claimed by Roman autocrats dating back to Julius Caesar, so it makes sense that Tiberius would want to cultivate a reputation for it, but the framing is nonsensical.[58] Even as he claims credit for mercy, Tiberius reiterates Libo's guilt (*quamuis nocenti*), and reinforces the Senate's responsibility for the trial by implying that he was about to ask the Senate for clemency (*petiturum*). Tiberius' statement overlooks his previous coldness toward Libo when he asked the Senate to postpone his trial for a day (same verb: *petiuit*) before begging the emperor for mercy and being instructed to plead with the Senate instead (2.30.4). Tacitus deflates the end of Tiberius' comment with his expression that he would have spared Libo had he not hastened to kill himself. The sentence would have been complete had it ended with *nocenti*, and both Tacitus' and Tiberius' audiences already know how Libo died. By repeating that information, Tacitus makes it explicit that Tiberius' sudden mercy was both useless (because too late) and false, because the offer of clemency was belated. Had Tiberius offered to spare Libo earlier, Libo might not have killed himself. Thus, Tacitus reiterates the injustices of the trial. Tiberius' offer of clemency compounds the inconsistencies of the proceedings with a final touch of pretense.

---

57. Plass cites this passage as one in which Tacitus points out the absurdity of emperors offering clemency when they are themselves responsible for the punishment (1988, 119).

58. Cowan argues that *clementia* was an important but controversial virtue in Tiberius' reign. The correct application of *clementia* might have been out of fashion with some factions of Tiberius' supporters, but it remained a central virtue professed by the principate. Cowan also notes that *clementia* could, in situations like this one, be resented because "it seemed to emphasize the condescension of the princeps" (2016, 80).

The Senate follows Libo's conviction with a flurry of proposals to erase his memory and declare thanksgivings for his death (2.32.1–2). These measures magnify Libo's menace beyond anything that even his prosecutors had suggested. The Senate's proposal that the date of Libo's death be made a public holiday (2.32.2) is especially extreme. Tacitus finds the senators' behavior so disgusting that he adds his explicit opinion: "I recorded those men's sycophantic suggestions so that the chronic nature of that evil in the state should be known"[59] (*quorum auctoritates adulationesque rettuli, ut sciretur uetus id in re publica malum*, 2.32.2). Tacitus insinuates that the Senate was responsible for a great part of the injustice of Libo's trial, and this, too, is supported by the contrast that he has repeatedly drawn between Libo and his prosecutors. Tacitus' readers have been repeatedly reminded of Libo's uselessness and inability to damage the state. The senators, in contrast, are a source of "chronic" evil that is not defeated but rather encouraged at this trial. Ironically, the Senate instantiates the threat to good government that they have just blamed on Libo. Again, the irony of the situation emphasizes Tacitus' points about injustice.

Humor helps Tacitus illustrate that Libo was not a serious threat without confirming Libo's innocence or guilt. Although Tacitus' use of humor is subtle and occasionally cruel, it serves as a consistent background for this narrative. By portraying Libo as farcically incapable of treason, Tacitus makes both Libo and his accusers seem foolish, while also encouraging contempt for the accusers' opportunism. This portrayal might not have been as persuasive had Tacitus written a simple condemnation of either party. By using humor, he underlines the absurdity of the trial and implies rather than states the legal injustices that will come to plague Rome during the rule of Tiberius.

Because Tacitus employs humor in this overtly programmatic episode, his use of humor here has implications for later events. Tacitus' Tiberius will continue to manipulate justice, conceal his true intentions, and encourage unscrupulous *delatores* (and the Senate will let him get away with it).[60] Because the Libo Drusus episode stands as a paradigm, Tacitus' use of humor creates a framework for injustice in later episodes. Not every informer is as devious as Catus, nor is every defendant as pathetic as Libo, nor is the Senate as indolent in other trials. Despite these differences, the humorous aspects of this episode

59. I have changed Woodman's rendering of *malum* as "disease" to "evil."

60. For example, Tiberius reacts to the death of Germanicus with either superhuman reserve or secret glee (3.3.1). In another example, Tiberius seems more interested in revenge than justice during the trial of the same Vibius Serenus who was involved with Libo's prosecution (4.28–29).

regularly reappear later. Repetition saps humor but supports the sense of injustice that must accompany such disparities between perception and reality. In this episode, Tacitus uses humor to cement a perception of Libo as a dupe, his prosecutors as schemers, the Senate as complacent, and the treason trials as unjust. By using humor to accomplish this, Tacitus leaves a strong but malleable impression of the hypocrisy involved in the later treason trials.

THREE

The Wedding of Messalina and Silius

Most Tacitean humor tends toward the ironic, sarcastic, and dryly absurd. This strain of humor derives from ancient rhetoric, and is, I argue, the most common kind of humor used by Tacitus. Other types of humor do appear, however. Tacitus' use of comedy in the reign of Claudius is an especially well-studied example.[1] I agree with this assessment and expand upon it by examining Messalina's marriage to Silius, an episode in which humor has often been identified but less frequently treated as significant. In this episode, Tacitus uses humor to illustrate Claudius' inability to control his wife and freedmen, as previous scholars have argued.[2] In addition, however, I argue that Tacitus uses humor to characterize the elite men in this episode negatively, thereby explaining how non-elites and women came to dominate politics. Tacitus presents a parallel

1. Syme says Claudius "deepened and widened [Tacitus'] sense of humor" (1958, 539). Vessey calls Tacitus' portrayal of Claudius a "subtle satire, verging at times on broad comedy" with "ferocious humor and bitter irony" (1971, 385-86). He finds Messalina's death reminiscent of "the coarser Plautine dramas," although he unfortunately does not specify which dramas those might be (1971, 400). Dickison argues that when Tacitus says Claudius "provoked laughter" in his contemporaries, he expects his audience to join in (1977, 634). For Dickison, Tacitus makes reference to comic archetypes to promote the sense that all roles are reversed in the court of Claudius (1977, 635).
2. Tacitus is frequently dismayed by the political influence of freedmen, and Claudius' principate provides an extreme case study. Vessey discusses Narcissus' dominance in the Messalina episode (1971, 399–400). Dickison says Claudius "makes almost no impression at all" because his subordinates overshadow him (1977, 642). Griffin comments on a later episode that Claudius appears helpless to do anything without his freedmen's advice (1984, 54), and that Tacitus rarely allows Claudius to be the center or even the subject of his own reign; someone else always wields power on his behalf (1990, 483, 488). Fagan refers to Claudius' "pliancy" (2002, 567). Malloch expands on the same idea (2009, 1–2). Similar observations on Claudius go back as far as Ryberg (1942, 404n83).

between Claudius' inability to control his court and Silius' lack of agency, drawing an ironic contrast between their abandoned authority and the usurpation of their authority by others.

Tacitus' introduction of Messalina has been lost in the lacuna between Books 6 and 11. In what survives, our first impression of her occurs when she is already empress (11.2.1–2). Silius is mentioned twice before the episode in which he marries Messalina: first at 11.5.3, where Tacitus calls him *consul designatus* and hints about his later "power and extermination" (*potentia et exitio*).[3] Initially, Tacitus encourages a somewhat positive portrait of Silius, who proposes to revive a law that would promote lost principles of legal ethics (11.5.3–11.6.2).[4] Elsewhere, Tacitus appears sympathetic to similar efforts.[5]

Messalina becomes so erotically obsessed with him that she is distracted from a plot against Agrippina and Nero: "She had become so inflamed for C. Silius, the finest of the Roman youth, that she evicted Junia Silana, a noble lady, from her marriage with him and took control of a now available adulterer" (*nam in C. Silium, iuuentutis Romanae pulcherrimum, ita exarserat, ut Iuniam Silanam, nobilem feminam, matrimonio eius exturbaret uacuoque adultero poteretur*, 11.12.2).[6] Tacitus presents Messalina's lustfulness as a surprise.[7] The beginning of the sentence is entirely taken up by her hatred for Agrippina, but the emphasis then shifts to her passion. The passion that distracts Messalina is further delayed by Tacitus' word order: *nouo et furori proximo amore* ("by a new love which bordered on madness," 11.12.1). By delaying the word *amor* (it is the penultimate one in the sentence), Tacitus creates suspense and surprise. He has not yet set up a strong opposition between scripts, but this phrase indicates a shift from typical aristocratic infighting to a new and shocking event. Although the relationship between Messalina and Silius has not yet been established, the

3. I have altered Woodman's "powerfulness" to "power." This passage seems to be Tacitus' first mention of Silius. He notes his status and situates him in the narrative (Malloch 2013, 11.5.3).
4. Malloch suggests that Silius' proposal was excessively naïve and foreshadows his later "detachment from reality" (2013, 11.5.3), so a negative impression of Silius is also possible.
5. Here, Claudius accepts a limited version of the proposal (11.7.4), and later Tacitus presents the same issue as an early, positive, act of Nero (13.5.1). Woodman notes that the same law had been revived by Augustus (2004, 197n15).
6. Koestermann sees this paragraph as the culmination of an elegant transition to a narrative about competition between imperial women (1963, 11.12.1). The comparison between Nero and Britannicus foreshadows Messalina's downfall by mentioning the woman who will succeed her as Claudius' wife.
7. It is a surprise because it is so extreme, not because it is uncharacteristic of Messalina. Ancient characterizations of Messalina focus on her lust, and Tacitus treats it as almost incredible (Wyke 2002, 323–26). Tacitus also frames Messalina's lust in masculine terms, which make it more transgressive (von Stackelberg 2009, 602).

circumstances of their affair will depart so far from the typical subject matter of Roman history that Tacitus will use comic motifs to underscore the strangeness of this part in his narrative.

Tacitus' new portrait of Silius is more frivolous than the one provided a few chapters ago. He was *consul designatus* at 11.5.3, but here he is "the most beautiful of the Roman youth" (*iuuentutis Romanae pulcherrimum*, 11.12.2).[8] Tacitus does not normally provide details about the appearance of his characters, but this passage is focalized through Messalina. The gender reversal in Messalina's pursuit of Silius has been noted in prior scholarship,[9] as has the similarity between Messalina and Sallust's Sempronia,[10] who pursued men more often than she was pursued by them (*saepius peteret uiros quam peteretur, Bellum Catilinae* 25.3). Roman historians found lustful women not merely disturbing but also anomalous.[11] Messalina is so intent on adultery with Silius that she ousts his current wife, Junia Silana.[12] Messalina has little reason to eliminate Silius' wife because she should have no hope of marrying him while married to Claudius. Indeed, sexual jealousy between women is not a particularly common trope in Roman literature. Situations of sexual competition between women rarely devolve into direct conflicts. Jealous women are frequently more

---

8. I have changed Woodman's translation of *pulcherrimum* from "finest" to "most beautiful" because "finest" frequently connotes nobility and decency as well as a pleasant physical appearance. Although *pulcher* has a similar range of available connotations, I believe that the most superficial sense applies here. (Messalina was not attracted to Silius' nobility of spirit.) In Tacitus, *pulcher* appears more often in a metaphorical sense than a literal one (*pulcher, Lexicon Taciteum*), which makes its literal application to Silius even more pointed.
9. On Messalina's usurpation of masculine roles: Santoro L'Hoir (1994, 24–25); von Stackelberg (2009, 602).
10. Santoro L'Hoir (1994, 24) and Milnor (2009) comment on Sempronia's influence on Roman historiography. Santoro L'Hoir positions Sempronia as an influential example of a masculine woman whose influence represents a threat to the traditional role of Roman men. Milnor sees Sempronia as a complex ancestor of many of the influential women portrayed by Roman historians.
11. Some of Tacitus' most fully elaborated female villains are associated with sexual indecency, but usually without an emphasis on sexual appetite. Tacitus accuses Agrippina of sexual relationships with her uncle (the emperor Claudius, 12.3.1, 12.5.1), a freedman (Pallas, 12.25.1), and possibly her son Nero (14.2.1), but he centers Agrippina's desire for power, not for sex. Her sexuality is a tool of her evil, never its root cause. A few female characters even deviate from elite female chastity without being portrayed as evil. Of these, the most prominent is Epicharis, the freedwoman whose participation in the Pisonian conspiracy culminates in her gruesome, heroic death (15.57.1–2). Although Epicharis is the mistress of a conspirator, sexual behavior is not a factor in Tacitus' construction of her character. (As a non-elite woman, Epicharis may also be held to a different standard.) Similarly, the *matronae* of comedy, who often attempt to control their lecherous husbands, tend to be more concerned with restoring the stability of their households than with sexual jealousy (Christenson 2016, 221).
12. Junia Silana reappears as a vengeful enemy of Agrippina (13.19.2–3), so she was probably no pushover.

focused on securing their men than on settling a personal grudge against another woman.[13] For example, when, at the end of Plautus' *Asinaria*, the *matrona* Artemona crashes a dinner party that her husband and son are attending at the house of the *meretrix* Philaenium, she says almost nothing to the hostess but drags her husband out in a rage (920–940).[14] In another example, the *meretrix* Bacchis in Terence's *Hecyra* explains that she has discouraged the *adulescens* Pamphilus from seeing her after his marriage, even though their relationship would not be adulterous by the Roman definition and his departure diminishes her income (750–760). Messalina's behavior is therefore unusual even for a character in a comic drama. It is more unusual in history, where such conflicts are rarely pertinent.[15]

In addition, Silius almost disappears from this section of the narrative. Messalina and Junia Silana fight over him before he has any say in the matter. While Messalina takes on unnervingly masculine qualities, Silius is made irrelevant more than he is feminized.[16] In the comic framework that Tacitus has established, Silius, the consul designate, takes the ingenue role. His positions as ingenue and future consul are not compatible, but instead constitute opposed scripts. Messalina and Silius have each accepted roles that are inappropriate for their status.

In a final farcical touch, Messalina has imperial property delivered to Silius' house (11.12.3). Messalina visits Silius' house accompanied by her attendants as

13. One unusual instance of jealous conflict between women occurs in Propertius, who describes a scene in which an enraged Cynthia physically attacks two sex workers whom the narrator has hired in her absence (4.8). Similarly, Ovid imagines that Delia and Nemesis will snipe at each other during Tibullus' funeral (*Amores* 3.9.55–58). Both these examples come from Roman love elegy, a genre which portrays nonnormative relationships.

14. Artemona briefly addresses Philaenium (920), but she has little animus against her and much rage against her husband.

15. One possible example from history is Livy's treatment of Tullia, the wife of Tarquinius Superbus. She was originally married to Tarquinius' brother Arruns while her sister was married to Tarquinius. This arrangement was unacceptable to Tullia because she and Tarquin were obviously more suited to each other because of their similarly violent temperaments. Livy claims that there was, if not jealousy, at least dislike between the sisters, too (1.46). Overall, however, Livy is less concerned with the conflict between women and more with the congruence of Tullia and Tarquinius. Another useful parallel is a passage where Tacitus minimizes the possibility of female sexual jealousy. Agrippina did not separate Junia Silana from her prospective husband to acquire him for herself but to curtail the political influence that a husband would acquire with her money (13.19.2). Although this incident exemplifies the awfulness of both women, Tacitus averts the notion that their competition was about personal jealousy.

16. For Silius occupying the feminine or passive role in their relationship, see Malloch 2013, 11.12.2. I agree that Silius is somewhat feminized, but not that his occupying a feminine role is sufficient to explain his meager part in the narrative.

part of her masculine pursuit of him.[17] This detail is not exclusive to Tacitus,[18] but he emphasizes it here and returns to it later (11.30.2), making it a substantial thread in his narrative. Messalina's gift-giving resembles that of comedy's unfaithful husband, who sometimes brings his wife's property to his mistress as a gift.[19] Tacitus presents this information as more shocking than laughable, but it nevertheless underlines a variety of strong contrasts in his characterization of both Messalina and Silius.[20] Most obviously, "empress" and "adulteress" are not supposed to be compatible roles, but that is only an ideal separation, not a necessary one. The roles of "empress" and "comedy character" (and more particularly "male lover" or *adulescens*) are similarly opposed but are united here in Messalina. The episode does not end like a comedy, nor does Tacitus keep his focus on Messalina's pseudo-comic qualities, but her behavior indicates that other aspects of the principate have become contradictory, more like fiction than reality. Messalina does not behave entirely like either a comedy character or an empress, but the interplay between the two roles is humorous and crucial to her characterization in Tacitus.

At this point, Tacitus returns to Silius' perspective. This Silius has greatly devolved from the consul designate of his first appearance. He considers the affair with Messalina a political steppingstone, albeit a high-risk one. Tacitus spares a single sentence to explain that Silius accommodated Messalina's all-consuming lust because he predicted death if he refused her and potential

17. Malloch detects an ironic or mocking note in Silius' hope for secrecy being dashed by Messalina's constant public display (2013, 11.12.3). This dynamic makes their relationship more ridiculous and also presages Tacitus' descriptions of Nero, who often appears unable to distinguish between good and bad publicity.
18. Cassius Dio also mentions that Messalina gave Silius many of Claudius' possessions (epitome 61a.31.3). He adds, however, that Messalina was responsible for making Silius consul, which adds a different emphasis.
19. One example is in *Menaechmi*, where Menaechmus enters with his wife's clothing concealed beneath his own so that he can smuggle it out of his house as a gift for the *meretrix* next door (130–134). Another is in *Asinaria*, in which the *senex*'s wife discovers that he was responsible for multiple thefts that she blamed on her enslaved maids (884–889). In addition, there is at least one example of a similar motif in ancient history. Herodotus' Xerxes receives a distinctive garment from his wife but gives it to his mistress when she asks for it. When his wife finds out, she blames his mistress' mother and has her disfigured. Because the mistress' mother's family is powerful (her husband is Xerxes' brother), her disfigurement leads to an attempted revolt that Xerxes quashes (the full episode is at Herodotus 9.108–113). This is a close ancient historical parallel for a member of the ruling family causing trouble by transferring possessions from a spouse to a concubine. The comparison shows how disastrous such behavior can be. I do not see any of these examples as directly in dialogue with Tacitus, but together they illustrate the existence of an ancient motif in which a husband gives a wife's clothes to a mistress.
20. Koestermann detects frivolity in this passage, which Tacitus has enhanced by his use of chiasmus and asyndeton (1963, 11.12.3).

benefit should he accept (11.12.2).[21] Silius does not display qualities associated with female characters in comedy, but that is in part because he does not display much of a personality. In his compliance Silius resembles Claudius, another stunningly passive character, whose next marriage will be arranged in a debate that his freedmen advisers dominate (Griffin 1984, 54). In the Silius episode, Claudius plays the roles of both the emperor and the unsuspecting *matrona* whose household goods are being carried off as gifts to a girlfriend.[22] Tacitus also comments on Claudius' hypocrisy in exercising the office of censor while his own household violated traditional morals and mentions his attempt to curtail verbal abuse of elites at the theater (11.13.1). Here, Tacitus spells out the untenable tensions in the imperial household. Although not all the qualities ascribed to Claudius or Silius are entirely incompatible with being emperor, Tacitus shows their lack of fitness for the job through humorous and ironic patterns.

Messalina decides suddenly to marry Silius: "Messalina, having become sated with the simplicity of her adultery, was already drifting to hitherto unrecognized lusts when Silius himself, whether by some fatal derangement or deeming that the remedy for looming danger was danger itself, urged an abrupt end to dissembling" (*Iam Messalina facilitate adulterorum in fastidium uersa ad incognitas libidines profluebat, cum abrumpi dissimulationem etiam Silius, siue fatali uecordia an imminentium periculorum remedium ipsa pericula ratus, urguebat*, 11.26.1). For once, Silius expresses an opinion. If he is already taking a risk, he may as well make it a profitable one. Still, Silius misjudges, in Tacitus' opinion, because he displays "fatal derangement" (*fatali uecordia*, 11.26.1).[23] His desire to end the charade (*abrumpi dissimulationem*) is questionable because he intends not to abandon Messalina for a less precarious life but to end their deception by becoming her husband in truth and therefore making the lie into

21. This is not unlike Otho's rationale for becoming emperor (*Hist.* 1.21). Both characters assume that death is more imminent and power more easily obtained than either is.

22. Dickison sees him as a foolish *senex*, deceived by his wife and freedmen (1977, 644). I agree that Claudius is gullible but suggest that we can name possible comic parallels beyond the *senex*. Claudius is, however, less canny than several of comedy's *matronae*, who often do realize their husbands' infidelity and take steps against it (e.g., *Casina*'s Cleostrata, *Menaechmi*'s anonymous *matrona*, or even *Mercator*'s Dorippa, who suspects her husband mistakenly). Even clueless *matronae* are, unlike Claudius, often capable of decisive action once informed (e.g., *Asinaria*'s Artemona and *Phormio*'s Nausistrata).

23. *Vecordia* also appears during the trial of Libo Drusus (2.30.1), where it refers to the absurdity of the evidence against Libo. It will also appear later when Nero encounters the insane Caesellius Bassus (16.3.2). Perhaps "derangement" implies a separation between perception and reality that is relevant to both humor and politics.

a reality. Nor does Silius have a plan to overthrow Claudius.[24] Although some of Silius' language might imply a conspiracy or assume that Claudius will be murdered, he asks explicitly only to marry Messalina, a last-minute reversal of the expectation that he would prioritize Claudius' murder.

Although Silius appears to have planned far enough in advance that he offers to adopt Messalina's son Britannicus and to maintain her power (11.26.2), he does not acknowledge Claudius, the obvious obstacle to their marriage. Silius refers to Claudius' death,[25] but he does not propose any method by which they could kill him nor any way to legitimize himself as emperor. Like Libo Drusus in Tiberius' reign, Silius presents a minimal threat to the emperor, despite his outrageous behavior. Because Tacitus presents Silius as ambitious, however, the contrasts in his character tend to demonstrate his personal incompetence rather than imperial injustice. Claudius, in contrast, is notably less cunning than his counterpart Tiberius, but he instead fits into the picture of incompetence in the principate that Tacitus builds in this episode.

Messalina's reaction to Silius' plan reinforces the comic archetypes that define their relationship. Unlike Silius, who was introduced as *consul designatus* before he doubled as a comic *meretrix*, Messalina is never shown to be capable of political action that extends beyond her own gratification.[26] Like Silius, Messalina fails to anticipate the difficulties that they will immediately encounter. Her reason for accepting the marriage proposal is outlandish: "yet she desired the name of 'matrimony' by reason of that magnitude of notoriety which is the ultimate pleasure for the prodigal" (*nomen tamen matrimonii concupiuit ob magnitudinem infamiae, cuius apud prodigos nouissima uoluptas est*, 11.26.3). This recalls the start of the passage, where Messalina began to lose interest in

24. Fagan observes that if Messalina and Silius did have a plan, it must have been an extremely poor one, given how little it was concealed (2002, 573–74).

25. He reminds Messalina that they should not "wait upon the princeps's old age" (*senectam principis opperirentur*) and even more vaguely that "accomplices with similar dreads were available" (*adesse conscios paria metuentes*, 11.26.1–2). Neither he nor Messalina suggests that she should divorce Claudius.

26. Tacitus credits Messalina with instigating the trial of Valerius Asiaticus (11.1–2), but that incident is directly connected to her desire to take his property, and elsewhere she asserts power almost exclusively in service of her sex life. Although Tacitus' portrayal of Messalina is fragmentary, there is no reason to believe that she developed more focused political schemes in lost passages. Cassius Dio's Messalina also lacks clear motivations—at one point he says she married men other than Claudius simply because she wanted to be married to many men (epitome 61a.31.1–2)—so there may have been no transmitted reason for her behavior, or none beyond the ancient stereotype of female lust running out of control. On the other hand, Rutledge has reconstructed plausible reasons that Asiaticus presented a political threat (2001, 107–8), so it may be that Tacitus concealed Messalina's political awareness.

Silius in favor of "unrecognized lusts" (*incognitas libidines*, 11.26.1). Silius' marriage proposal supplies enough novelty to rekindle her interest. Although the most obviously shocking thing about their marriage is that Messalina was already married to Claudius, Tacitus presents the concept of marriage itself as the thing that appealed to Messalina. She desired to be infamous and therefore wanted to marry Silius, because it would be scandalous to marry Silius while married to Claudius. Marriage, however, is traditionally meant to legitimize relationships, not to make them more scandalous. Messalina wishes instead for a marriage that will be more scandalous than her adultery, a plan that turns the idea of marriage on its head. Again, Tacitus emphasizes the incongruities central to the characters' reasoning.

It is also significant that Messalina desires her wrongdoings to be known.[27] She seeks to publicize her affair although her power depends on her marriage to the emperor.[28] Claudius is apparently not the only person in his court with a confused and lazy approach to politics, because Messalina is also confused about what will benefit her and what will not.

Tacitus ends the chapter on this ironic note: "and, waiting merely until Claudius set off for Ostia to sacrifice, [Messalina] celebrated all the solemnities of a wedding" (*nec ultra exspectato, quam dum sacrificii gratia Claudius Ostiam proficisceretur, cuncta nuptiarum sollemnia celebrat*, 11.26.3). Clearly, Messalina and Silius do not celebrate their wedding correctly, because Messalina remains married to Claudius, which would normally be a serious obstacle. Tacitus has already called their marriage shocking, so by saying that they decided to do everything correctly despite the one glaring omission, he turns their wedding into an ironic joke.

In his description of the wedding, Tacitus is explicitly incredulous (11.27):

> As I am not unaware, it will seem fantastic that any mortals felt such unconcern in a community aware of everything and silent on nothing, still less that a consul designate, on a predicted day and in the presence of signatories, came together with a princeps's wife as if for the purpose of begetting children; that she

27. This is a central theme also in Tacitus' treatment of Nero (discussed in chapters 4 and 5), who sometimes appears eager to spread knowledge of his crimes, but, unlike Messalina, he appears to have been able to make his notoriety benefit him.

28. Tacitus portrays Messalina as more politically active than Claudius, but her political activity mainly consists of threats to obey her or face Claudius' anger. For example, Tacitus implies that she would have threatened Silius with death if he had not agreed to have an affair with her (11.12.2).

for her part listened to the words of the officials and sacrificed before the gods; that they reclined at table among party guests; and that there were kisses, embraces, and, finally, a night spent in spousal license. Yet none of this has been compiled to promote a marvel, but I am transmitting what was heard and written by my elders.

Haud sum ignarus fabulosum uisum iri tantum ullis mortalium securitatis fuisse in ciuitate omnium gnara et nihil reticente, nedum consulem designatum cum uxore principis praedicta die, adhibitis qui obsignarent, uelut suscipiendorum liberorum causa conuenisse, atque illam audisse auspicium, uota subisse, sacrificasse apud deos; discubitum inter conuiuas, oscula complexus, noctem denique actam licentia coniugali. sed nihil compositum miraculi causa, uerum audita scriptaque senioribus tradam.

Tacitus offers his own opinions at the start, along with a warning that the episode will seem incredible. In doing so, he averts one common feature of humor: surprise or suddenness that forces a reader to work though the humorous thought process on their own. Humor appears instead in the enumeration of normal but contextually inappropriate things that Messalina and Silius did at their wedding. For Tacitus, their actions are worthy not merely of strong disapproval but are incongruous to the point of humor, and he goes so far as to halt the narrative to emphasize these incongruities.

Tacitus warns that the whole escapade may seem *fabulosum*, especially because the scandalous marriage happens in view of an audience at a prearranged time and accompanied by religious rituals, all of which are characteristic of Roman theater. *Fabulosus* is related to *fabula*, a theatrical play.[29] By invoking the *fabula*, Tacitus reinforces the impression that the entire situation is unbelievable and recalls the comic motifs used earlier in the episode. Although *fabula* can indicate any genre of play, the events of the episode invite parallels with comedy, and Tacitus emphasizes the irrationality of the situation, a characteristic that lends itself to humor.[30] He expands on the theatricality of the

29. Koestermann calls the sequence from 11.26 to the end of Book 11 a "marriage tragedy" (*Ehetragödie*) that Tacitus embellishes for artistic more than historical reasons (1963, 11.26.1). Dickison notes parallels between this episode and Roman comedy, specifically commenting that *fabulosus* is a sign that Tacitus intends to communicate theatricality in this episode (1977, 645). Nappa (2010, 191–95) discusses this episode including its links to theatrical and mime performance.

30. On the significance of *fabulosus*, see also Plass (1988, 83) and O'Gorman (2000, 116), who make

characters' behavior by emphasizing the large audience that Messalina and Silius had at their marriage. Tacitus provides no explanation, not even a possible motivation for why Messalina and Silius were so rash. Instead, he cites the prominence of their wedding as a prime example of something hard to believe. Humor arises from the contrast between their public wedding and its obvious illegality. Messalina and Silius appear to believe that their marriage will remain discreet despite their active attempts to publicize it. Their behavior is so bizarre that it is difficult to square with reality. A public audience at such a private event also evokes theater.[31] As before, Messalina and Silius are engaged in behavior more typical of comic characters than serious politicians. The implicit comparison between wedding and comedy disturbs the dignity for which Tacitus wishes imperial politics would strive.

Tacitus furthers the humorous tone by introducing serious political and legal terms along with behavior that is absurd, theatrical, or unrealistic. Silius is again called *consul designatus* (11.27), a reminder of his official status that heightens the inappropriateness of his behavior (Malloch 2013, *ad loc*). Messalina and Silius are married "as if for the purpose of begetting children" (*uelut suscipiendorum liberorum causa*, 11.27), a traditional or at least Augustan marriage formula (Koestermann 1963, *ad loc*; Malloch 2013, *ad loc*). Without expatiating on the problems that could have arisen from their having a child, Tacitus illustrates the difference between them and a conventional married couple by adding terms that would be appropriate in a normal marriage but are incongruous here.[32] The conjunction *uelut* can be read as indicating either equivalence or pretense. They might be married exactly in the manner of a normal couple, or they might be married merely "as if" they were. Messalina and Silius also perform at least two formal rituals (auspices and sacrifice) during their wedding, a considerable effort toward legitimating their marriage despite Messalina's ongoing marriage to Claudius.

Finally, the last word in the narrative of their marriage is a punchline: "a night spent in spousal license" (*noctem denique actam licentia coniugali*, 11.27).

---

the connection to theatrical comedy and comment on Tacitus' difficulty in explaining this bizarre episode.

31. In this episode, Tacitus repeatedly suggests that Silius and Messalina are engaged in a theatrical performance to bridge the gap between their behavior and their goals. Tacitus also draws parallels to comedy, which are humorous in themselves, but the events have an overarching formal connection to theatrical performance.

32. *Suscipiendorum liberorum causa* is associated with Roman marriage, and *subisse* might have been a marriage word or the transmitted text might be a corruption of *nupsisse* (Furneaux 1907, *ad loc*). Koestermann details possible emendations, which include *subscripsisse* (1963, *ad loc*).

Although the word order cannot be preserved in translation, in Latin "spousal" (*coniugali*) is the last word in the sentence. *Noctem denique actam licentia* would have been a sufficient close to Tacitus' description of the marriage—the final part of the chapter was already moving in a scurrilous direction. The addition of *coniugali* is not technically a surprise—the paragraph describes a marriage—but it is a reminder that Messalina and Silius conceived of their relationship not merely as licentious (which it was) but as a marriage (which it was within their shared fiction). Although Tacitus' tone is shocked and contemptuous, he encourages the idea that their relationship was not simply an affair. The final *coniugali* confirms both the essential incongruity of the situation (sex that is both marital and adulterous) and the facticity of their marriage. The overall impression is of humor in the absurdity of situation and the gravity of its repercussions. Tacitus draws on comedic tropes to explain Messalina and Silius' relationship because the wedding cannot be explained without acknowledging that it was unlikely, incredible, and absurd. On the other hand, Tacitus does not allow humor to overwhelm his serious concerns. His introductory and concluding remarks on the wedding accentuate its absurdity by emphasizing that it really happened and that therefore its implausibility should be overlooked. Humor helps unite the theatrical absurdity of the scene with its facticity, even as Tacitus includes a straight-faced warning that his audience will have difficulty bridging such disparate ideas.

These contrasts become more varied and chaotic as Tacitus expands on public reactions to Messalina's marriage (11.28.1):

> Therefore the princeps's household shuddered; and in particular those with whom power lay—and upon whom, if things should change,[33] alarm would descend—no longer muttered in secret exchanges, but openly: when it was an actor who trampled over the princeps's bedroom, they said, humiliation had certainly been inflicted but actual extirpation had been only a remote possibility; but, as things were now, a young noble with dignified good looks, with strength of mind, and with an approaching consulship, was girding himself for a greater prospect: for there was no concealing what remained after such a marriage.

33. I have kept Woodman's somewhat vague translation of "if things should change" for *si res uerterentur* because the Latin is also vague. Furneaux, however, translates the clause as "if a revolution ensued," which is its likely sense (1907, *ad loc*). I use Woodman's translation because "revolution" implies a significant and organized change, which is likely but not necessary in the Latin. It is also notable that Claudius' freedmen are thinking further ahead than anyone else in the narrative when they anticipate that Silius must plan to overthrow Claudius.

> *Igitur domus principis inhorruerat, maximeque quos penes potentia et, si res uerterentur, formido, non iam secretis colloquiis, sed aperte fremere, dum histrio intra cubiculum principis exultat adulterio, dedecus quidem inlatum, sed excidium procul afuisse: nunc iuuenem nobilem dignitate forma, ui mentis ac propinquo consulatu maiorem ad spem accingi; nec enim occultum, quid post tale matrimonium superesset*

The subject of the sentence is the emperor's household, a group that would usually include the empress. Instead, she is at odds with the rest of the household. The other members of Claudius' household anticipate a dramatic reversal that would ruin their power: *potentia et, si res uerterentur, formido* builds tension by delaying *formido*. Power turns to fear when there is a danger that Silius might wrest control from Claudius. The freedmen have changed their typical habits from persuading secretly to complaining openly (11.28.1), which mirrors Messalina and Silius' decision to make their marriage public instead of hiding their affair. Although the change in the freedmen's behavior is not as extreme as the change in Messalina's and Silius', it parallels their desire to suddenly publicize things that would normally be kept secret. The freedmen's fears pick up on Tacitus' implication that Rome was never ignorant nor quiet about anything (11.27) and on the sudden revelation of information that had previously been kept secret.

In addition, the comparison between reality and drama reappears. The mention of an "actor" (*histrio*) is literal and not directly related to comedy[34] but it resonates with the comic archetypes to which Messalina and Silius have been compared. Messalina's bedroom is both the literal location of a theatrical performer and the metaphorical location of the great comedy of her affairs.[35] The contrast between *histrio* and *consul designatus* is similarly humorous in that it builds on the contrasts that characterize Silius. Although the actor and the consul designate are distinct men, and although the freedmen know that, the

---

34. *Histrio* refers to another of Messalina's adulterers, Mnester, who was a professional mime performer, not an actor (Furneaux 1907, *ad loc* and 11.4.1). The word is further problematical because it is an emendation for *histruo* in M, emended to *instruo* and *industruo* in early printed editions. *Histrio* seems to have been preferred as both similar to the text of M and for making sense in context. Despite the difficulty here, I think it is likely that Tacitus meant to introduce theatrical vocabulary.

35. Santoro L'Hoir also points out the irony of Claudius writing legislation to control morality in theater while an actor sleeps with his wife (2006, 233), as does O'Gorman, who further comments that even Tacitus indicates that he has struggled to fit such a strange story into his historical narrative (2000, 115–16).

implicit comparison emphasizes their substantial similarities and how inappropriate those similarities are. A professional actor committing adultery with an empress is a source of shame, but a future consul who behaves in the same way becomes a political threat.[36]

The freedmen's analysis of Silius, however, is inconsistent with what Tacitus has said about him. His "dignified good looks" (*dignitate forma*) are consistent but not synonymous with Tacitus' initial description of Silius as *pulcherrimus* (11.12.2), but "strength of mind" (*ui mentis*) has not been mentioned. His ambition was addressed briefly (11.26.1–2), but not demonstrated by anything aside from his being caught up in Messalina's lust. That Silius must have had greater plans after the marriage conforms to the Tacitean trope that ambitious young men all want to become emperor,[37] but this notion remains unsupported in Silius' case. Claudius' freedmen assume that Silius must have a plan, but Tacitus gives no hint of it, and Messalina has no strategy beyond alleviating her boredom. The freedmen's suspicions might be reasonable in circumstances where predictable political norms prevailed, but that is not the case here. The gaps in the freedmen's reasoning further illustrate the distance between the main characters' behavior in this episode and the conduct that would normally be expected of them.

Claudius' freedmen think more cogently when they note the weakness of the current emperor. Claudius is "a dullard and shackled to his wife" (*hebetem Claudium et uxori deuinctum*, 11.28.2).[38] Messalina seems at least as likely to order executions as he is, which lends credence to the idea that she could transfer power.[39] Nevertheless, they believe that Claudius' sluggishness will give them the power to foil Silius' (largely imaginary) schemes. Because Claudius is unaware of his wife's antics or indeed anything at all, they can push through the accusation against Messalina with minimal fuss (11.28.2). Tacitus never implies that Claudius' freedmen were right to fear a potential coup by Silius, but they

36. Claudius' freedmen appear to believe that Silius is a real threat, perhaps even that he is organizing a coup. Although Tacitus suggests that Silius never made such a plan, his characters seem to believe it.

37. Tacitus employs this assumption with Otho (*Histories* 1.21) and with Torquatus Silanus, one of Nero's perceived enemies (15.35). Some of the characteristics that made Libo Drusus susceptible to a treason charge also feed into this assumption.

38. Tacitus will later use *deuinctum* to describe Nero's attachment to his concubine Acte in a passage focalized through Poppaea (13.46.2, discussed in chapter 4). In both passages, *deuinctum* has a negative connotation and describes an emperor brought low by an inappropriate romantic relationship (Malloch 2013, 11.28.2).

39. Tacitus suggests that Messalina was not interested in elevating Silius and that their marriage was not her idea, but the freedmen through whom this passage is focalized do not know that.

seem to believe that Silius is a threat to imperial power. The comparison between Silius and Claudius points out their real similarities; both were passive dupes of Messalina and inadequate as emperors.

The freedmen debate their options and, when they cannot agree, Narcissus acts independently to bribe two of Claudius' concubines into breaking the news of Messalina's marriage to him (11.29). The ensuing scene has long been recognized as humorous.[40] Tacitus begins with language appropriate to a more official situation. Narcissus summons Calpurnia and Cleopatra, the two concubines, "to compel the denouncement to be undertaken" (*perpulit delationem subire*, 11.29.3). Tacitus combines opposites here by applying *delatio*, a technical term for political accusations, to Calpurnia and Cleopatra, atypical *delatores* in that they are *infames* women who bring their accusation in a private space rather than a court.[41] Their social roles are traditionally incompatible with legal accusation, yet that is what they do in this ridiculous moment.[42] Like the freedmen and many other figures who come to prominence during Claudius' principate, Calpurnia and Cleopatra are too low in status to participate in traditional politics. Tacitus does not voice disapproval of their participation here, perhaps because desperate times call for desperate measures, or perhaps because Narcissus is Tacitus' chosen villain in this episode.[43] Nevertheless, it is highly unusual that Narcissus asks Calpurnia and Cleopatra to act as *delatores*, and Tacitus' choice of words shows the gap between the official and actual roles performed by imperial courtiers.

Calpurnia's approach to Claudius comes off as ridiculous: "Calpurnia (that was the concubine's name), groveling at Caesar's knees when they had been granted some privacy, cried out that Messalina had wedded Silius" (*Exin Cal-*

40. This scene's theatrical qualities have been remarked on by Koestermann (1963, 11.30.1) who compares Narcissus to a theatrical director. Dickison sees Narcissus playing the role of the Plautine comic slave who orchestrates deceptions (1977, 638–39).

41. In his study of delation, Rutledge identifies Calpurnia and Cleopatra as two of the only known female *delatores*. He understands their role in the episode as potentially reflecting a larger phenomenon of women exercising power through personal relationships (2001, 35). If that is so, Tacitus' decision to acknowledge the influence of women here and in few other legal proceedings is perhaps even more striking.

42. In her argument for comedy in this episode, Dickison notes that Tacitus gives Narcissus a more prominent role here than he has during the same events in Suetonius (1977, 639). By emphasizing the role of freedmen and concubines, Tacitus maximizes the opportunities to bring up discrepancies between the ideal and real government of Rome.

43. Tacitus presents Narcissus' increase in power as threatening. The *paelices*, in contrast, seem to be of such a low social status that their increase in power is negligible. Similarly, Tacitus will present Nero's freedwoman concubine Acte as an influence on him, but never as a political menace on a par with noblewomen like Poppaea and Agrippina.

purnia (id paelici nomen), ubi datum secretum, genibus Caesaris prouoluta nupsisse Messalinam Silio exclamat, 11.30.1). Ironically, the announcement of this news is less public than Messalina's marriage was. Calpurnia conveys the news privately (*secretum*) while Messalina and Silius married in public. Calpurnia adds further drama to the scene by throwing herself down at Claudius' knees and "crying out" the news (*exclamat*). The similarity to a comic scene is increased by the fact that Cleopatra "was standing by, waiting for this very thing" (*id opperiens adstabat*) like an actor waiting for a cue (11.30.1). The women's theatrical blocking adds to the impression that each side of this conflict (Messalina's vs. Claudius' supporters) is producing a rival play (Malloch 2013, *ad loc*). Claudius is notably without agency. Although physically present, he does not react to the news yet, and Calpurnia gives more direct commands than he does.[44] Claudius is almost as indifferent to politics as Messalina is. Both are more interested in indulging the political opinions of their sexual partners than in the implications of those opinions. The principate looks rather empty at the center.[45]

Narcissus' exhortation to Claudius is marked as self-serving and expands on the ironic, comedic elements that Tacitus established earlier. Narcissus lists the "house, slaves, and the other trappings of his fortune" (*domum seruitia et ceteros fortunae paratus*, 11.30.2) that Claudius has lost to Silius, a reminder that Messalina had palace furnishings removed to Silius' house as if she were a comic cheating husband (11.12.3). Narcissus exclaims that Claudius' possessions have been turned over to Silius, comically suggesting that they were the crux of the matter, despite their insignificance compared to the empire. Although Claudius' possessions might symbolize Rome, his household furniture is not of primary importance. Narcissus focuses on details that correspond to comedy rather than *imperium*. Although Narcissus implies that Silius plotted to usurp Claudius, he focuses on trivial details. This is in part because he is speaking to the uncomprehending Claudius and in part because there is no noncomedic way to explain the absurd situation. In addition, Narcissus has no motivation to differentiate between threats to the imperial household and threats to Rome because his own influence is tied to his position in the household, and because

44. Calpurnia is the subject of the verb *postulat* when she asks that Narcissus be summoned (Koestermann 1963, 11.30.1).

45. Haynes comments that in Tacitus, Julio-Claudian rule, and particularly Nero, hollowed out imperial power into an insubstantial fiction (2003, 6–7). Although Haynes focuses on the aftermath of the Julio-Claudian dynasty in Tacitus' *Histories*, her observation about the void at the center of the principate is also applicable to Claudius' reign.

imperium is more or less a moveable possession of Claudius' household.[46] By comparing state power and household goods, Tacitus makes the hereditary nature of the principate seem ridiculous.

Narcissus further frightens Claudius by asking sarcastically if he was aware that he had been divorced and reminding him that Silius is a potential threat to his principate: "'Do you know of your divorce?' he said; 'the people, the senate, and the soldiery saw her marriage to Silius, and unless you act quickly, her husband holds the city!'"[47] (*'an discidium' inquit 'tuum nosti? nam matrimonium Silii uidit populus et senatus et miles; ac ni propere agis, tenet Vrbem maritus,'* 11.30.2). Narcissus' comment highlights several humorous contrasts that Tacitus has already used. First, Narcissus plays on Claudius' obliviousness, a chronic issue that has hampered his government and allowed others to effectively usurp his *imperium*, and which makes him resemble comedy's *senex* (Dickison 1977, 644). Second, Narcissus invokes serious political concerns in a milieu that does not immediately evoke them. The Senate and people represent the traditional political order of Rome, and their invocation is a reminder of the mess that the principate has made of traditional politics. Narcissus does not go so far as to claim that all these groups sanctioned Messalina's wedding to Silius and supported him as emperor, but by saying they witnessed the marriage he implies that they were aware of Claudius' weakness and awaiting his reaction. Again, the comical and serious parts of these episodes have become commingled.

In addition, Narcissus implies that *imperium* is in Messalina's gift. Claudius appears to believe this. It has been implied before that Messalina could take Claudius' power and bestow it on another man,[48] and Narcissus reinforces that

46. This interpretation resonates with the speech of Galba in *Histories* 1, where he compares *imperium* under the Julio-Claudians to "the heirloom of a single family" (*unius familiae quasi hereditas*, 1.16.1, trans. Fyfe and Levene).

47. I have altered Woodman's translation to retain the active voice of *vidit*. Woodman's passive translation preserves the Latin word order, which is usually of great benefit, but in this sentence it throws off the emphasis. In Latin, the emphasis falls on the final part of the sentence—all the elements of the Roman government who witnessed the marriage, rather than the marriage itself. Emphasis on the last part of the sentence is natural in Latin, but in English, the agent construction with a passive verb relegates the agent to a syntactical backwater. Because I do not consider *populus et senatus et miles* a punchline, I prefer to preserve the emphasis rather than the original word order.

48. Silius assumed Messalina would elevate him as part of his calculation in the beginning of their affair (11.12.2) and later (11.26.2), and Claudius' freedmen took the possibility seriously (11.28.1). Messalina's self-mythologizing also could have impinged on the privileges usually exercised by Julio-Claudian emperors, given that manipulation of myth was their special right (von Stackelberg 2009, 617–18).

idea here by the final word *maritus*, not strictly new information, but a surprise word choice. Claudius' rival is neither "Silius" nor "consul designate" but "the husband," a disconcerting appellation because it binds him to Messalina. It is also destabilizing because Claudius still believes he is Messalina's husband, therefore the husband who controls Rome ought to be him.[49] Messalina has no official claim to imperial power (nor does she seem to covet it), yet her husband, whoever that is, will control Rome. This is humorous because it requires a leap of logic to be understood (although the tractable Claudius has no trouble with it),[50] and because it equates *imperium* with the furnishings of the palace which Messalina brought to Silius' house. This is not only an improper but also an improbable way to transfer imperial power. The humor lies in the absurdity of repeatedly comparing imperial power to household furniture, which emphasizes Claudius' and Narcissus' bad reasoning, adding to the absurdity of Claudius' principate and to readers' presumed indignation at Narcissus' influence.[51]

Claudius' reaction to this news is also humorous because he requires confirmation from two more officials. These are the prefect in charge of the *annona* and the praetorian prefect, Turranius and Lusius Geta, respectively (11.31.1).[52] There is humor in the fact that Claudius consults his court from the bottom of the social scale up. His concubine Calpurnia brought him the news, his other concubine Cleopatra confirmed it, his freedman Narcissus confirmed it again, and finally two public officials confirm it. That Claudius must be told five times implies foolishness rather than caution. Also, these officials represent two of the emperor's most important political resources (the grain distribution and the praetorians), but they are called in merely to confirm that Messalina married Silius. The officials devise a series of plans, but Claudius is not ready even to hear them: "It is generally agreed that Claudius was deluged by such panic that

49. Although Messalina has married Silius, she has not notified Claudius of their divorce. Thus, "who is married to Messalina?" is a complex legal question. Treggiari draws out the implications of Cicero's description of a case in which a husband remarried without notifying his first wife. Cicero suggests that the second marriage could have invalidated the first but also allows that a specific legal formula might be necessary for divorce (*De Orat.* 1.183–184). Different traditions argued for and against the legality of a new marriage contracted without a formal divorce from a previous spouse (Treggiari 1991, 35–36). Claudius' confusion is still foolish, however, because this legal question is not central to the main problem.

50. The logical mechanism here is closest to "reasoning from false premises" (Attardo et al. 2002, 10). If Messalina's marriage did bestow imperial power, Claudius would be in more trouble than he is.

51. Dickison identifies the source of humor in Narcissus' speech as the contrast between "superior behavior" and "inferior character" (1977, 636).

52. It is probably a coincidence that Geta is a common name of comic slaves in Menander.

he asked repeatedly whether he himself was in control of the empire and whether Silius was a private citizen" (*satis constat eo pauore offusum Claudium, ut identidem interrogaret, an ipse imperii potens, an Silius priuatus esset*, 11.31.1). Claudius has bought into the idea that Silius could become emperor simply by marrying Messalina.[53] This is another reminder that Claudius rarely exercised imperial power, and the emperor's confusion reflects his indifference to politics. He appears almost neutral in his failure to influence who is in power. Instead of instructing his advisers to be sure that he remains emperor, he merely asks to be informed who is emperor, and he does so multiple times (*identidem*). His uncertainty persists after his question has been answered. Silius and Claudius are thus in comparable positions, even though Claudius is emperor and Silius is not. Both depend on others for their authority and neither has consolidated his authority on purpose. Claudius' advisers seem by turns competent and distracted by trivial concerns. He requires the prefects of the *annona* and the praetorian guard to confirm that his wife has remarried, a duty that they would not normally be called upon to perform. Claudius' foolishness naturally affects the way others act, drawing them into his humorously disordered administration.[54]

Messalina and Silius, meanwhile, step up their theatrical antics by celebrating a Bacchic festival (11.31.2–3). Von Stackelberg notes that this passage is suffused with references to Bacchus and maenadism, motifs which emphasize potentially subversive behavior (2009, 615–16). The overall effect is chaotic, with gestures to theatricality. The Bacchic costume worn by Silius includes buskins, and the attendees are called a chorus (11.31.2).[55] The most direct theatrical comparison is to Euripides' *Bacchae* (von Stackelberg 2009, 616).[56] It is not clear, however, who occupies which role in the play. Messalina is among the bacchants, and Silius is decked out in buskins and ivy.[57] If she were to elevate Silius to the position of emperor, Messalina would confirm the existence of a

53. Koestermann compares this passage to the tension between *priuatus* and *princeps* connected to Otho at *Histories* 1.21.1 (1963, 11.31.1).
54. Nappa understands the episode as focused on the instability of Claudius' regime but sees Silius as a contrast to Claudius rather than an ironic twin (2010, 202–3).
55. Syme recognizes this episode as a locus of "gaiety" and "parody" but also calls it "cruel" and "ominous" (1958, 539).
56. See also Santoro L'Hoir (2006, 235–36) for Tacitus' use of Euripides, which she notes is a departure from his preference for Aeschylean motifs.
57. Von Stackelberg interprets these details and another about a man keeping watch in a tree as references to *Bacchae* (2009, 616).

new imperial god, a Dionysus Silius.[58] Tacitus' readers already know, however, that Silius was never emperor and that he and Messalina both would suffer the fate of Pentheus instead. Yet by the same comparison, Claudius is an aged, vacillating, pathetic Dionysus who must be encouraged to defend his power. In fact, Claudius better resembles Cadmus, the elderly bacchant and former king who witnesses the tragedy but participates only peripherally. The image of Messalina and her new husband acting like bacchants is absurd enough by itself, but the implicit comparison between Claudius and Bacchus is even more humorous because it evokes a contrast between the old, indolent emperor who cannot act to defend his authority and the young, vengeful god. Tacitus has repeatedly shown Claudius to be inadequate to the task of emperorship let alone godhood, so the suggestion that he could take that role is humorous. Furthermore, when Messalina's lookout suggests that Claudius is like a "storm" (*tempestatem*, 11.31.3) on his way from Ostia, the comparison minimizes Claudius rather than flattering him. Coming as it does from the mouth of Messalina's wedding guest, this quip relies on a comparison between Claudius and a storm to imply that Messalina and her friends need not fear Claudius' vengeance. Although the speaker turns out to be wrong, Tacitus has included a comment apparently intended to make light of Claudius' authority.

This marks the end of Messalina's and Silius' presence in the narrative. Silius, never particularly prominent, nearly disappears after parting from Messalina (11.32.1). The next mention of him is at an *ad hoc* military trial where he makes no defense but asks to be killed quickly (11.35.2). Whatever substance there was in his alleged attempt to become emperor, Silius had neither resources to draw upon nor a concrete plan. There is irony in Messalina's asking a Vestal Virgin to speak for her (11.32.2), but her high status makes it less unlikely and therefore less humorous that she would attempt to enlist the chastity of the Vestals in her defense. There is more humor in Claudius' continued fear for himself, which causes him to veer into overreaction. Claudius considers Geta, the praetorian prefect, a shifty character, and so Narcissus is able to persuade the emperor to transfer Geta's military post to him (11.33). Tacitus considers this decision shocking because it puts a freedman in command of a crucial group of soldiers instead of assigning the responsibility to an elite man. Indeed, this

58. Conversely, Silius is "bound" by ivy and has no thyrsus, signs that he is subordinated to Messalina (Malloch 2013, 11.31.2). Silius is more like Pentheus than Dionysus. Despite that, it seems likely that Messalina meant for Silius to represent Dionysus rather than the bacchants' next victim. Still, his impending doom adds irony for Tacitus' readers.

seems to have shocked Tacitus more than it did other ancient historians. Cassius Dio also suggests that Narcissus dominated the reaction to Messalina's marriage but does not mention that Narcissus took on military power (epitome 61a.31.5). By contrast, Tacitus seems concerned about Narcissus' accumulation of powers that would not normally have been available to him. Instead of focusing on Messalina, Tacitus moves on to Claudius' freedmen.

Tacitus adds another touch of absurdity among Claudius' counsellors by reporting the reaction of Lucius Vitellius, who makes an ambiguous comment: "Vitellius' only exclamation was 'Oh, the deed! Oh, the crime!' Narcissus kept hounding him to clear up its ambiguity and to provide them with access to its meaning; but he still failed to prevail upon him, except to the extent that the man's replies were weighed and likely to come down on whichever side one tipped the scales" (*non aliud prolocutum Vitellium quam 'o facinus! o scelus!'. instabat quidem Narcissus aperiret ambages et ueri copiam faceret; sed non ideo peruicit, quin suspensa et quo ducerentur inclinatura responderet*, 11.34.1). As Tacitus comments, Vitellius' utterance is literally ambiguous because the "crime" could be either Messalina's marriage to Silius or Narcissus' opportunism in usurping power over the troops (Woodman 2004, 212n65; Malloch 2013, *ad loc*).[59] There is further humor, however, in Vitellius' rhetoric. *O facinus o scelus* is an ostentatious pronouncement on the model of *o tempora o mores*, not a normal way to converse in a small group of people.[60] Although the overblown sentiment is less strange in the extreme circumstances, it remains an exaggerated turn of phrase, even if Vitellius meant to convey only the single, safe political meaning (i.e., that Messalina's wedding was a crime). Vitellius' ulterior meaning, that Narcissus had assumed powers to which he had no right, is recognized by Narcissus who asks insistently for clarification. Claudius, who does and says nothing of interest here, appears not to comprehend the second meaning (and perhaps not the first, either). If Vitellius wanted Claudius to understand both meanings, he has not managed to convey his message.

Tacitus uses this remark to set up a contrast between Vitellius' Ciceronian moralizing and his recognition that he cannot directly criticize Claudius' freedmen. The contrast between indignation at the neglect of old virtues and the necessity of self-preservation are contrasted with each other here. There is further absurdity in Narcissus asking Vitellius to clarify what he meant, because it

59. Koestermann notices sarcasm in this passage (1963, 11.34.1).

60. Claudius appears to be accompanied by three people: Narcissus, Vitellius, and Largus Caecina.

implies that when Narcissus asked Vitellius what he meant by *o facinus o scelus*, Vitellius either repeated the phrase or remained silent, neither of which provide a satisfactory answer. Vitellius' evasiveness suggests that he wanted to have an excuse ready to show his support for whichever faction happened to triumph. Furthermore, this is the second time Claudius has had to ask repeatedly for clarification (the other is 11.31.1). His ignorance seems more incompetent the more he fails to correct it.

Unfortunately for Vitellius, his grand pronouncement made neither of the impressions that he might have meant it to, because it neither convinces Narcissus that he was speaking generally nor enlightens Claudius about his unwise delegation of power. Because Narcissus does not belong to the social class that would usually fill such a position, his status and office conflict with each other. As a freedman, he should not command Rome's urban cohort. This discrepancy is not humorous in itself but rather introduces a contradiction that portends disaster. By showing that Vitellius failed to make Claudius aware of this incongruity, however, Tacitus erases the difference between freedmen politicians and those of senatorial status. First, the failure of communication between Vitellius and Claudius suggests that there is no longer a conflict between Narcissus' political position and social status, or at least that the emperor does not care about it. Second, Vitellius' toothless objection to Narcissus' power casts doubt on the idea that aristocratic elites are more useful than freedmen are. Vitellius has social rights that Narcissus does not, but they are irrelevant to the emperor. This dovetails with Tacitus' other uses of humor in this episode by setting up an unstable comparison between elite and non-elite politicians in which the groups are at once contrasted and equated.

Tacitus is more indignant than humorous about Narcissus' abuse of power. Narcissus organizes everything so that Claudius has no chance to interfere and even gives orders that Messalina be removed as far from the emperor as possible and calls for her children to be kept away lest they appeal on their mother's behalf (11.34.2–3). Tacitus builds up the horror of Narcissus taking control: "During all this there was an amazing silence from Claudius; Vitellius was close to incomprehension: there was universal obedience to the freedman" (*Mirum inter haec silentium Claudi, Vitellius ignaro propior: omnia liberto oboediebant*, 11.35.1).[61] Where Tacitus initially used humor to illustrate the flaws of Claudius

61. Tacitus' condemnation of Narcissus parallels a later comment on Agrippina: "there was universal obedience to a female" (*cuncta feminae oboediebant*, 12.7.3). This similarity has been noted by Benario (1983, 150) and Santoro L'Hoir (1994, 19). Besides reinforcing Tacitus' contempt for impe-

and Silius, here he shifts to emphasize the upheavals that their uselessness could create. Although the incompetence of high-status men can be humorous, their inability allows lower-status people to take control.[62] Narcissus' dominance is in some ways a surprise, postponed as it is to the end of the sentence, but if this is a final joke, its humor is nearly overwhelmed by its serious political implications. Claudius' failures of leadership have been repeated so often that Tacitus must explain who stepped into that power vacuum. Messalina was not a major danger to Claudius because she had no political ambition (when she exercises political influence, it is to serve her lusts), but there are other figures, notably Narcissus, who control Rome in the absence of a strong emperor.

The rest of Tacitus' narration of this episode (and the whole of Book 11) consists mainly of a list of punishments meted out to Messalina's adulterers.[63] Humor drops out entirely. Tacitus' use of humor is concentrated in the parts of the episode that describe Messalina's and Silius' behavior, and it therefore dissipates when they are killed. Humor here is entwined and balanced with indignant moralizing against the scandalous acts of some characters and others' lackadaisical reactions to them. It establishes the circumstances of the political fallout of Messalina and Silius' wedding. At first, their decision to get married is attributed mostly to their personal follies. Messalina pursues new lusts and Silius convinces himself that a relationship with Messalina will prove advantageous to him. Tacitus uses humor to describe their relationship because it illustrates the incompatibility between their actions and a functioning principate. The humorous tone also supports the veracity of Tacitus' narration, because, as Tacitus points out, much of this sequence of events is difficult to believe. If Tacitus did not acknowledge the absurdity of the material, it would have been more difficult to accept it as true. By using humor, Tacitus acknowledges that Messalina's marriage was improbable, implicitly asking readers to suspend their

---

rial women and freedmen, the parallel is significant because in the later passage Agrippina's control is compared favorably to Messalina's. Agrippina is one of Tacitus' villains, but she is a determined tyrant, not a lust-driven opportunist. The application of similar language to Narcissus and Agrippina emphasizes Claudius' powerlessness and Messalina's lack of control.

62. In this episode, Narcissus also acts as a *delator*, the accuser who exposes Messalina's crimes and is rewarded for bringing them to the emperor's attention (Rutledge 2001, 31). Tacitus often expresses contempt for *delatores*, who were often characterized as lowly or foreign, although some were of distinguished status (Rutledge 2001, 22–23). That characterization provides yet another reason for Tacitus to present Narcissus as a grave threat to elite power.

63. There may be humor in Tacitus' comment that Suilius Caesonius escaped death because of his reputation for deviant but feminine sexual behavior (11.36.4), but Tacitus does not emphasize the irony of Caesonius being saved by a trait usually considered a flaw. In any case, Caesonius is not central to the narrative.

disbelief. Tacitus continues to use humor in his characterization of Claudius, creating the impression that Claudius and Silius are rough equivalents as Messalina's husbands and powerless pseudo-emperors. As soon as Narcissus begins to take control of the narrative, however, Tacitus' tone veers toward the sinister, because Narcissus' participation in these events is the type of swift and decisive assertion of control that Tacitus expects from high-status men, not from freedmen. Narcissus waited until Messalina's behavior had gotten out of hand before he acted and did not actively undermine Claudius. Nevertheless, Tacitus treats Narcissus' activity as highly sinister in a judgment that seems to be based almost entirely on his status. Vessey has noted that Narcissus appears as "a sinister caricature of the *fallax servus* [i.e., the *servus callidus*]" (1971, 400).[64] This connects Narcissus to comedy while also presenting him in a negative light. The humor that Tacitus uses to describe these episodes serves as an illustration of the failures of Roman elites as compared to the freedpeople who are running Rome.

64. See also Nappa (2010, 194).

FOUR

Humor in Nero's Consolidation of Power

In the early Neronian books of the *Annals*, Tacitus uses humor to illustrate how Nero consolidated power. For much of his early reign, Nero claimed powers that were only nominally his while the principate was managed by more competent politicians. Although Nero gradually wrested power from them, Tacitus never credits Nero with traditional political competence.[1] Instead, Tacitus' Nero gains attention and power by doing bizarre things and making unbelievable claims, playing the emperor rather than grappling with imperial responsibilities. Although Nero is frequently ridiculous and rarely behaves like an emperor, he manages to accumulate authority, murder political rivals, and control the behavior of his despicable courtiers. He is effective not despite his absurdity but because of it.[2]

In this chapter, I argue that Tacitus portrays Nero's theatrical, absurd behavior as a strategy—frequently an effective one—for solidifying his position as emperor.[3] In addition, Tacitus uses the absurd humor inherent in Nero's behav-

1. Modern historians dispute the narrative that Nero gained power over time. Drinkwater (2019) makes a thorough argument that Nero was never in power in his own principate.
2. Joy Connolly connects Lucan's depiction of Neronian Rome to a grotesque dynamic derived from Bakhtin's grotesque through Achille Mbembe's analysis of grotesque power in postcolonial Africa. In essence, mockery of the ruler's grotesque body does not undermine his power but instead reinforces it (Connolly 2016, 292–94). Connolly reframes Lucan's bloody dismemberments as "farce or irony" meant to demonstrate the attraction of violence while also warning the audience about the danger of these displays (2016, 288). Connolly's reading of Lucan is persuasive and suggests that such a power dynamic could have operated in Neronian Rome. Tacitus, however, is so wary of referring to the body that the grotesque rarely has a chance to emerge. (One exception may be at *An.* 16.4.3, discussed in chapter 5.) Nero's regime may have relied on a kind of grotesque power, but Tacitus rarely addresses that possibility.
3. This is not a new argument about Nero, nor is it specific to Tacitus' treatment of Nero. Champlin

ior to show that Nero exercised power in an unusual and disturbing way. Because his spectacles involve other members of the political elite in his fictive world, nobody can remain untainted by the aura of absurdity that Nero creates around himself. In Tacitus' depiction of Nero, absurdity influences both elites and common people to accept Nero's power. Tacitus' use of humor in the Neronian books also implies that the principate is not merely prone to absurdity but requires it.[4] Tacitus creates humor out of the gap between perception and reality that produces the disorienting mental effects of Nero's rule.

The humorous strands in Tacitus' discussion of Nero are not concentrated around a single script opposition. Tacitus' characterization of Nero relies not on one contradiction but on the issues that consistently appear around performance. Instead of picking a single script opposition,[5] I focus on absurdity and performance to highlight the humor in the Neronian books of the *Annals*. Because Tacitus' Nero narrative is long and diffuse, I do not argue that all invocations of performance create humor, nor is my analysis of humor comprehensive. Instead, I highlight one major humorous strand in Tacitus' discussion of Nero's reign.

Starting from his introduction of Nero, Tacitus portrays the emperor as interested in controlling his public image, often at the expense of political concerns. Humor arises from the disconnect between Nero's reality and his appearances, an opposition that dogs many characters in Tacitus and reaches a pinnacle in Nero.[6] Tacitus suggests that Nero attempted to cultivate a reputation for being competent and powerful, but that when he failed to create that impression, his failure to deceive others was better evidence of his power than a successful deception would have been.[7] For example, although Nero could

argues that Nero often "combin[ed] pointed, often extravagant, gestures with effective measures" (2003, 2–3). My contribution is that Tacitus uses humor to illustrate and explain Nero's unusual style of governance.

4. Tacitus makes a similar point in his characterization of Otho, discussed above in chapter 1. Otho's power, too, is paradoxically reinforced by his incompetence.

5. Raskin names real/unreal as an overarching script opposition (1985, 114), and Nero's performances can overtake reality.

6. Bartsch (1994) and Haynes (2003) address the disconnect between reality and imperial pronouncements at length. Bartsch argues that Tacitus, Suetonius, and Cassius Dio all characterize Nero as a performer who scrutinized his audience's reactions and thereby forced others to perform (1994, 2–3). Haynes argues that Nero created illusions to make his power seem more real, but that he was not convincing and that after his death the idea of inherent power in the principate was discredited (2003, 40–42).

7. It is also possible that Nero was simply bad at deceiving people and that his failure to deceive his subjects happened to benefit him by accident. I argue that Tacitus implies Nero meant to turn his absurd deceptions to his advantage, and that even if he did not display much competence as a schemer, his unconvincing deceptions nevertheless benefited him.

not conceal his murder of Agrippina, his authority was proved by his having gotten away with matricide. Nero tries to seem like a good emperor while also making unthinkable demands, and that tension creates humor as it forces Nero's subjects to bow to a version of reality that they know to be untrue.[8]

Tacitus' Initial Characterization of Nero

According to Tacitus, Nero began his reign under the supervision of a group of advisers. The most important of these were Seneca, Burrus, and especially Agrippina, who had striven to make her son emperor.[9] In his earliest appearances, Tacitus' Nero is a political pawn rather than a player in his own right, but he gradually accumulates political power by murdering or simply ignoring everyone who exercises influence over him. This process culminates in the murder of Agrippina, whose death marks the point when Nero ceases to listen to any of his original advisers. Although the murder is a grave crime, Tacitus portrays it as born of the performance and absurdity that are typical of Nero.

Tacitus' Nero first appears at *Annals* 11.11.2 among noble boys performing the *lusus Troiae*. Performance and perception are central to this first appearance. Although the *lusus Troiae* is a socially acceptable performance, Nero still comes off as an object of spectacle.[10] At the game, the *plebs* prefer Nero to Britannicus so much that their favor was later understood as an omen that Nero would be emperor (11.11.2). Thus, Nero is reliant upon performance from his earliest public appearances. Public visibility—and perhaps even performance—were important affirmations of imperial power in the early principate,[11] but in

8. My argument is similar to Barry Baldwin's, who posits that Tacitus' Nero generates humor by "alternating between inane depravities and industrious concern for the minutiae of state affairs" (1977, 129). I see less "industrious concern" than Baldwin does, but I agree that the contradictions of Nero's character create humor.
9. Ancient sources disagree on which of Nero's early councilors was most prominent and for how long. Griffin provides a concise analysis of possible arrangements of power early in Nero's reign (1984, 37–39). Drinkwater argues that Agrippina dominated until February of 55 (2019, 54).
10. Although *ludicrum* and *lusus* are related to *inludere* and *ludibrium* (both of which are related to humor), the use of *lusus* in "*lusus Troiae*" does not have a humorous connotation. *Ludicrum* and *lusus* both have a connotation that means "spectacle" and were used to refer to the Troy Game (*OLD lusus, ludicrum*). Nevertheless, the overlap between the language of humor and the language of spectacle should be noted.
11. Geoffrey Sumi has argued strongly for continuity between the public ceremonies of the Roman Republic and those of the principate, noting that Augustus himself was compared to an actor (2005, 7–8). Augustus also debuted young imperial men at the *lusus Troiae* (Sumi 2005, 238), so Nero's presentation to the public followed tradition. Nero's performances will soon overstep traditional boundaries, however, and Tacitus' choice to narrate a relatively mundane public appearance is significant in itself for his construction of Nero's character.

Nero's case his public appearances seem to have been his only qualification to be emperor. Later, Nero will begin to perform in inappropriate ways that ought to undermine his authority but do not.

Tacitus adds details to foreshadow Nero's later mythmaking by recounting a rumor that snakes guarded the infant Nero: "And it was publicized that serpents had been present at his infancy in the manner of guards—a fantasy which was assimilated to foreign wonders, for he personally, no detractor of himself, was accustomed to describe how only one snake had been seen in his bedroom" (*uulgabaturque adfuisse infantiae eius dracones in modum custodum, fabulosa et externis miraculis adsimilata; nam ipse, haudquaquam sui detractor, unam omnino anguem in cubiculo uisam narrare solitus est*, 11.11.3).[12] By attaching this rumor to the *lusus Troiae*, Tacitus highlights Nero's interest in crafting public reputation through performance. Nero participates in creating this image of himself; Tacitus says that he downplayed the story about the snakes (11.11.3).[13] Tacitus suggests that it was uncharacteristic of Nero to forgo the opportunity to brag, and that not bragging must have been a deliberate strategy. Here Nero does not, however, manipulate public opinion on a serious matter but about trivial details. Nero's story deflates the supernatural implications of the original rumor (Koestermann 1963, *ad loc* provides august comparisons),[14] but Nero does not dismiss the entire story. Instead, he replaces a version in which the snakes symbolized a god with one in which there was a single snake which may or may not have been an omen. Despite the insignificance of this story, Tacitus uses it to introduce Nero. I argue that he does so because the story illuminates the combination of political calculation and frivolous display that continues to be central to his characterization of Nero and that gradually develops into a major humorous motif that Tacitus uses to describe Nero's reign.[15]

Despite Nero's personal interest in his image, he initially remains under

12. All translations of the *Annals* are Woodman's (2004) unless otherwise indicated.
13. I assume that Nero later denied that he was guarded by snakes, but Tacitus leaves the timeline unclear. The rumor about snakes might appear simultaneously with the Troy Game (the verb, *uulgabatur*, is imperfect, and the Troy Game ignites public interest in Nero). In addition, a story about a young man would naturally discuss his childhood, whereas an adult emperor would be able to fabricate a wider range of false histories. Tacitus does not specify when the rumor emerged, nor when Nero addressed it.
14. See also O'Gorman (2000, 168–70) for the significance of Tacitus' reworking of a similar story in Livy about Scipio Africanus and Plass (1988, 70–71) for the later parallel of Commodus' performances being understood as omens and Dio's treatment of Commodus strangling snakes as a metaphor for killing his brothers.
15. Syme associates this episode also with "bathos" and "credulity" (1958, 349), both of which will be important parts of Tacitus' portrayal of Nero's reign.

Agrippina's control, while she treats his principate as her principate.[16] Nero's few appearances so far have had only minor effects on the narrative, but Agrippina also seems to understand the importance of performance in her son's rule. For example, Tacitus underlines the publicity that Nero gained from his marriage to Octavia (12.3.1–2), elevating the boost to Nero's visibility above other political advantages that Nero gained. Tacitus' comments on Octavia's previous fiancé (whom Agrippina had to get out of the way) are telling: "Caesar had betrothed Octavia to L. Silanus and by means of triumphal insignia and the magnificence of a gladiatorial show had brought the young man, brilliant as he was in other respects too, to the enthusiastic attention of the public" (*quia L. Silano desponderat Octauiam Caesar iuuenemque et alias clarum insigni triumphalium et gladiatorii muneris magnificentia protulerat ad studia uulgi*, 12.3.2). The benefits of marrying the emperor's daughter are many, but Tacitus singles out publicity as the most important of them. More attention implicitly means a better chance at imperial power.[17]

At the *lusus Troiae* and at Nero's wedding, imperial aspirants compete for public attention. At the *lusus Troiae*, Nero is compared favorably to Britannicus, his rival as a potential emperor.[18] Tacitus foreshadows Nero's triumph by mentioning Britannicus briefly and then dwelling on the public's ecstatic reception of Nero. Nero's marriage to Octavia shows that a good reputation is important, but also that it is completely transferable, unrelated to personal qualities. Although Silanus perhaps had other good qualities, triumphal insignia and credit for a gladiatorial show (sponsored by Claudius) are immediate political benefits that any husband of Octavia's would have received. Nero, or any other young male aristocrat, could replace Silanus without it making a difference. This popularity contest allows Agrippina to promote her son simply by putting him in the public eye. Although his popularity allows Nero to become emperor

---

16. Griffin argues that Tacitus characterizes the early years of Nero's rule as dominated by multiple councilors (including Seneca) rather than by Agrippina alone (1984, 39–40). Drinkwater argues that Agrippina was the dominant influence on Nero, but only until early in the year 55 (2019, 54). I focus on Agrippina to the exclusion of Burrus and Seneca because Tacitus uses humor to demonstrate how Nero dismantled Agrippina's power and does not use the same rhetorical technique with Nero's other advisers.
17. Claudius may also be a target of humor here. Plass comments that Tacitus explains Claudius' decision to marry Nero to Octavia in terms of "political irrationality" because Claudius advances Nero without a good reason (1988, 125).
18. In his version of the same episode, Suetonius does not mention that Britannicus appeared in the *lusus Troiae* but does record other episodes of rivalry between the two (*Nero* 7). Tacitus' placement of Britannicus at the *lusus Troiae* strengthens the sense of competition between them even before Agrippina's marriage to Claudius.

and remains part of his justification for his rule, popular attention will prove to be a flimsy basis for power and will repeatedly make him appear absurd to both his contemporaries and Tacitus' audience. Tacitus does not believe that transferable public attention can provide a stable basis for rule.

Of course, political spectacle was not new to Rome.[19] Nero did not introduce spectacle to politics, but Tacitus' Nero has a special commitment to courting public attention. Few of Tacitus' Julio-Claudian emperors would have won popularity contests. Tiberius conspicuously avoided public life before he became Augustus' successor and later feared Germanicus' popularity as a threat to his authority.[20] Caligula may have been popular (Tacitus' opinions on this point are lost), but his accession depended on an insider scheme supported by the praetorian captain Macro.[21] Although Tacitus' narrative of Claudius' accession has also been lost, it seems unlikely that he portrayed him as making an active effort to become emperor. Nero is therefore the first Roman emperor to publicly campaign for the job.[22] According to Tacitus, Nero gained political advantages from his public showmanship.

Yet Nero's early exploits are not his own but Agrippina's. Nero is too young to act independently; his mother rules him. Although she is not the center of attention in either episode, she is the producer to Nero's performer. Her comparative reserve and judgment are one reason that Tacitus does not yet use humor here. Nero's management of spectacles will be considerably less measured, more exaggerated, and more absurd.[23]

Nero's majority affords him another moment of public visibility. Tacitus begins the episode in foreboding terms: "the time was ripe for Nero's toga of manhood to be speeded up for him, so that he should seem adapted to under-

19. Public spectacles were one of the few circumstances in which the emperor would encounter the people (Griffin 1984, 110). Nero's innovation, says Bartsch, was making himself the spectacle rather than a fellow spectator. Although all the ancient sources connect Nero with theatrical spectacle, Tacitus especially connects innovations in spectacle to innovations in politics (Bartsch 1994, 2–3).

20. Tacitus' narration of Germanicus' death emphasizes his popularity (*Annals* 2.82.1–2.83.4).

21. Suetonius says that Caligula became Tiberius' successor because Tiberius disliked him and because he conspired to murder Tiberius by seducing Macro's wife (*Caligula* 12). Neither of these plans required public support.

22. Augustus might be a competitor for this dubious title, given that he fought a civil war to put himself in power. Nevertheless, because Tacitus did not include Augustus in the *Annals*, and because Augustus did not merely win the principate but invented it, Nero still takes a unique approach to becoming emperor.

23. Agrippina is not always an exemplar of subtlety, but Tacitus characterizes her as an architect of secret deals rather than a focus of public spectacle. Attracting attention would have been even less acceptable for a woman than it was for Nero himself.

take political life" (*uirilis toga Neroni maturata, quo capessendae rei publicae habilis uideretur*, 12.41.1). Although Nero is granted significant political power, the process starts with the desire that he seem (*uideretur*) capable without discussion of whether he was capable. Tacitus implies that Nero was too young to wear the *toga uirilis*, much less take on adult responsibilities,[24] and hints that Agrippina was responsible for Nero's apparent good luck.[25] Agrippina reveals her interest later in the episode when she complains that Britannicus has slighted Nero in public (12.41.3). Nero himself does not yet seem concerned about his reputation. Agrippina continues to manage his public appearances and does a creditable job of making him well-known. Nero's early appearances are not notably humorous, but they establish public appearances as a foundation of Nero's power.[26] Tacitus develops this theme later with humor.

The Murder of Britannicus

As Nero begins to consolidate power, Tacitus puts great emphasis on his competition with his stepbrother Britannicus. Significantly, Nero appears to understand this competition as centered on absurd performance rather than practical concerns. Nero's constant performance makes him appear ridiculous but can also make others appear ridiculous. At times, Nero seems to have a sense of humor of his own, and he accompanies his most drastic crimes with theatrical spectacles that hover between horror and farce. This motif finds its earliest expression in the murder of Britannicus.

According to Tacitus, Agrippina had threatened Nero that she would support Britannicus if Nero disobeyed her, and Nero concluded that Britannicus was a threat to him (13.14.2–3).[27] Although Agrippina's murder remains far off

24. Nero would have been 12, about a year younger than any other Roman known to have taken up the *toga uirilis* aside from Commodus and Caracalla, and even they may have been about a year older than Nero (Furneaux 1907 and Koestermann 1963, 12.41.1).
25. Tacitus uses a passive construction in which the *toga uirilis* is the subject of the main verb, but from the previous discussion of Nero, it seems that Agrippina demanded this honor for her son. Tacitus does not say why Claudius and the Senate wanted to bestow privileges on Nero, but Agrippina would presumably have supported her son's advancement. It is also telling that Nero is honored more than Britannicus, whom neither Claudius nor the Senate had reason to disfavor.
26. In another example, Nero delivers Claudius' funeral oration in a text written by Seneca (*An.* 13.3.1–3). Reciting Seneca's words diminishes Nero's political agency and literary originality (O'Gorman 2000, 148–49), but the emperor remains the object of spectacle, a quality that Nero will consistently value above native eloquence.
27. Tacitus implies that this conflict was sparked when Nero demoted Agrippina's ally Pallas. He

(she dies at the start of Book 14), and Nero's advisers, Seneca and Burrus, retain their influence, this episode constitutes an early assertion of Nero's power. After he realizes that Britannicus could become a threat (13.15.1–3),[28] he acts without the knowledge of Agrippina or Octavia, although both are present when Britannicus is poisoned (13.16.3–4).

Tacitus begins the episode with Nero recalling an earlier confrontation in a frivolous yet ominous setting: "On the festival days for Saturn, amid the general disporting of his contemporaries, during the sport of drawing lots for 'king' that particular lot had fallen to Nero" (*festis Saturno diebus inter alia aequalium ludicra regnum lusu sortientium euenerat ea sors Neroni*, 13.15.2). Crucially, these circumstances are ironic. Nero, who has recently become emperor of Rome in reality, becomes the temporary king of festivities by chance.[29] Tacitus puts Nero's name at the end of the sentence, setting up a violation of expectations (a punchline) that never materializes. Language related to play and reversal of fortune (*ludicra*, *lusu*, *sortientium*, and *sors*, arranged in parallel for better effect) leads not to a surprise, but to a restatement of what everyone must already have known; Nero attained a position of power in a frivolous game through no effort of his own (Schulz 2019, 76). Tacitus does not stress the eerie

---

refers to Nero's comment that Pallas was "on his way to forswear" (*ire Pallantem, ut eiuraret*, 13.14.1), that is resign his office or perjure himself. Woodman understands this passage as a joke (2004, 251n27, 216n8), and Martin sees "sarcasm" in Pallas resigning his magistracy when, as a freedman, he could have had no official magistracy to resign (1981, 165n6). This may be an example of Tacitus and a character using humor at the same time. (Martin connects it to Tacitus' general contempt for freedpeople.) Most instances of humor in Tacitus, however, work from only one perspective—the historian recoils from the emperors' sick sense of humor and the emperors cannot perceive that the historians of the future will find them grotesquely humorous.

28. Britannicus might actually have threatened Nero had Agrippina transferred the praetorian guard's support to him. Britannicus was also about to come of age (Griffin 1984, 68–69, 73–74). Cassius Dio writes as if Britannicus had an obviously better right to the principate than Nero did (epitome 61b.1.1, by the Leunclavian book division). Drinkwater doubts Agrippina would really have supported Britannicus over Nero but agrees that Britannicus could have become a threat (2019, 175). None of this makes Nero's course of action any less humorous in Tacitus' telling.

29. These circumstances correspond to a logical mechanism called "differential potency mapping," in which elements of one script are mapped onto another script that connotes a different level of power (Attardo et al. 2002, 6). In this example, the role of emperor and the role of game king are united in Nero. Both scripts indicate monarchic power, imaginary in the latter and real in the former. Part of Tacitus' joke is that even though Nero is the real emperor, his ability to exercise his power is not much different from that of the game king. The other half of the joke is that the façade of power, present in both scripts, turns out to be part of what grants the emperor real power. In addition, the setting is ominous and significant. Pearce argues that Tacitus uses the banquet setting to demonstrate Rome's decline into tyranny and "death and disaster, dramatising the ways in which harsh political realities intrude upon and disrupt tableaux of pleasure and relaxation" (2010, 58). Transgression of the rules of dining can represent transgression of more serious rules (Pearce 2010, 62).

congruity between Nero's actual and fictive positions as emperor and game king but merely draws the parallel. Nero's good fortune in being allotted the role of ruler in the party game recalls his appearance at the *lusus Troiae*, where he was applauded more than Britannicus and where his good fortune was interpreted as a sign that he would become emperor (11.11.2). Although Tacitus does not endorse the idea that the applause at the Troy Game constituted an omen, these coincidences nevertheless bolster Nero's reputation and make his authority seem destined.

Nothing is indubitably humorous yet, but Tacitus and Nero are both setting the stage for humor: Tacitus by laying out the ironies of the situation, Nero by commanding Britannicus to sing because he is "hoping for ridicule" of Britannicus (*inrisum [. . .] sperans pueri*, 13.15.2). Instead of embarrassing himself as Nero expected him to, Britannicus sings a song that evokes his situation as a deposed imperial prince (13.15.2). Nero fails to effectively mock Britannicus because he has underestimated him. His plan backfires when Britannicus' performance induces pity rather than scorn. Nero has violated Cicero's advice against mocking a pitiable opponent (*De Orat.* 2.237). Although Nero chose a convivial setting because he thought it would give him the advantage, it, too, undermines Nero's plot, "because night and its recklessness had removed dissembling" (*quia dissimulationem nox et lasciuia exemerat*, 13.15.2). In Tacitus' introduction of Britannicus and Nero, the internal audience (the crowd) perceived Nero's prominence as effortless or destined. In this episode, Britannicus not only usurps the attention that Nero believes is due to him, but does so in the domain of musical performance, one in which Nero has asserted primacy.[30] Britannicus' deft handling of Nero's boozy party is another encroachment on Nero's area of expertise. Neither singing nor conviviality are serious areas of competition, nor should skills in either area make Britannicus a political threat to Nero.[31] Britannicus' behavior has nothing to do with Agrippina's threats (which focused on the loyalty of the praetorians). Britannicus has not become more of a threat to Nero than

30. Tacitus establishes Nero's interest in music and other performing arts early (13.3.3). Suetonius, in his version of the same episode, claims that Nero had Britannicus killed primarily out of envy over his singing voice (*Nero* 33), although Griffin thinks Suetonius projected Nero's later behavior onto earlier events (1984, 114).

31. Nero repeatedly uses *convivia* to stage serious political business, including multiple murders of family members. Thus, he violates the rules of both politics and *convivia* (Schulz 2019, 27–28). Britannicus also makes musical performance a political issue, and musical performance will continue to be significant throughout Nero's principate (Schmitzer 2005, 345).

he was already.[32] Tacitus, however, suggests that Nero understood Britannicus' performance as a threat to his power.

Nero quickly decides to have his stepbrother murdered.[33] His decision contains elements of absurdity. After Agrippina berates him and threatens to support Britannicus, Nero recalls that Britannicus' singing and convivial skills are on a par with his own and concludes that he must eliminate Britannicus. Although Agrippina's threats prompt Nero to reevaluate Britannicus, Tacitus suggests that Nero concluded Britannicus was a threat to him only after he reflected that his hostility was displayed in musical performance in a convivial setting.[34] Tacitus implies a relationship between showmanship and holding the principate. By suggesting that Nero understood Britannicus' threat in terms of his performance, Tacitus implies that Nero understood his own power as based upon performance. It is, of course, not true that Britannicus' behavior at a single party is the most potentially subversive thing about him, but it is the thing on which Nero focuses. Nero, either through a misunderstanding or because he already intends to construct his principate as a mandatory performance, has decided that the performative aspect of being emperor is an essential part of *imperium* in which he needs to best Britannicus.[35]

The parallel tradition provides informative contrasts. Suetonius agrees that Nero's primary motivation for murdering Britannicus had to do with Britannicus' singing, but he separates Britannicus' voice from his lineage. In Suetonius' version, Britannicus' voice and lineage are balanced on either side of a comparative *quam* (*Nero* 33). Suetonius treats vocal performance as unrelated to political power, whereas Tacitus suggests that Nero considered them related domains. Cassius Dio, on the other hand, gives almost no details on Britannicus' death but describes his funeral, which he says revealed that Nero had caused his murder

32. Bartsch asserts that the internal audience's pity for Britannicus seals his fate by showing their sympathy with him (1994, 14). Although Nero might have worried about others' sympathy to Britannicus, Tacitus does not emphasize it as a factor in the murder.

33. Tacitus emphasizes Nero's changed opinion on Britannicus rather than any substantial change in circumstances ("Nero, realizing the resentment, redoubled his hatred," *Nero intellecta inuidia odium intendit*, 13.15.3). Nero already hated Britannicus (the *Lexicon Taciteum* identifies this use of *intendit* as roughly equivalent to *augeo*), and this incident reinforced his convictions.

34. Nero may understand Britannicus as a potential threat as soon as he hears his mother's threats and calculates Britannicus' age (13.15.1), but Tacitus does not provide an explicit statement of Nero's opinion on Britannicus until 13.15.2, which suggests that the material described in the intervening space helped Nero to this conclusion.

35. Tacitus does not say whether Nero acts out of strategy or simply does what he wants and occasionally stumbles upon sound political strategies. I argue in chapter 5 that later, Tacitus suggests that Nero's mockery of opponents was an intentional strategy, but that later strategy cannot necessarily be read back into this passage.

(epitome 61b.7.4). Dio does not connect the murder to performance, but only to politics. Tacitus is our only source that is interested in the internal audience to Nero's conflict with Britannicus (Schmitzer 2005, 343, 345–46).

From Nero's absurd reasoning comes an absurd and theatrical murder. Nero's first attempt to poison Britannicus fails (13.15.4), and although Tacitus provides plausible reasons for the failure, Nero's reaction is unreasonable to the point of absurdity. Tacitus repeatedly points out the discrepancies between Nero's expression of his wishes and what he actually desires to be done. The language of crime is warped here. Nero is "impatient at the slowness of the crime" (*lenti sceleris impatiens*, 13.15.5),[36] disturbed not by the crime itself but how long it is taking, and he "ordered reprisals for the poisoner" (*iubere supplicium ueneficae*, 13.15.5), not for the crime of poisoning (for which she had previously been convicted) but for failing to repeat it. He accuses his agents (Julius Pollio, a tribune in the praetorian guard, and Locusta, the poisoner) of "delaying his security" (*securitatem morarentur*, 13.15.5) by being too cautious in performing the murder, even though he ostensibly wants the murder to be kept secret.[37] Nero's impatience reflects his sense of how to assert authority. He considers it more secure to be known as his stepbrother's murderer than to delay the murder long enough to make Britannicus' death appear accidental. This is ironic because Nero ought to be mistaken (fratricide should not increase his security) but he is correct, as Britannicus' death will defang Agrippina by removing the only other obvious imperial candidate.[38] Tacitus does not mention that any moral opprobrium attached to Nero for this crime,[39] and the moral apathy of Nero's contemporaries reflects poorly on the senatorial elite as well as the emperor.

---

36. Santoro L'Hoir connects the "customary vocabulary of haste and delay" to the tragic language that Tacitus uses to describe other murderers. Among these, Britannicus' death is distinguished by its swiftness—he dies immediately and unexpectedly—and by its clarity; Nero's murderous power is well understood by observers as well as perpetrators (2006, 189–91). Tragic vocabulary therefore contributes to the humorous contrast in this episode by reminding readers of previous secretive murders to compare with Nero's blatant crime.

37. Koestermann opines that Nero's concerns seem ill-considered even before this passage. The *quia* clause at 13.15.3 gives an impression of hasty thinking, while earlier clauses emphasize Nero's strong emotions (1963, *ad loc*). In addition, the use of *securitas* as a euphemism for "murder" corresponds to Cicero's contention that assigning positive euphemisms to bad behavior is one way to create irony (*De Orat.* 2.272). Nero is not aware of creating irony, but Tacitus certainly is.

38. Schmitzer sees this element of the episode as part of a larger narrative about Agrippina's attempts to get and keep power. That narrative is framed and enhanced by theatrical motifs (2005, 339–40).

39. Drinkwater argues that emperors could justify killing family members whose existence threatened Rome's stability (2019, 175).

Nero's agents obey his demands, and the section ends with the jarring image of them brewing a fast-acting poison "next to Caesar's bedroom" (*cubiculum Caesaris iuxta*, 13.15.5). Juxtaposition of the poisoners and Nero's bedroom emphasizes the physical and metaphorical closeness between the emperor and the people who carry out his sordid work.[40] Tacitus suggests that the two poisoners are not the type who ought to influence politics, but by a perverse twist, these two inappropriate people are the emperor's only confidants at a pivotal moment.

If Nero's preparations for the murder were transgressive, the murder itself reaches a humorous level of absurdity. Nero's previous attempt to have Britannicus murdered seems to have taken place in a private setting.[41] The second attempt is carried out in a remarkably public context, at a dinner attended by senatorial elites and their children. Tacitus gives no count of the guests and names only a few individuals but shows that Nero's crime had an audience: "the other nobles of the same age" (*ceteris idem aetatis nobilibus*) constitute a crowd and are "in the sight of their relatives" (*in adspectu propinquorum*, 13.16.1), which suggests that many people witnessed the poisoning. Tacitus' focus on the audience confirms the difficulty of keeping the murder secret and calls attention to a major issue from earlier in this episode. Nero does not want to be found out as a fratricide, but he is willing to incur that reputation if he can guarantee that he will be the central performer in his principate. In contrast to the poisoners' first attempt, which was so secret that even Agrippina seems not to have known about it (13.16.4), the second attempt displays Nero, the emperor, as much and as prominently as possible.

The contrast between Nero's conflicting impulses to conceal his crimes and to attract attention to his power creates humor because emperors are not supposed to base their power merely on their capacity to attract attention, regardless of whether it is positive or negative. Public appearances at the games or in the Senate could elevate a ruler's reputation, but a public poisoning ought to be a stain. Yet Nero courts attention with a crime, something that earlier emperors might at least have tried to conceal. Two models of power (that of concealing crimes for the sake of legitimacy and that of flamboyancy for its own sake) come into conflict here because Nero's contradictory decision to both conceal

40. Juxtaposition of disparate elements can serve as a logical mechanism of humor in script theory (Attardo et al. 2002, 5).

41. Tacitus says Britannicus was first poisoned by "his actual tutors" (*ab ipsis educatoribus*, 13.15.4), who presumably poisoned him in secret.

and publicize Britannicus' death should fail or should at least seriously undermine him. In fact, as Tacitus' readers already know, Britannicus' murder would lead to the expansion of Nero's authority. Tacitus creates humor out of the contrast between Nero's insistence on secrecy and his desire to publicize his crime. Nero cannot convincingly maintain both façades at once. In this way, Tacitus introduces humor by bringing together incompatible courses of action that nevertheless reinforce each other. The basis of Nero's power is shown to be performance rather than anything concrete.

The poisoners' plan is meant to conceal that Britannicus was poisoned. Although the plan goes without a hitch, the more intelligent members of the internal audience stare fixedly at Nero (13.16.3). Tacitus reports nothing suspicious except for Britannicus' obvious physical distress. Although Nero and his co-conspirators made a serious effort to conceal their plot, the crime itself takes place in public and is immediately detected by those wise enough to make an educated guess.[42] Ostensibly, Nero wants to avoid their attention, yet their focus on Nero confirms his primacy over Britannicus. In other circumstances, a young man having a sudden, inexplicable physical crisis might command all attention, but those who have guessed what is going on immediately turn to Nero.[43] Secrecy is broken, but Nero's power is confirmed by attention, as it was at the *lusus Troiae* when he was favored over Britannicus. His reputation still matters—he seems to consider his public image paramount—but he does not seem to care that he is attracting negative attention so long as he is attracting attention.[44] The contrast between the need for concealment (because Nero is committing a heinous crime) and for display (because power and display of power are synonymous for Nero) conflict with each other here. The overlap between what should be advertised and what is too terrible to be mentioned in public is an animating contrast in much of Nero's reign and also a fertile ground

42. Tacitus calls this group *quibus altior intellectus* ("those of a deeper understanding") and does not explain why they stared at Nero. Furneaux interprets the opposite group, whom Tacitus calls *imprudentes*, as having no idea what was going on (1907, *ad loc*). Koestermann suggests that the more sagacious group were frozen in terror because they understood (1963, *ad loc*). I assume that the smarter group intuited that Nero was the person most likely to have harmed Britannicus.

43. Another powerful figure, Agrippina, is also present. That the more intelligent people do not look to her is a sign that her influence is declining.

44. The elite audience here presumably has a more sophisticated understanding of the politics of the court than do the masses at the *lusus Troiae*. The populace may turn toward Nero out of ignorance and desire for spectacle, but the elite are forced to pay attention to him because they run serious, even mortal, risks if they displease him. Nero's demand for attention is consistent over multiple social orders, but the nature of that attention varies.

for humor.[45] The contrast here is not necessarily humorous, because the opposed scripts confront each other subtly at this point, but the absurdity of Nero's principate is becoming apparent.

Nero's reaction to Britannicus' poisoning heightens the absurdity of the scene. Having obtained the spotlight, he plays his role competently, appearing nonchalant, "reclining and apparently unwitting" (*ut erat reclinis et nescio similis*, 13.16.3). Nero's performance is convincing. His excuse, however, is not: "[Nero] said that this was usual, owing to the epileptic illness with which Britannicus had been afflicted since early boyhood, and that his vision and feeling would return gradually" (*ait per comitialem morbum, quo prima ab infantia adflictaretur Britannicus, et redituros paulatim uisus sensusque*, 13.16.3). Although technically possible, this explanation is extremely unlikely. Suetonius records the same excuse with the specification that Nero lied (*ementitus*, *Nero* 33), a more pointed verb than Tacitus' colorless *ait*.[46] Tacitus' description suggests that the poison induced a response similar to a seizure, but it is incongruous that Nero should mention Britannicus' alleged epilepsy to a roomful of people who were already acquainted with Britannicus. Even if the Roman senatorial elite had somehow remained ignorant of a serious illness that had manifested in one of the previous emperor's children, Britannicus' stepmother and sister would have known the truth of such a claim. Octavia expresses no emotion, but Agrippina briefly shows her fear and dismay (13.16.4), emotions which she would not have displayed were this truly a routine occurrence.[47] Notwithstanding Nero's cool delivery, the lie convinces neither his audience nor Tacitus'.

---

45. Bartsch comments on another episode that, "Tacitus' Nero thus emerges as a man whose power is characterized by his ability to decide what the truth in the public realm will be," and that "for us [Tacitus' audience] to draw a distinction between this false but public script and the reality behind appearances, we must be made privy to the (putative) unspoken truth that Nero is perverting into his (putative) lies for public consumption" (1994, 22). I agree with Bartsch's assessment of Tacitus' Nero and add that characters in Tacitus are often aware of Nero's manipulations of reality even if they cannot confront him about them. Bartsch mentions that Nero appears "as the victim rather than the dictator of his audience's acting or as the unavenging addressee of oddly nuanced performances" but says that this occurs in other sources, not in Tacitus (1994, 24, 190).

46. Koestermann says Britannicus really did have epilepsy and that Nero lied only by implication (1963, 13.16.3), and Griffin suggests Nero's excuse was "credible" (1984, 74). Pearce, on the contrary, calls the excuse "implausible" and calculated to humiliate the dinner guests (2010, 64). Drinkwater provides a brief survey of modern historians, many of whom agree that Britannicus died of epilepsy (2019, 175–76n38). I advance no opinion on the historical reason for Britannicus' death but assert that Tacitus presents the death as a murder and does not support the epilepsy theory.

47. Agrippina's fear is for her own well-being rather than Britannicus'. Still, her shock indicates both that she was unaware of the plot and that she did not believe Nero's excuse.

As with Otho's claim that the support of the Senate would bring him victory,[48] Nero's assertion that Britannicus is merely suffering from epilepsy becomes absurd because nobody believes the excuse, but everyone acts as though they do: "So, after a brief silence, the delightful party resumed" (*ita post breue silentium repetita conuiuii laetitia*, 13.16.4). The situation is horrific, but the observers' frightened reactions take on a darkly humorous tone. Despite their instincts, and despite the disturbing event they have just witnessed, the spectators succumb to Nero's authority because they are accustomed to concealing emotions that might be unwelcome to the emperor. *Laetitia* is an especially significant term because it is extraneous and comes at the end of the sentence. The contrast between the initial stunned horror and the subsequent convivial joy makes the joy stand out as a grim punchline. Tacitus could have said that the *conuiuium* itself resumed, or that false expressions of joy were taken up. Instead, *laetitia* is an incongruous surprise at the end of the paragraph, because it foregrounds the emotional whiplash of the situation[49] and because it appears disconcertingly real. This joy adds to both the demonstration of Nero's power and the surreality of the scene because Nero is apparently able to command changes in emotion that are, if not genuine, impossible to distinguish from reality.[50] Elsewhere, Tacitus mentions joy (*laetitia*) in connection to murders when he wants to demonstrate that a character exercised power tyrannically.[51] A joyful reaction to death (or at least a crisis—Tacitus never makes it clear if Britannicus died in the room or was removed to die elsewhere) supports Nero in the moment, but makes him look ridiculous in the long term, as his guests' joy reflects their coercion into a fabricated reality that they did not truly believe.

This episode can be illuminated by comparison to Suetonius' version of the same events. Suetonius' interest throughout is with a few named characters directly involved in the action. He describes Nero personally flogging Lucusta

48. *Hist.* 1.84.3, discussed in chapter 1.

49. Despite the shock, emotional display is not inevitable. Octavia reacts with apparent equanimity, and the silence Tacitus mentions right before the joy resumes (*breue silentium*, 13.16.4) suggests that Nero required merely a compliant and not a demonstratively joyful reaction.

50. Haynes draws a distinction between actual reality, which cannot be expressed in language, and "the symbolically structured 'reality' in which Roman society actually operates" (2003, 34–35). She understands Nero's power as largely fictive, a demonstration of the way that all power is propped up by unreality (2003, 75). Although I have not adopted Haynes' terminology, my use of the word "reality" here refers to social reality and not the unreachable actual reality.

51. For example, Tacitus comments that Otho was happy when the head of Piso was delivered to him (*Hist.* 1.44.1), discussed in Keitel (2006, 237–38). Similarly, Vitellius is delighted to see the corpses of citizens abandoned on the field at Bedriacum (*Hist.* 2.70.4).

(Locusta in Tacitus) when her first poison failed to kill Britannicus and wraps up the episode by describing how Nero rewarded her when the next attempt succeeded (*Nero* 33). The guests who saw Britannicus poisoned are mentioned once and only as "guests" (*convivae*, 33). Suetonius mentions neither Agrippina nor Octavia. His is an emperor's-eye view of the episode; readers have access to privileged information about Nero but not about the reactions of those who witnessed Britannicus' death. In contrast, Tacitus' narrative inhabits the minds of multiple witnesses, increasing narrative uncertainty even while Nero's guilt is certain. By treating Britannicus' murder from multiple perspectives, Tacitus highlights the discrepancy between perception and reality and thus creates suitable conditions for humor.

At the beginning of the episode, Tacitus suggested that the most advantageous course of action was for Nero to conceal that he murdered Britannicus, and that Nero knew this. At the end, however, Tacitus suggests that Nero asserted his power by displaying his crime, because all the witnesses quietly sat through the murder as if it was not a murder. There is humor in the seamless shift from instinctual to politically advantageous reactions,[52] and with the strong contrast of humor Tacitus also illustrates one facet of Nero's power. Nero himself may be deluded or obsessed with performance, but whether he has accidentally stumbled upon a sound political strategy or skillfully plotted a show, he displays his ability to get away with murder.[53]

It is also significant that Nero's victory diminishes Agrippina's power. She controls Nero before this episode, and in later episodes she remains an obstacle to Nero taking sole control of Rome. At the fatal dinner, however, she is as shocked as anyone and cannot conceal her surprise. Instead of looking to her, the guests look to Nero. The humorous contrasts that Tacitus uses to describe Nero illuminate his effort to wrest control from Agrippina and his other councilors, thereby demonstrating both the fact of his power and how he wielded it against his political opponents.

---

52. The opposed scripts correspond to Raskin's most general opposed pair, real/unreal (1985, 113–14). There are other scripts involved, including powerful/powerless (the senatorial elite are powerful in theory, but less so in reality) and terrified/relaxed. I consider the real/unreal script opposition the most apt because this episode has broad implications for Nero's regime and for Tacitus' narrative, in which reality is often at issue. Britannicus' death marks the beginning of Nero's effort to force everyone else to inhabit the fictive reality upon which his power depends.

53. In addition, Schulz (2019, 113) notes a final irony in Nero's lamenting that he has been deprived of the help of his brother in governing the empire after he had him killed (13.17.3).

Nero as Petty Criminal

Tacitus continues to portray Nero as engaged in a combination of concealment and spectacle.[54] He opens the next year with another episode in which Nero's power alters the perceptions and behavior of others: "Nero wander[ed] through the streets of the City and its love-lairs and distractions in servile apparel, accoutered to dissemble his identity" (*qua Nero itinera Vrbis et lupanaria et deuerticula ueste seruili in dissimulationem sui compositus pererrabat*, 13.25.1). Nero's choices here are even more inscrutable than they were during the murder of Britannicus. Presumably Nero is driven by his own "foul recklessness" (*foeda [. . .] lasciuia*), but even while dressed like a slave and meaning to conceal his identity, he is accompanied by people authorized to assault passersby (13.25.1). Nero's disguise must be faulty because by the next sentence, word has gotten out that the emperor sneaks out of the palace at night to assault distinguished Romans (13.25.2). The consequences are predictably bizarre. Nero's habit of mugging elites encourages others to do the same because they expect to be protected by the possibility that anyone doing violence at night might be the emperor and therefore must not be punished (13.25.2). The situation is absurd because the emperor's behavior is imitated by people who do not hold positions of power. Although Nero's behavior is inappropriate for a person of any social role and although his identity is not well concealed, the professional muggers end up being treated as if they, like Nero, have the right to beat up strangers.[55] Imperial immunity is distributed over a large group of opportunists, mainly minor criminals whose actual occupation contrasts strongly with that of an emperor.

People who defend themselves against Nero run great risks. Julius Montanus, after having counterattacked the disguised Nero, pleaded his innocence on the grounds that he had not recognized him, but "was driven to die—exactly as though he had remonstrated" (*quasi exprobrasset, mori adactus est*, 13.25.2). It is difficult to reflect in English, but in Latin *mori adactus est* appears at the end of

54. Concealment and spectacle are opposed scripts because you cannot simultaneously display and conceal an event. This opposition, which continues to be important throughout Tacitus' characterization of Nero, also corresponds to the real/unreal script opposition because it demands that witnesses to Nero's antics treat them as simultaneously true (because they saw them) and fictive (because it is unacceptable to admit that they happened).

55. It is also possible that Nero's behavior was typical of rowdy aristocratic youths and that it would not have been a blemish on his reputation (Champlin 2003, 152–53). Tacitus does not refer to this possibility, however, but emphasizes the inappropriateness of Nero's behavior.

an involved sentence that describes the entire Montanus incident. Putting this information at the end of the sentence makes it an ironic surprise if not an outright punchline. In addition, Tacitus omits a detail that might have made Montanus' punishment seem slightly more reasonable; Cassius Dio suggests that Nero interpreted Montanus' request for a pardon as an admission that he had known that he was attacking Nero (epitome 61b.9.3–61b.9.4). By omitting Nero's reasoning, Tacitus obfuscates the reason for Nero's anger, which makes him seem irrational.[56]

Tacitus presents this event as ominous, yet it has a futility that makes it absurd as well. Nobody in the episode acts in a way that might be expected in a normal situation,[57] and that adds an element of humor. The further contrast between Nero the emperor, Nero the mugger, and Nero's imitators also exploits the contradiction between high and low status. Although Nero has the authority to initiate larger projects (including wars, a more traditional choice for emperors looking to do violence), he disguises himself to commit petty violence against Romans. The opportunistic pseudo-Neros are granted part of the privilege of the emperor because they cannot be distinguished from him.

This confusion of roles is humorous also because it necessitates a reversal of normal thinking. Usually, an emperor would be content to exercise power as an emperor, not by assaulting people in secret. Nor would regular muggers be empowered to behave as though they were emperors in disguise—the excuse would be too implausible, applied to most emperors. Finally, Tacitus shows that Nero's behavior caused a major change in the behavior of other elites. Where before they were empowered to fight off attackers with impunity, they can no longer, as any assailant might be the emperor in disguise. Their consternation reverses normal class dynamics and provides a vivid illustration of their subjection to Nero. The nexus of secrecy and performance is further complicated because everybody must participate in the deception that is generally known to be taking place because they are unable to avoid damage unless they play along. Tacitus says Nero was known to be putting on a false display, but his behavior encouraged others to perform in order to secure their places in the alternate

56. Bartsch notes that Tacitus' is the only account of these events in which Montanus does not know Nero's identity in the moment, and that Tacitus' version contradicts itself (1994, 18–20).

57. The possible exception is Montanus. His failure to conceal Nero's involvement makes him an insufficiently compliant audience member, which encourages Nero to condemn him (Bartsch 1994, 16).

reality he created. Nero amuses himself with half-staged street fights[58] while others are forced to participate in the spectacle as if it were real.

This episode introduces new complications to the absurd contrast between Nero's behavior and the way that Nero expects people to react to his behavior. The fact that these two categories are different illustrates Nero's power; he can demand that people not only obey him but also that they engage in the complex process of interpreting his explicit pronouncements to divine his implied wishes. Nero's subjects must frequently do bizarre things because the alternative is for him to clarify his desires by exercising conventional power, as he did with Montanus. Nero's subjects must understand that he wishes to be allowed to assault them without their resistance, but they must consent to this without acknowledging that their attacker is Nero. In addition to continuing the concealment/display theme from the Britannicus episode, Tacitus adds an opposition between the exalted position of an emperor and the lowly one of a mugger. The two scripts overlap in Nero, whose unexplained desire to exchange his role as emperor for a lowly one is both disconcerting and humorous. Although Tacitus does not mention future incidents in which Nero disguised himself as a mugger, Nero engages in non-imperial pursuits throughout the surviving books of the *Annals*.[59] This episode also provides an example of people other than Nero benefiting from his deceptions. The opportunistic muggers derive a clearer benefit from Nero's disguise than Nero does. Although Nero successfully asserts his power by telling unanswerable lies, that strategy is shown to be problematic because Nero cannot (or does not) stop the muggers from taking advantage of his fictions. Tacitus presents unconvincing but accepted falsehood as a problem of Nero's principate generally rather than as unique to Nero. The emperor starts the trend, but he is not the only person who benefits from it.

58. Tacitus says that Nero added a group of soldiers and gladiators to his entourage so that they could step in if the emperor's victims were getting the better of him (13.25.3). Nero's entourage lends a theatrical tone to the affair, as if the soldiers and gladiators are Nero's co-performers and the victims are an unfortunate audience.

59. Champlin argues that much of Nero's behavior is presented by ancient historians as merely unusual, not actually counterproductive for a Roman emperor. In fact, Champlin argues, some of Nero's apparently odd behavior would have made him more popular or enhanced his public image (2003, 237). Although Champlin presents compelling reasons that Nero was popular in his own time and later, Tacitus does not entertain the possibility that Nero acted rationally. Instead, Tacitus constructed a resoundingly negative portrait of the emperor and may indeed have overlooked rational explanations for Nero's behavior.

Poppaea

Poppaea takes such successful advantage of Nero's use of falsehood that she may be more paradigmatic of Nero's principate than Nero is himself. Tacitus treats Poppaea as a crisis in the making before he even mentions her name (13.45.1)[60] and describes her with considerable irony. "This woman had everything else except honorableness" (*huic mulieri cuncta alia fuere praeter honestum animum*, 13.45.2) is his initial pronouncement on her character.[61] Plass calls this comment a "bitter witticism" that "asserts the corruption of a society in which such a statement actually meets expectations because character is treated as optional" (1988, 29). Tacitus' tone is humorous, as indicated by the delay of *praeter honestum animum* to the end of the sentence, where it serves as an insult and as a punchline.

Tacitus emphasizes that Poppaea, like her most famous husband, relied on a combination of performance and concealment: "She paraded modestness and practiced recklessness, rarely emerging in public, and then only with part of her face screened by a veil, lest she satisfy people's gaze or because it became her" (*modestiam praeferre et lasciuia uti; rarus in publicum egressus, idque uelata parte oris, ne satiaret aspectum, uel quia sic decebat*, 13.45.3). Tacitus' Poppaea knows that her beauty is her best quality but keeps it hidden in order to better flaunt it.[62] This phrase also unites two opposed scripts (modesty and lasciviousness) in the character of Poppaea. Going out in public is not a performance on the same scale as sneaking out in disguise or giving musical recitals (as Nero does later), but for a Roman noblewoman cultivating a reputation for modesty, appearing in public would have approached as close to performance as was acceptable. Because Poppaea performs modesty, her display is paradoxically one of concealment. She reveals enough of her face to let people know that she is beautiful, but her concealment of her beauty is a vital part of her message.[63] Poppaea knows what she is

60. Tacitus also prepares the way for Poppaea by relating the murder of Pontia by Octavius Sagitta (13.44.1–5), a sordid story that conjures an atmosphere of lust and violence (Martin 1981, 168).

61. This passage is reminiscent of Sallust's comment in *Bellum Catilinae* that to Sempronia, "there was nothing she liked less than propriety and restraint" (*cariora semper omnia quam decus atque pudicitia fuit*, 25.3 trans. Batstone 2010. See also Martin 1981, 168). These comments reflect not only that the historians find these women immoral but also that they use them as illustrations of a total reversal of morality. In both cases, the woman represents a pattern of reversed values that reflects on a larger group of people (Catiline's rebellion in Sempronia's case; Nero's court in Poppaea's).

62. Koestermann comments that *modestiam praeferre et lasciuia uti* is a vivid demonstration of Poppaea's duality in ironic terms (1963, *ad loc*).

63. It is unclear how often Roman women wore veils or what veiling connoted. Hughes argues that

doing; she either believes that it is best to incite greater desire for her beauty by concealing it or that she looks more beautiful when partially veiled.[64] Neither Poppaea's false modesty nor her actual libidinousness are points in her favor, but her show of modesty makes her notable. Her display of concealment is a contradiction, as is Nero's, and it is effective, as is Nero's.

If Poppaea is a performer to rival Nero, the episodes that follow her arrival on the political scene are as close as Tacitus comes to comedy.[65] Her first marriage is dissolved as her relationship with Otho smoothly transitions from adultery into marriage (*adulterio matrimonium iungeretur*, 13.45.4). Two opposed scripts, marriage and adultery, are joined to each other by a single verb (*iungere*, a verb that connotes marriage, no less). Otho plays the role of the enamored *adulescens*, although he remains conscious of the political implications of their relationship: "Otho would praise his wife's good looks and elegance in the princeps's presence, whether being incautious through love or so that he might inflame him and, if they both possessed the same lady, that that bond might add to his power"[66] (*Otho siue amore incautus laudare formam elegantiamque uxoris apud principem, siue ut accenderet ac, si eadem femina potirentur, id quoque uinculum potentiam ei adiceret*, 13.46.1). Otho resembles the overenthusiastic lover from comedy,[67] if a comic *adulescens* were disastrously combined with a mature politician. Tacitus connects the imperial court to a set of tropes that would have been familiar from and hilarious in comedies and simultaneously likens the absurd machinations of comic lovers to those practiced by the emperor and his cronies.[68] By combining a comic premise with political con-

---

veiling was not typical for women of any status in the imperial period and cites the depictions of women on the *Ara Pacis* as evidence that imperial women were not necessarily veiled (2007, 221, 229). Whatever was the typical custom of elite Roman women, Tacitus implies that Poppaea's veiling was in some way ostentatious.

64. In his study of Tacitus' "loaded alternative," David Whitehead suggests that most binary alternatives in Tacitus are not weighted one way or another (1979, 475–76) and names this passage among the majority of unweighted alternatives (485). In this case, the alternative need not be loaded either way because both options suggest that Poppaea intended manipulation.
65. Messalina's wedding in Book 11 (discussed in chapter 3) is comparable in its use of comedy.
66. I have changed the last word in Woodman's translation of this sentence from "powerfulness" for the sake of simplicity.
67. He is young and eager to brag about his love affair, which contributes to the love triangle. In *Histories* 1, Tacitus draws a comparison between Otho and the *adulescens* in Plautus' *Mostellaria* (Fraser 2007, 624).
68. The version of this story that Tacitus tells in the *Annals* differs from all other sources, including his own in the *Histories* (Champlin 2003, 47–48). In all other versions, Nero encourages the marriage between Otho and Poppaea and therefore presumably knew her before she married Otho. The version in the *Annals* puts Nero and Otho in direct conflict over a canny, ambitious woman, a situation which ancient Romans would have recognized from comedy.

cerns, Tacitus makes the situation both more humorous (because of the overlap between imperial court and comic stage) and more sinister, because it is inappropriate for a ruler to behave like a comic archetype. The doubled perspective required to understand Otho as both a scheming courtier and a foolish young lover increases the ominous tension in the situation while also increasing its absurdity.[69]

It is Poppaea, however, who stars in the imperial comedy. Tacitus suggests that she either caught on to Otho's plan or realized the opportunity of her own accord, because she advances the deception: "Poppaea first achieved influence by means of skillful blandishments, pretending that she was unequal to her desire and captured by Nero's good looks" (*Poppaea primum per blandimenta et artes ualescere, imparem cupidini et forma Neronis captam simulans*, 13.46.2). In English, the crucial participle must introduce the clause, but in Latin, *simulans* comes last, leaving the middle of the sentence ambiguous before the last word explains it. *Imparem cupidini* offers no clues about the gender of the person referred to by *imparem* and might at first be taken to describe Nero's reaction to Poppaea. The feminine participle in *forma Neronis captam simulans* corrects that impression and reiterates what Tacitus has already said—that Poppaea was not emotional in her choice of lovers but reconciled personal desire with political advantage.[70] Deception is an essential part of Poppaea's character, and here Tacitus conceals her machinations even from his readers until the last possible moment.[71] The discrepancy between Poppaea's ardent exterior and calculating mind is amusing in itself, and extra humorous because it resembles the behav-

---

69. Both of Otho's roles are partially true. Otho was ambitious, but elsewhere Tacitus suggests that he loved Poppaea despite their mutual shallowness (*Hist.* 1.78.2).

70. "Susceptible to neither her own nor another's emotion, she would transfer her lust wherever advantage showed" (*neque adfectui suo aut alieno obnoxia, unde utilitas ostenderetur, illuc libidinem transferebat*, 13.45.3), Syme calls this the main negative comment on Poppaea's character in her introduction (1981, 40).

71. It is significant that Tacitus attributes any machinations to her at all. Other sources pay less attention to her or emphasize apolitical aspects of her character. Suetonius, for example, says only that she was first beloved of Nero then kicked to death by him (*Nero* 35). Cassius Dio introduces her in a cursory fashion (epitome 62a.11.1), blames her in part for the murders of Agrippina and Octavia (epitome 62a.12.1; 62b.13.1), and complains about her luxurious lifestyle when she dies (62b.28.1), but attributes almost no mental activity to her. In her biography of Nero, Griffin derives her most detailed points on Poppaea's politics from Josephus, who describes her influence on Judea rather than Rome (1984, 101). Griffin finds it difficult to believe that Poppaea ever attained political influence equivalent to Agrippina's because she was originally of lower status and depended on Nero for political clout (1984, 103–4). Champlin understands all surviving characterizations of Poppaea as basically ahistorical, and Tacitus' in particular as a "ferocious caricature" (2003, 103). Still, Tacitus has taken the time to write a caricature where Suetonius and Cassius Dio provide little information.

ior of the money-grubbing comic *meretrix*, if the *meretrix* had turned her sights from money to imperial power. Poppaea understands the façade required by imperial power even better than Nero does, and her deception is more successful than his because it does not become public knowledge.

Tacitus shows that Poppaea's machinations became increasingly ridiculous after she was confident that she had hooked Nero (13.46.2):

> She changed to haughtiness, insisting, if she were detained beyond a night or two, that she was a wedded woman and could not give up her married state, bound as she was to Otho by the kind of life which no one could equal: he was a man of magnificent spirit and refinement, she said, in him she saw things deserving of the highest fortune; whereas Nero, bound by custom to a maidservant concubine, had derived nothing from his servile cohabitation except sordid abasement.

> *ad superbiam uertens, si ultra unam alteramque noctem attineretur, nuptam esse se dictitans, nec posse matrimonium amittere, deuinctam Othoni per genus uitae, quod nemo adaequaret: illum animo et cultu magnificum; ibi se summa fortuna digna uisere. at Neronem, paelice ancilla et adsuetudine Actes deuinctum, nihil e contubernio seruili nisi abiectum et sordidum traxisse.*

Tacitus reports Poppaea's speech indirectly, yet the passage approaches a comic monologue, given that Poppaea makes almost nonsensical arguments and implicitly compares Nero to a slave. The absurdity of Poppaea's protestation that she is a married woman should register as disingenuous immediately for any audience but the internal one, Nero. Her insistence on her marriage comes directly after she is asked to stay with Nero beyond "a night or two." Poppaea suddenly claims that her marriage is important to her when it wasn't the last night or the night before that.[72] Her repetition of this argument (*dictitans*) heightens its improbability. The reasons why she cannot leave Otho are equally bizarre. She claims that she is "bound" to him "by a type of life which no one could equal" and that he is "deserving of the highest fortune" (13.46.2). Without context, these might be good reasons to stay with a husband, but given that

72. Perhaps Poppaea wants to avoid a three-night separation from her husband, which was significant in Roman marriage law but not equivalent to divorce (Koestermann 1963, 13.46.2). It is unclear why a three-day separation from Otho would disadvantage Poppaea when she apparently wants to marry Nero.

Nero is the emperor, it is at best odd to claim that he maintains an insufficiently magnificent lifestyle.[73] In addition, if Otho seemed worthy of "the highest fortune," Nero was already its conspicuous beneficiary.[74] For Tacitus' readers, Poppaea's argument against marrying Nero is humorous because it demonstrates that her resistance is false and her arguments are concocted to achieve marriage to Nero despite her overt argument that she should remain married to Otho. The fact that Nero believes Poppaea confirms that deceptive appearances are paramount in his principate.

Poppaea also implicitly connects Nero's power to appearances. Several of her objections to marrying him imply threats to an emperor who enjoys demonstrating his power through performance and excess. The comparison between him and Otho is unflattering in that it exalts Otho above the emperor, but worse is Poppaea's implication that Nero has been infected by the status of his freedwoman concubine, Acte. Poppaea describes herself as bound (*deuinctam*) to Otho, while Nero is bound to Acte. Acte has already been a political problem for Nero,[75] but Poppaea argues that Acte's status could rub off on Nero, a claim with little validity. Poppaea first calls Acte a *paelex* (which suggests a relationship congruent with the difference between her status and Nero's), but she later refers to their relationship as a *contubernium seruile*,[76] and the parallel between Poppaea's marriage to Otho and Nero's relationship with Acte suggests that Acte's low status made Nero less aristocratic.

Poppaea also argues that Nero gains nothing from a relationship with Acte. By this point, Poppaea has dropped her pretense of not wanting to marry Nero and begun to make the case that they should marry. (She does not acknowledge the change in her argument.) Acte offers Nero nothing but "sordid abasement" (*abiectum et sordidum*, 13.46.2), while Poppaea presumably offers him the possibility of a legitimate child.[77] Although Poppaea's argument is disingenuous

73. In the *Histories*, Tacitus says that Otho competed with Nero over who could be more luxurious (1.13.3), so perhaps Otho did offer Poppaea a more hedonistic life than Nero did. Nevertheless, Poppaea's claim that Nero could not equal Otho's style seems exaggerated.

74. There is dramatic irony here as well because Otho later became emperor.

75. Tacitus reports that Agrippina found it unacceptable for her son to associate with a freedwoman (13.13.1). Given Tacitus' contempt for influential freedpeople, Agrippina's disdain for Acte may reflect his own assessment.

76. *Contubernium* indicates cohabitation, and when it refers to a marital relationship, as it does here, it exclusively refers to marriage between slaves (*OLD*). Tacitus overdetermines this connotation by calling the relationship a *contubernium seruile*. The marital sense of *contubernium* occurs nowhere else in Tacitus (*Lexicon Taciteum*), so it is striking that Tacitus introduces the concept here. Koestermann calls Poppaea's use of *contubernium* an example of her power over the emperor (1963, 13.46.2).

77. Later, Poppaea names the possibility of legitimate children as a primary reason for their marriage (14.1.2, 14.61.4).

because Acte could not have married Nero, Poppaea's criticisms of her are significant because they reverse Poppaea's role and Nero's. Poppaea is deciding between husbands by weighing the benefit of each.[78] Nero is already married to Octavia, who garners no mention here but was a better political prospect than either Poppaea or Acte. In Poppaea's speech, however, the choice is between Acte (not useful) and Poppaea (presumably useful, but for unspecified reasons). Poppaea's speech demonstrates that performance, including lying, is important in politics because it has real influence, especially because Nero cannot separate imperial concerns from trivial ones.

Poppaea is an empress to fit Nero's principate. She makes a careful spectacle of herself and finds in Acte a weakened rival to defeat in a fictive competition, as Nero did with Britannicus.[79] Nero is apparently fooled by her lies, but Tacitus' narrative presents them as well matched. Poppaea's courtship of Nero is ridiculous for its resemblance to theatrical comedy (in which romantic competition is typical) and for her falsehoods that pass for the truth.[80] Simultaneously, Poppaea's behavior demonstrates that absurd performance is currency in Nero's principate and that the performance/concealment script opposition will continue to be relevant, perhaps even crucial for determining who wields power. Tacitus uses this episode to expand on the reversal of the values of truth and falsehood. Poppaea's excuses carry weight, even though they seem absurd from the perspective of Tacitus' readers. Falsehood has become important because Nero encouraged it, but other political figures can take advantage of the value he puts on performance. In this instance, Nero himself is taken in by a distortion of reality that his style of governance has made possible.

The Murder of Agrippina

Tacitus' humorous characterization of Nero peaks in his narration of the death of Agrippina. Previous episodes used humor to point out Nero's consolidation of power, while Agrippina remained an obstacle, although her influence had declined.[81] Tacitus credits Poppaea with instigating the murder plot, and again

78. Tacitus referred to her capacity for calculation earlier, saying that Poppaea could subordinate her lusts to her advantage (*utilitas*, 13.45.3).
79. In addition, Poppaea's introduction foreshadows Agrippina's downfall because her influence is in inverse proportion to Agrippina's (Koestermann 1963, 13.45.2), so Poppaea is a key figure not only in her own rise but also in Nero's consolidation of power.
80. I discuss Tacitus' use of the conventions of comedy in chapter 3 also.
81. Especially significant is Agrippina's reaction to the murder of Britannicus, where Tacitus suggests that her influence waned as Nero became more prominent (13.16.4).

her arguments are implausible but believed.[82] She incites Nero to murder his mother with accusations (*criminationibus*) and "by way of a witticism" (*per facetias*, 14.1.1). According to Tacitus, these "witticisms" consisted of her calling the emperor "the ward" (*pupillum uocare*, 14.1.1) and claiming that he had neither power (*imperium*) nor freedom (*libertas*). These *facetiae* do not sound particularly humorous—the funniest formal element in them is the alliteration between *principem* and *pupillum*—and they tend toward straightforward criticism, but Poppaea's blatant falsehoods recall Nero's requirement that others recognize his power by treating his fictions seriously. Poppaea implies that Nero could become the object of mockery because his power is fictive, and this prospect is more terrifying to him than his mother's actual influence.

Poppaea also repeats threats she used earlier, including her threat to return to Otho (14.1.2).[83] By bringing up Otho, she revisits her first objection to being married to Nero, and it rings as hollow here as it did earlier. Tacitus specifies that she accompanied her speech with "the artful tears of an adulteress" (*lacrimis et arte adulterae*, 14.1.3), a contrivance which deceives Nero but reveals her insincerity to Tacitus' readers. As it was earlier, Poppaea's performance is humorous for Tacitus' readers because it is so obviously false. Nevertheless, her unconvincing complaints touch off Agrippina's murder and may have alarmed Agrippina enough that she attempted to seduce her own son as a countermeasure.[84]

Tacitus depicts Nero's decision to murder Agrippina as almost casual: "Deeming her overburdensome wherever she was, he decided to kill her, debating only whether by poison or the sword or some other violence" (*postremo, ubicumque haberetur, praegrauem ratus interficere constituit, hactenus consultans, ueneno an ferro uel qua alia ui*, 14.3.1). Despite having attributed many flaws to Agrippina elsewhere, Tacitus does not name Nero's reason for murdering her. Possibly Agrippina's attempts to commit incest with him made her presence unpalatable (14.2.1–2).[85] Possibly Nero was convinced by Poppaea.[86]

82. Despite his antipathy to Poppaea, Tacitus blames her for only a few specific crimes. This and the death of Octavia are the most pivotal of those crimes.

83. Syme notes "satiric or comic effects" in this passage (1981, 41).

84. Tacitus hesitates to confirm or deny the rumors that Agrippina tried to seduce Nero (14.2.1–2). Although Tacitus does not clarify the reason, he says that Nero started avoiding Agrippina and soon decided to have her murdered (14.3.1).

85. Baldwin sees humor in the passage where Agrippina attempts to commit incest with Nero because of the implication that Agrippina was too old to be attractive (1977, 131). I do not discuss this passage because I find it unlikely that Tacitus is making a disapproving comment about Agrippina's physical attractiveness, a characteristic that is rarely a focus of his judgment.

86. If Poppaea actually did convince Nero to kill his mother so they could marry, Nero did not follow through, as he would not divorce Octavia for another three years (Martin 1981, 170).

Possibly Agrippina's murder became inevitable at her son's accession. Rather than settling on an answer, Tacitus presents Nero's decision without explanation and moves on to the problem of the method of death. The fussiness of *ueneno an ferro uel qua alia ui* contrasts with the enormity of Nero's decision to kill his mother, a more shocking and significant choice than his selection of a method. Through much of the episode, Tacitus uses humor while communicating the details of Agrippina's death even though the deed is a horror.

As in the murder of Britannicus, Nero focuses on public spectacle to the exclusion of practical matters.[87] Nero's plan to kill his mother relies on his and his courtiers' expertise in putting on a show, with predictably absurd results. By calling attention to how public the murder was, Tacitus again draws out the contrast between performance and secrecy. The murder is obvious even though the emperor and his advisers intend to keep it secret.[88] Their final plan to drown Agrippina on a collapsing boat is more showy than practical or deceptive. Tacitus attributes the shipwreck plan to Anicetus, perhaps an appropriate person to propose a plan involving a ship because he was prefect of the fleet (14.3.3).[89]

Tacitus presents this plan as theatrical rather than plausible. It relies on a faulty boat and proposes that after Agrippina's death, Nero can prove his piety by constructing a temple to her (14.3.3). If anyone in Nero's circle foresaw problems with the plan, Tacitus does not mention it.[90] Tacitus presents the plan as ridiculous. Nero's concern over the method rather than the fact of the murder is repeated by Anicetus' summary articulation of the murder plot and his interest in pretending that Agrippina was not murdered at all. Anicetus glosses over practical issues to focus on the appearance of the deed once it has been accom-

87. Haynes considers this episode to be highly theatrical, while also suggesting that theater is an inadequate metaphor for Nero's behavior (2003, 73–74). Antonio Marchetta makes a detailed argument that Tacitus based the episode on a play, Seneca's *Thyestes* (2004, 97–586), and cites ways that Tacitus builds up the theatricality of the episode. Trevor Luke is suspicious of the story because it is too thematically convenient with Tacitus' portrayal of Nero as obsessed with performance (2013, 209).

88. Tacitus says that they were motivated to cover up their crimes not because they feared a bad reputation but because they worried that Agrippina's supporters would figure out their plot in advance and foil it (14.3.2). In this episode, secrecy is a matter of efficacy at least as much as deception, and it is therefore even stranger that Nero insists on theatricality.

89. Baldwin finds Anicetus' deadpan cynicism humorous (1977, 132). Marchetta finds Tacitus' introduction of Anicetus sarcastic because it shows that Anicetus, Nero's former teacher, was still educating him in vice (2004, 222).

90. Although the plan is ridiculous enough in Tacitus, Suetonius provides an even more bizarre account in which Nero first wants Agrippina's bedroom ceiling to collapse on her, then settles for the collapsible boat plan after the ceiling plan is discovered (*Nero* 34). In Suetonius, Nero is the originator of both plans.

plished, and in doing so he ignores the potential snags in his plot. To a reader, the plot is obviously bizarre, and indeed it goes wrong almost immediately.[91] Nero deceives Agrippina into believing that he wants to make amends (14.4.1)[92] and later assuages her suspicions in order to persuade her onto the boat (14.4.4). This is the only part of the plan that works as intended.

In the sequence that leads to Agrippina's death, Tacitus employs a considerable amount of irony and humor. He begins with some uncharacteristic scene-setting, describing the calm night and sea with cosmic irony: "as if the gods had provided it to prove criminality" (*quasi conuincendum ad scelus dii praebuere*, 14.5.1).[93] The gods have picked an ironic setting for Nero's great crime. The contrast between Nero's and the gods' goals plays up the dramatic irony between the knowledge of the historian and the reader, who know Nero's plan, and the characters in the narrative, most of whom do not. While readers may interpret the weather as the gods' way of revealing Nero's crime, Nero's victims would have understood it as a good night for sailing. And if the gods mean to reveal Nero's plot, they also lend Agrippina false confidence.[94] While hardly uproarious, the passage begins with dramatic irony in the contrast between characters' impressions of reality and reality as Tacitus presents it to his readers.

At the beginning of the scene, Agrippina's freedwoman Acerronia reflects happily on Agrippina's reconciliation with her apparently penitent son when part of the boat collapses almost on top of them (14.5.1).[95] Although the boat

---

91. Nero's plot is so unlikely that at least one modern scholar has proposed it was a garbled reflection of a theatrical plot (Dawson 1969), and even in disagreeing with that interpretation, Plass describes the assassination as a "comic opera plot" (1988, 82).
92. Tacitus attributes Agrippina's susceptibility to Nero's deception to "the credulity of females being responsive to joyful news" (*facili feminarum credulitate ad gaudia*, 14.4.1). Credulity is an atypical element in Tacitus' characterization of Agrippina, who just a chapter ago was so suspicious that poison could not be relied upon in the plot against her. Agrippina's sudden credulity does, however, explain why this part of Nero's plot succeeded.
93. My translation departs from Woodman's because Woodman puts the gods in an agent construction ("ensured by the gods"). I make the gods the subject of the clause, as they are in Latin, because it better reflects how unusual it is for Tacitus to bring the gods directly into the narrative. Cassius Dio does something similar in his narration of the same event, saying that the sea itself was unwilling to be blamed for the crime (epitome 62a.13.3). Koestermann comments on the tragic tone of this passage and the personification of the sea (1963, *ad loc*), as does Mendell, who calls it a "melodramatic flourish" (1957, 61). Shannon considers this comment a serious sign that the gods disapprove of Nero (2012, 749).
94. Schulz interprets this passage as an example of "mutual understanding between the emperor and his non-human surroundings," a reflection on his imperial divinity. That is contrasted, however, by 14.10.3, where Nero finds the sea oppressive (Schulz 2019, 85). Tacitus is probably not sincerely portraying Nero as a deity, but Nero was identified with several gods, so the comparison is reasonable.
95. Tacitus describes the arrangement of Agrippina's retinue on the boat in the same long sentence in

collapses as planned, the people charged with executing the plot experience a range of mechanical failures. They have not predicted that Agrippina and Acerronia would be protected by the high sides of the couch on which they were sitting, and they are unable to trigger a further failure of the boat because the other passengers (who are not in the know) panic and prevent them from doing so (14.5.1–3). The rowers (who must have been in on the plot) attempt to capsize the ship by leaning to one side but fail because they cannot decide which side to lean toward and because the ignorant passengers unwittingly counteract them (14.5.2).[96] Tacitus draws an implicit contrast between the concern for secrecy in the planning stage and the incompetence with which Nero's agents carry out the plot. Tacitus introduces humor in the contrast between the plotters' expectations and their abilities and finds more humor in his characterization of these events as a performance gone wrong. By laying out first the ideal (but unlikely) course of the plot and then detailing what actually happened, Tacitus demonstrates the gap between expectation and reality, significant opposed scripts.[97] The initial deception, performed by Nero himself, went better than it needed to, but the murder attempt is so chaotic that Agrippina survives it. Nero's deception is initially successful and enables the first murder attempt, but in retrospect it seems pointless because the obviousness of the murder made deception impossible.

In the chaos of the half-failed murder, Acerronia is finished off "while she misguidedly kept shouting that she was Agrippina and that the princeps's mother must be rescued" (*imprudentia dum se Agrippinam esse utque subueniretur matri principis clamitat*, 14.5.3).[98] Tacitus frontloads Acerronia's lack of

---

which the trap is triggered. The first independent clause says the ship had not gone far. Acerronia's misguided joy about the reconciliation is the second independent clause, followed by a subordinate clause in which the trap is sprung, then a final independent clause saying that Crepereius, another of Agrippina's attendants, died immediately. This sequence is not especially humorous (Crepereius' death is not much of a punchline), but it is surprising and emphasizes the disconnect between what happened and what was expected. Marchetta comments that Tacitus meant to imply that Agrippina did not believe Acerronia's optimism (2004, 265–66).

96. Baldwin suggests this passage could be "a piece of deliberate farce" (1977, 133).

97. Again, Raskin's real/unreal script opposition is evoked (1985, 113–14). Tacitus' narrative strategy in describing first the plan and then the facts corresponds to a simple logical mechanism, juxtaposition (Attardo 1994, 225–26).

98. Woodman allows *imprudentia* to refer loosely to Acerronia but puts it outside the parentheses that describe Acerronia's misjudgment (2004, 277). I think a less ambiguous translation is justified. Furneaux interprets *imprudentia* as a causal ablative referring to Acerronia's misjudgment (1907, *ad loc*). Koestermann suggests that, although the placement of *dum* would be unique, Tacitus has displaced *imprudentia* because it explains the entire clause and is therefore a necessary preface to it (1963, *ad loc*). I have altered Woodman's translation to attach *imprudentia* more surely to Acerronia.

judgment by saying she acted misguidedly (*imprudentia*). Tacitus separates *imprudentia* from the behavior it describes. We read that Acerronia misjudged before we learn that it was a mistake to claim to be the emperor's mother. The revelation that Acerronia's *imprudentia* was part of a reasonable (if deceptive) strategy creates a punchline. In other circumstances, Acerronia's ploy might have been successful. Tacitus, his readers, and many of the other characters know that claiming to be Agrippina will get Acerronia killed, but Acerronia is ignorant of her circumstances and believes that it will help her.[99] The joke is at Acerronia's expense, but the humor comes from the contrast between the expectations of characters in the narrative and those of readers who know Nero's plans.

Tacitus contrasts the fatally credulous Acerronia with Agrippina, who does not draw attention to herself. She is silent, which keeps her concealed (*minus agnita*, 14.5.3). Agrippina's silence provides a variation on the humor associated with Acerronia. Agrippina survives the first attempt on her life because she does not advertise that she is the emperor's mother, even though she is. The humor here turns on the contrast between the fictive affection connecting the imperial family members and their actual murderous antipathy for each other. The emperor's mother (and, for that matter, his stepbrother) are owed filial favor, but they are murdered instead. Tacitus uses this contrast to illustrate the lengths to which Nero's subjects must go in order to lie correctly. Acerronia gives the performance that she believes is required of her. She thinks that her deception will benefit her, but she unwittingly assumes a disadvantageous role. Her reasoning is sound, but she is missing essential information. Tacitus presents Acerronia's predicament as humorous to demonstrate that an advantageous lie can quickly become an absurd one. Agrippina, unlike Acerronia, initially refuses to perform. Tacitus does not explicitly say that she understood in the moment that her son wanted to kill her, but the contrast between her reaction and Acerronia's suggests that she had guessed.

In this scene, humor allows Tacitus to show that both women's strategies were reasonable while simultaneously explaining why one escaped and the other was killed. Acerronia's reaction follows one dictum of Nero's principate because she engages in deceit to try to gain an advantage. Agrippina acts on another dictum of Nero's principate, which is that when a crime is being com-

99. A few sentences ago, Acerronia was rehearsing the joys of mother-son reconciliation (14.5.1). She was thoroughly duped by Nero's performance.

mitted, it is better to make sure you know what the emperor expects before resuming your performance. (Nero's murder of Britannicus establishes this rule.) These two dicta are confusing for the victims of the crime as well as for its perpetrators. According to Tacitus, Nero's power was supported by performance, but he exercised it to accomplish crimes that needed to be covered up. Acerronia understands performance as a way to placate Nero (and it is) while Agrippina understands that if she wants to escape, she must engage in a different type of performance by concealing her knowledge of the plot, which she does by keeping silent during the crisis and sending a deceptive message later.

By bringing together these two responses to the shipwreck, Tacitus shows that both characters are at once rational and ridiculous. Falsely claiming to be Agrippina would not be a good strategy in less chaotic circumstances, but strategic lies are often required in Nero's court. Remaining silent in the face of disaster would be dangerous under normal circumstances, but it is correct here, although it preserves Agrippina's life only temporarily. Tacitus has framed the whole narrative as a show gone wrong, in which Acerronia's and Agrippina's behavior illustrates the peculiarities of Nero's regime. Although Nero is a tyrant, he communicates his wishes without making explicit commands. Instead, he demands that others support his version of reality, which Tacitus presents as absurd. People must comprehend both what Nero actually wants and what he wants them to believe he wants. Plenty of courtiers fail at this difficult task (like Acerronia), and even success at reading Nero does not guarantee a good outcome. In this episode, Tacitus uses humor to illustrate this complex dynamic of performance and to show that the uncertainty Nero has cultivated benefits him because it is difficult for his courtiers to mount a coherent response to it. Tacitus exploits the difference between Agrippina's and Acerronia's responses to point out both the unlikeliness and the durability of Nero's power. Tacitus uses humor to suggest that Nero's rule is not merely contradictory, but also supported by its own contradictions.[100]

The humor in this episode centers on the chaotic response of Nero's court in the face of a disaster, as it did in the murder of Britannicus.[101] Nero expects people to play along when he exercises his powers, even when he does so in a

100. Nero's regime mirrors a joke structure because it depends on opposed, overlapping scripts. Like a joke in script theory, Nero's power is supported by a system of contradictions that paradoxically reinforce each other.

101. Luke sees Agrippina's death as the culmination of a power struggle that reaches back to Britannicus' murder (2013, 208).

laughable way. People must recognize his power, but also pretend that they cannot detect his plots. The shipwreck is evidence of Nero's power and the apparently irrational way he exercises it. Tacitus disapproves of both and treats them as uncomfortably intertwined; if Nero were not reckless enough to display his crimes, he might not be able to demonstrate his power as starkly. Nero's absurd demands prove his power to command more than his conventional demands do.

Agrippina keeps Nero's criminal intent concealed after she has arrived at her villa. Tacitus says that by combining her knowledge of the ship collapsing, Acerronia's death, and her own injury, she concluded that Nero was up to something (14.6.1).[102] She decides to pretend not to understand that she was attacked because she recognizes the importance of both performance and concealment.[103] Instead of challenging her son, she sends him a message that he should not be afraid for her (14.6.2). Agrippina's deliberations are more ironic than humorous because her life is at stake and much of the scene is focalized through her.[104]

Instead, Tacitus extends the humorous strand to other characters. He describes a group of people who rush the beach near Agrippina's house: "the assumption being that [the shipwreck] had happened by accident, and each person on hearing of it ran down to the shore" (*quasi casu euenisset, ut quisque acceperat, decurrere ad litus*, 14.8.1). Their misperception is humorous because they are victims of dramatic irony, and their subsequent behavior reinforces this impression: "The whole beach was filled with the complaints, vows, and shouting of those asking their different questions or answering in uncertain terms. A mighty multitude with lights streamed down, and, when it became known that she had been preserved, they prepared themselves to offer

102. This passage calls the collapsing ship a *machinamentum*, a word with theatrical overtones that match the episode's performance motif. Although *machinamentum* does not have a special theatrical significance, it is a variant on the more common *machina*, which does have a specific theatrical sense (*OLD*). In addition, Cassius Dio says that the mechanism in question was inspired by a theatrical device (epitome 62a.12.2). Tacitus does not mention this detail, but it may have been implied by his vocabulary. Griffin calls the *machinamentum* "part of a tendency for theater to invade [Nero's] life" (1984, 164). Marchetta distances Tacitus' *machinamentum* from theater machinery but notes a pronounced connection between theater and the collapsing boat in Suetonius' and Cassius Dio's accounts of the same events (2004, 223).

103. Plass sees Agrippina's decision to conceal her knowledge as an example of "political irrationality," specifically the type that uses contradiction to produce "wittily empty sentences" (1988, 123–24).

104. Bartsch understands this as the moment Agrippina submits to Nero's control of the spectacle (1994, 20–21).

congratulations—until they scattered at the sight of an armed and menacing column" (*questibus uotis clamore diuersa rogitantium aut incerta respondentium omnis ora compleri; adfluere ingens multitudo cum luminibus, atque ubi incolumem esse pernotuit, ut ad gratandum sese expedire, donec adspectu armati et minitantis agminis deiecti sunt*, 14.8.1). Tacitus does not identify the people on the beach beyond saying that they heard the story and believed the shipwreck was an accident. Their ignorance makes sense because they are not typical participants in politics.[105] The humor comes from the fact that they are forced to change their behavior extremely quickly when the soldiers arrive, and the crowd realizes they have badly mistaken their assigned role. They feel concern for Agrippina for the better part of two sentences (three independent verbs), in which they fill all available space on the beach and attempt to congratulate Agrippina on her escape, but in the *donec* clause, they forget all that and vanish from the narrative.[106] The first part of this passage is set up as a joke with a punchline, the target of which is the crowd who appear on Agrippina's beach. The punchline underscores the opposed scripts that operate simultaneously on this group. On the one hand, it is correct to support the emperor's mother. On the other, it is correct to obey the emperor's wishes and not to cross his soldiers.

The hapless well-wishers are hardly the most reprehensible people in this episode, especially not compared to Nero, Anicetus, and Agrippina. They are, however, misinterpreting the situation, an amusing mistake from the perspective of Tacitus' readers. While Tacitus has discussed the impact of Nero's lies mainly on his courtiers and others close to him, the people on the beach are insignificant yet still struggle to cope with Nero's fictions. Tacitus criticizes the credulity of the *vulgus* using similar themes as he does when he skewers the flagrant crimes of the emperor and his cronies.[107] The humor is complicated, however, because the internal audience on the beach are understandably ignorant. Tacitus' audience can find humor in the crowd's premature exuberance and sudden reversal, but the crowd's mistakes are not the results of an informed but illogical view of the situation, but of total misinformation. Instead of understanding the entire situation, they hear only fictions without having access to

105. Although Tacitus does not specify who they are, it seems unlikely that they are influential. Galtier says they are ordinary people who happen to notice the shipwreck (2014, 311).

106. Galtier theorizes that they never even lay eyes on Agrippina (2014, 312).

107. The people on the beach are not the Roman *vulgus* because they are at Bauli, but their imprudence and recklessness are consistent with Tacitus' other depictions of common people. In any case, they are a contrast from the secret plots of Nero's court (Galtier 2014, 313).

the reality that would temper their reaction to these fictions. Unlike the elites, they do not have the means to understand what Nero really wants.[108] Their unmitigated support for Agrippina, the emperor's mother, aligns with Nero's representation that he loved his mother, but conflicts with the way he actually wants them to act. Tacitus shows that Nero counted on those in the know to recognize his deceptions, and that uninformed outsiders might accidentally believe his fictions in their entirety.[109] Because recognizing deception required an insider's perspective (limited to elites, freedmen, and perhaps careful historians), Nero's messages that he is in power become garbled whenever people are legitimately confused by his official fictions.

Despite the ignorance of the people on the beach, Nero remains the most prominent target of humor. At this phase of the plot, he improvises desperately. Nero imagines the coup that Agrippina might still organize (14.7.2) and summons Burrus and Seneca, whom he has not yet told about the conspiracy against Agrippina, although Tacitus doubts that they were ignorant of it ("it being doubtful whether they were ignorant even before this," *incertum an et ante gnaros*, 14.7.2). The contrast between the calculated calm of Nero's advisers and his own frenzy is humorous because the character who ought to be in control has again lost control of events that he himself set in motion.

Despite the presence of Seneca and Burrus, Nero, according to Tacitus, came up with a plan to finish off Agrippina. He pretends that Agrippina's messenger Agerinus[110] was part of a plot to kill him (14.7.6). Tacitus reminds readers of the performance motif by saying Nero "set the stage for an accusation of his own" (*scaenam ultro criminis parat*, 14.7.6). Because there is no literal stage, this figure of speech repeats the idea that Nero draws on theatrical performance (Baldwin 1977, 134; Bartsch 1994, 21). Although Tacitus credits Nero with excellent powers of deception earlier in the episode, he portrays his gambit here as truly wretched. Nero "threw down a sword at [Agerinus'] feet" (*gladiumque [. . .] abicit inter pedes eius*, 14.7.6), apparently with no attempt at concealment. This plan is conspicuously awful. *Gladium* appears a few words before the

108. Marchetta contends that the people on the beach are dupes of Agrippina rather than of Nero because she pretended not to realize Nero wanted her murdered, and because many of Nero's deceptions were begun by Agrippina (2004, 175–76). Marchetta's point is reasonable, but I am less concerned with the fine distinction between deceptions associated with Nero and with Agrippina than with deception in Nero's court generally.

109. Julius Montanus (discussed above) provides a similar example. He defended himself on the charge of assaulting the emperor by claiming not to have seen through Nero's disguise and was commanded to kill himself regardless (13.25.2).

110. Suetonius calls the same figure Agermus (*Nero* 34).

clause to which it belongs, setting up an expectation of violence on which Nero's plan does not deliver. Tacitus does not even credit Nero with attempting to plant the sword discreetly (if such a thing were possible), nor does he offer any explanation of why an interrupted assassin would have a sword at his feet rather than in his hands. Although Nero intended to fabricate a pretext for having Agrippina killed by soldiers under Anicetus' command, his attempt to frame the messenger is presented as entirely unconvincing.[111] Tacitus presents Nero's encounter with Agerinus as happening almost at random and so emphasizes the strange and theatrical elements of Nero's rule to such a degree that they overshadow the ostensibly convincing excuse for Agrippina's murder, which encourages a humorous interpretation of the nonsensical plan.[112]

For Tacitus' readers, Nero's behavior here is familiar from the murder of Britannicus, which also entailed a failed first attempt and a second attempt during which it became obvious that Nero was trying to murder his relative. In both episodes, Nero intends to maintain secrecy, but then abandons it, and in both he refuses to acknowledge his guilt, even when his actions make him obviously guilty. Nero's acting is unimpeachable on both occasions. He betrays no alarm at Britannicus' collapse and displays a false *pietas* that deceives Agrippina. His plans, however, are superbly ill-considered.[113] The contrast between Nero's ability to deceive in person and his inability to plan a deception is humorous because it plays into an established script opposition between Nero's role as emperor and his role as actor. The two scripts are opposed because they are traditionally incompatible roles, but they overlap in Nero.[114] Moreover, Tac-

111. Burrus has already said that the praetorians would not kill Agrippina even if they were commanded to (14.7.4), so perhaps Nero needed a pretext for killing her. Anicetus' soldiers, however, are apparently from the fleet that he commanded, not from the praetorians, and their loyalty to Nero does not depend on his mother; Nero had independent ties to the fleet at Misenum. Only the praetorians loyally supported Agrippina (Griffin 1984, 68–69). Tacitus claims that Anicetus' men killed her without hesitation. If Nero was sure of Anicetus' troops, he might not have needed to fabricate an excuse but chose to invent a flimsy one out of habit.

112. Luke does not see the plot as ridiculous because there is nothing inherently unlikely about an agent of Agrippina being sent to stab the emperor (2013, 220–21), which is true. That interpretation, however, explicitly challenges the impression that Tacitus has cultivated. If he wanted Nero's excuse to seem plausible, he would have lent it a modicum of dignity.

113. Neither murder is planned entirely by Nero. Julius Pollio and Locusta do most of the practical work in Britannicus' murder (13.15.3–5), and Anicetus comes up with the flashier part of Agrippina's (14.3.3). Nevertheless, Tacitus credits Nero with some of the worst ideas in both schemes because he demanded a rapid and public poisoning with Britannicus and insisted Agerinus was menacing him with a sword during Agrippina's murder.

114. Haynes notes that Nero's rule was disconcerting because people were forced to acknowledge him as both an emperor and an actor (2003, 72–73). I argue that there is humor as well as menace in Nero's dual roles.

itus suggests that Nero's behavior as an actor actually contributed to his power as emperor, thus uniting the opposed scripts in a humorous yet ominous way. Because Nero does not convince people that his claims are literally true, he is like an actor, but because people obey him anyway, he is all the more clearly an emperor. Like a theatrical actor, Nero puts on a façade that people must recognize as false if they want to interpret him correctly. As a play would suffer from being understood as reality, so the world of the imperial court needs to be understood as fiction.

Tacitus suggests that although Nero successfully cultivated falsehood to secure his power, his system of falsehood simultaneously exposed him to ridicule, because those who understood the extent of his power also understood the extent to which it was propped up by falsehoods. Tacitus does not yet name any serious consequences that Nero experienced from appearing ridiculous, but he has hinted that Nero was vulnerable to being deceived by others (notably Poppaea). Tacitus also points out the limitations of Nero's control in the scene on the beach at Bauli. Nero purposely refuses to make his desires comprehensible to many of the people he aspires to control. Because they do not have enough information to understand what is and is not a performance, the ignorant majority believe in Nero's *pietas* toward his mother. Nero's façade usually supports his authority, but here and in the Britannicus episode, Tacitus makes him a target of humor because of his insistence on maintaining a public appearance that is obviously false. The Agrippina episode ends with Nero at the height of his powers, but also at a height of absurdity. Tacitus suggests that Nero's absurd deceptions forced people to confirm his authority (because nobody less powerful could get away with such bizarre lies), but Nero's lies also put his power on an unstable foundation, as Tacitus demonstrates by portraying Nero's principate with absurd humor.

After Nero's wild plots have played out, Agrippina's death itself contains little humor. Tacitus treats Agrippina as a terrifying figure rather than a humorous one.[115] Nero's performance, however, is not over. Tacitus says that after Agrippina's murder Nero reflected on his crime and realized he had done something very wrong (14.10.1). His supporters, however, still followed the false ver-

115. Her last words, "stab my belly" (*uentrem feri*, 14.8.5), and an earlier response to a prophecy of Nero's matricidal destiny, "let him slaughter, provided he achieves command" (*occidat [. . .] dum imperet*, 14.9.3) suggest that Agrippina perceived the irony of her situation. Despite the irony, I see little humor because both utterances make sense of the situation without introducing an opposed script. Tacitus confirms that Agrippina was ambitious and suffered predictable consequences.

sion of events that he had established. They congratulated him on avoiding his mother's supposed attempt to kill him and on her death (14.10.3–14.11.1, 14.13.1). In this way, Tacitus shows that Nero's fiction (that Agrippina tried to kill him first) was accepted (although perhaps not believed) and perpetuated by people other than Nero. Tacitus suggests that many of those who repeated Nero's fictions knew the truth even when they did not admit it, because if they had not known about the murder they might not have been so quick to assuage Nero's guilt for it.

Tacitus further illustrates the absurdity of the situation by recounting Nero's unbelievable excuses that appeared in a letter written by Seneca to the Senate (14.11.1–3).[116] Seneca's letter advances Nero's version of events but contains obvious falsehoods. The letter reveals that Nero was responsible for the murder even though it was meant to exculpate him.[117] This letter was met with strong incredulity. Seneca's account was not merely difficult to believe but incredible. Tacitus focalizes the reactions in two rhetorical questions which suggest that only a very "dull" (*hebes*) person could have believed Seneca's excuses. Because even Seneca's letter cannot provide a reasonable excuse, Nero's attempts to conceal his crimes seem all the more futile.[118]

The contrast between intent and result is, again, humorous only for Tacitus' audience—all the characters in the narrative treat the matter seriously. Tacitus, however, uses the humorous play between reality and fiction to emphasize that Nero's deceptions were not believable. The Senate sees Nero for what he is, which is a monster. Tacitus' readers, who have the benefit of hindsight, see a

---

116. "For [Seneca] narrated the shipwreck also; but who could be found so dull as to believe that it had been a chance occurrence? Or that a shipwrecked woman had sent a single man with a weapon to break through the cohorts and fleets of the Commander? Therefore it was no longer Nero, whose monstrousness outstripped the complaints of all, but Seneca who was the subject of adverse rumor, because in such a speech he had inscribed a confession." (*namque et naufragium narrabat: quod fortuitum fuisse, quis adeo hebes inueniretur, ut crederet? aut a muliere naufraga missum cum telo unum, qui cohortes et classes imperatoris perfringeret? ergo non iam Nero, cuius immanitas omnium questus anteibat, sed Seneca aduerso rumore erat, quod oratione tali confessionem scripsisset*, 14.11.2–3).

117. Seneca's reputation suffers more from the letter than Nero's does because Seneca has more of a reputation to lose.

118. I disagree with O'Gorman's interpretation that Nero is rendered "voiceless" here, or at least with her implication that Seneca's control over Nero's verbal presentation mattered to Nero (2000, 149–51). Seneca supplies the words, but they follow Nero's preferred version of the story, which he improvised when Agerinus arrived at his residence. Just as an actor expects to repeat a playwright's words, Nero conducts his principate as the starring actor/director who enjoys most of the attention and credit for the play regardless of its writer. Another Roman emperor might have cared that his words were subsumed by those of his adviser, but Tacitus' Nero prioritizes performance over nearly everything else.

monster who is also a laughingstock, impossible to take seriously for his ill-considered commands and his transparent plots. For his contemporaries, Nero's monstrosity (*immanitas*, 14.11.3) endangers the Roman political order, but readers can appreciate the absurdity of one of Nero's most taboo murders, in part because Nero's absurdity and impunity serve as a complex *exemplum* of tyrannical behavior. Because Tacitus wrote history, he had no need to keep Nero's secrets and could instead interpret Nero's behavior and perhaps even imply that it was reflected in contemporary emperors. As Tacitus makes clear, unsophisticated attempts to interpret Nero's behavior led to misunderstandings and sometimes to disaster, but readers can dissect the aftermath for a better understanding of how Nero manipulated the people around him.

In Tacitus, Agrippina's death confirms Nero's power over his advisers while simultaneously repeating the absurd methods of exercising power that Nero used to eliminate Britannicus. Tacitus pairs these episodes by using similar humorous motifs and explains how Nero came to exercise power in the way he did. Tacitus develops a humorous contrast between Nero's obviously false assertions and the reality that they cannot fully conceal. Nero demonstrates his authority by these performances rather than by using more typical means of coercion. Although Tacitus presents the process by which Nero's wishes are communicated as absurd and humorous, his regime is no less tyrannical for being supported by absurdity, and at times is more tyrannical because of its absurdities, which often transcend practical cruelty.[119] Nero's principate rewards humorous distortions of reality.

119. The humor of the contrast between Nero's desire to perform and to keep secrets is decreased in his murders of other political enemies because there is no need for an emperor to conceal the deaths of people who have plotted against him. (In fact, the opposite might be more advantageous.) Ordering the deaths of alleged traitors is compatible with an "emperor" script, perhaps even a "good emperor" script, while ordering the murder of close relatives, even ones like Agrippina, is not compatible with a "good emperor" script and requires the introduction of a different script.

FIVE

Humor as a Tool of Nero's Power

After Agrippina's death, Nero is the center of his own principate. Seneca and Burrus occasionally exert a benevolent influence, but their ability to advise Nero is severely diminished. Nero's confirmed authority manifests in an obsession with public performance that Tacitus portrays as both genuine and strategic. Nero persists in performance even when it makes him appear ridiculous, but absurd performance also supports his power.[1] Although Tacitus continues to make Nero a target of humor for the audience of the *Annals*, he also suggests that Nero and his courtiers began to take conscious advantage of the deceptive and political powers of humor. Some of Nero's courtiers realize that they can benefit from Nero's model of manipulating reality, while Nero himself increasingly uses mockery to combat his real and perceived rivals for imperial power. Although the absurd realities often benefit Nero, Tacitus shows the downsides of absurdity as a political strategy, especially later in Nero's reign, when his ridiculous behavior begins to discredit him with members of the senatorial class who understand they are being (incompetently) mocked and do not appreciate it.

1. Champlin argues that Nero's outrageous spectacles were, in fact, a practical way of courting the favor of nonelites, or that public performances at least facilitated a connection between him and the Roman people (2003, 62–63). Although the argument is compelling and illuminates the relationship between power and entertainment in ancient Rome, Tacitus does not emphasize the practical benefits of Nero's spectacles, preferring to focus on Nero's eccentricity. Tacitus constructs Nero's behavior as ridiculous despite historical reasons it might have made sense.

Nero as Charioteer

After Agrippina's murder, Nero immediately embarks on an absurd project: chariot racing. Tacitus calls Nero's desire to race and sing in public "foul" (*foedum*) and says that this desire was grudgingly indulged by Seneca and Burrus (14.14.1–2).[2] Nero's tendency to perform is in inverse proportion to the influence of his teachers. Seneca and Burrus arrange for Nero to race his chariot nearby Rome "without its becoming an indiscriminate spectacle" (*haud promisco spectaculo*, 14.14.2).[3] Nevertheless, the Roman people are invited to watch (14.14.2). While Nero's previous performances often focused on harming his enemies (e.g., Britannicus and Agrippina), chariot racing does not directly target anyone but allows Nero to show off and get his way despite his advisers' disapproval.

At this point, Nero had consolidated as much power as he ever would. The other members of the imperial family were dead or nonthreatening, and although Seneca and Burrus were still alive, neither exercised the influence they had earlier (Koestermann 1963, 14.14.2).[4] In the chariot racing episode, Nero appears less interested in performing virtues than in performing whatever gets most attention. Although Nero's advisers want his disgraceful behavior kept secret, Tacitus makes Nero appear less humorous as his public displays become more straightforward. Where Tacitus presented Nero's complex deceptions as terrifying for people who had to figure out how to react to them in real time, larger spectacles are presented as embarrassing but easy to comprehend.[5] Although Nero's deceptive behavior in the murders of Britannicus and Agrippina terrified elites and taxed their capacity to respond cogently to the emperor's behavior, Tacitus suggests that such behavior nevertheless fostered a privileged understanding between emperor and elites, excluding the ignorant common people. Less explicitly political displays, like chariot racing, are dis-

---

2. According to Griffin, their influence declined after Agrippina's death as Tigellinus assumed more power. Seneca continued to seem prominent for some time, but that was probably an illusion (1984, 80–81).
3. Tacitus says Nero desired to race and perform on the lyre not necessarily at public games but "as if at the games" (*ludicrum in modum*, 14.14.1). Later, he will perform publicly.
4. Later, Nero recognizes some other aristocrats as threats (notably members of the Pisonian conspiracy, which I discuss below), but immediately after Agrippina's death Nero does not seem to have worried about rivals.
5. Although Nero seems unaware that he should be embarrassed by his public performances, Tacitus often makes his internal and external audiences embarrassed on his behalf. Seneca's and Burrus' desire to prevent him from performing at 14.14.2 is representative.

graceful by traditional elite standards, but do not privilege the relationship between the emperor and the elites.[6]

Although Nero no longer needs to perform to secure his place as emperor, Tacitus suggests that absurd performance was not a temporary strategy but had become an integral part of the way Nero exercised power. Earlier, Nero performed to shore up his authority, but from this point Tacitus shows Nero engaging in absurd behavior to expose others to ridicule and to demonstrate his power. Tacitus implies that control over humor—specifically control over what was and was not mocked as absurd—constituted a significant part of Nero's authority.

Nero and Seneca

Tacitus uses Nero's break with Seneca to illustrate the changed norms of reality under Nero's principate. The episode contains two speeches in direct discourse. As Tacitus tells it, both Nero and Seneca attempt to shape reality by saying absurd things that the other must pretend to accept as true. Tacitus mentions several potential incitements to their conflict, including the possibility that Seneca was the last good counsellor Nero had not eliminated. Burrus' suspicious death left Seneca without an ally and coincided with the rise of Tigellinus, whom Tacitus introduces as a malign influence opposed to Seneca's good one. As Seneca's position weakened, bad people (*deteriores*) began to warn Nero that his impressive gardens and villas outshone the emperor's and that Seneca's eloquence and poetry might surpass his (14.52.1–3). Tacitus presents these as petty concerns ("bad people" voice them). Nero's court apparently evaluates loyalty based on real estate holdings and literary reputation.

The *deteriores* also accuse Seneca of mocking Nero's passions: "he was, they said, being openly prejudiced against the princeps's delectations, depreciating his power in controlling horses and making sport of his voice whenever he sang" (*nam oblectamentis principis palam iniquum detrectare uim eius equos regentis, inludere uocem, quoties caneret*, 14.52.3). They name a series of noncriminal acts as though they were crimes, and those acts, according to Tacitus,

6. Games gave the public a rare opportunity to observe the emperor in person and even to express their opinions to him (Griffin 1984, 110; Champlin 2003, 63). Although an emperor racing a chariot would have been different from an emperor sitting in the audience, the plebs may have understood enthusiasm for public games as a special imperial favor.

are their strongest evidence against Seneca. Their objections to Seneca would not seem serious and, Tacitus implies, would not have been taken seriously in a more virtuous Rome. In Nero's Rome, however, if Seneca mocked Nero for his artistic pursuits (*inludere*, 14.52.3), this criticism would insult the performances on which Nero's power relied. Guided by the *deteriores*' slander, Nero sees Seneca's mockery of his performances as a threat to his principate because the framing of the accusation encouraged him to take it seriously. Nero's disrespectable obsession with performance was well known, but by mocking it, Seneca comes close to exposing the absurdity that supports Nero's power. That awareness makes him a threat.

Inludere itself is an important word related to humor in Nero's reign. More often given as *illudere*, this verb refers both to mockery and to deception. Related words may refer to public games (*ludus*), play or public sport (*ludicrum*), and mockery or abuse (*ludibrium*). These and similar words appear frequently in contexts where Tacitus also uses humor. *Ludus* and *ludicrum* both often refer to public spectacles,[7] while *inludere* refers to mockery and therefore often indicates a maliciously humorous tone on the part of a character. *Ludibrium* seems to indicate public disgrace without explicit mockery, as when Tacitus applies it to Augustus' official inquiry about whether he could marry Livia while she was pregnant by her former husband (1.10.5) or when *ludibria* are added to Christians' executions (15.44.4). Although none of these words necessarily suggests humor, they describe a nexus between spectacle, play, deception, and mockery that often intersects with humor, especially in the Neronian books. Seneca's mockery of Nero here suggests some humor within the narrative and emphasizes the relevance of humor in this section.

Tacitus uses both Seneca's and Nero's speeches as demonstrations of the absurdity of power under Nero's regime. Seneca wants to retire without losing his life. In service of this goal, he makes an elaborate, self-deprecating speech. The speech is rife with irony because Tacitus has just described the real reasons Seneca wanted to retire, and they are not the same ones he gives in the speech. This dramatic irony makes Seneca's speech unconvincing, and even the format

7. Tacitus often uses *ludus* and *ludicrum* to discuss public games without any suggestion of humor, as, for example, at *An.* 1.54.1–2 where Tacitus describes the *ludos Augustales* and identifies disruptive competition between performers as a *ludicrum*. The latter form (a form of the adjective *ludicer, -a, -um*, often used substantively) also seems to have a contemptuous edge, as when the Senate attempts to prevent Nero competing in a musical contest in order to conceal the "disfiguring performance" (*ludicra deformitas*, 16.4.1). *Ludicrum* is therefore connected to public spectacle, but also to disgrace.

of paired speeches in direct discourse ironically highlights the pretense exercised on both sides (Martin 1981, 177, 233).[8] Because Tacitus insists on both the high stakes of the conversation and the obvious falsehood of Seneca's speech, readers are forced to consider why Seneca would adopt such an apparently flimsy argument, and to conclude that before Nero, a lie can be more convincing than the truth.[9] Serious argument and falsehood might overlap without humor in a simply deceptive speech, but here Tacitus introduces humor by showing that Nero accepts a known falsehood as if it were the truth.

In Nero's speech to Seneca, he addresses Seneca's false arguments as if they were true. Tacitus has set up the expectation that Seneca's speech was not believable and suggests that Nero knew it to be unbelievable.[10] Nero opens by giving Seneca credit for teaching him how to speak well ex tempore (14.55.1). Tacitus has already said that Seneca was Nero's teacher and that Nero's speech at his accession was written by Seneca (13.3.1). This passage reverses the teacher-student dynamic by proving that Nero can make his own speeches, while Seneca is forced to follow Nero's lead (Schulz 2019, 78–79).[11] This reversal frames the rest of Nero's speech and emphasizes the discrepancy between what Nero says and what he believes.

Both Nero's and Seneca's disingenuous speeches lend the episode a humorous edge, one that highlights the ways in which members of Nero's court maintain a serious façade even when all parties know their conversation has ascended to absurdity. Before and after the speeches, Tacitus reiterates that everything said at this meeting was disingenuous. I suggest that Tacitus turns the incongruity of their false speeches into humor to demonstrate why Nero was so wary of Seneca. Like Nero, Seneca is a consummate performer (that is, a liar). Seneca can also see through Nero's façade, and, as Tacitus suggests, he used his own ability to perform against Nero's. By making a speech that seems absurd to any-

8. Seneca also comes off as a tragic character who is ironically aware of his impending doom (Caviglia 2010, 333). The presence of humor does not erase the tragedy but merely adds another layer of emotion.
9. Syme is kinder in his assessment of Seneca in this passage, but his phrasing implies some slippage between truth and falsehood in his claims that the speech "had to be diplomatic and evasive," and that "hints or echoes can be caught of an authentic Seneca." He also calls one phrase a "platitude" (1958, 335). A truly authentic speech would give us more than "hints or echoes."
10. After Nero has finished speaking, Tacitus writes that he was "constituted by nature and trained by habit to screen his hatred by treacherous blandishments" (*facetus natura et consuetudine exercitus uelare odium fallacibus blanditiis*, 14.56.3). Woodman's translation apparently chooses the reading *factus* for *facetus*.
11. *Pace* O'Gorman, who argues that Seneca demonstrates his superior literary ability (2000, 151–53). Seneca is the grater talent and has significant successes, but he is playing by Nero's rules.

one who knows his true intentions, Seneca imitates Nero by constructing his own reality and attempting to trick others into going along with it. Many elites had to learn similar skills to survive Nero's principate, and here Tacitus connects that capacity to imperial power by framing this minor power struggle between Nero and Seneca as a speaking contest.

In his response to Seneca, Nero is temporarily placed in the position of a courtier who must recognize an authority's speech as false but then reply as if it were true. This type of performance occurs in earlier incidents, notably the death of Agrippina, in which victims (and bystanders) must recognize Nero's fictions without ignoring his literal power. The recurrence of the humorous contrast between fiction and reality alerts Tacitus' readers to the similarities between this and earlier contests over power and shows that performance continues to be a key factor in retaining influence in Nero's principate.[12] Neither Seneca nor Nero deceives the other, but neither tells the truth because not only Nero but also many of those around him remained committed to lies even after they had become obvious. By constructing his request as he does, Seneca appears absurd to Tacitus' readers because his claims are obvious lies that are nevertheless accepted by characters within the narrative. If the deception works, all the better, and if it does not, then being known to have given false reasons is less dangerous than it would be for Seneca to acknowledge and attempt to openly refute the rumors against him. In addition, Seneca knows the game from his previous support of Nero.[13] Tacitus illustrates the necessity of deception among the powerful by using humor in the construction of this exchange.

Nero forbids Seneca to retire. After their conversation, however, "[Seneca] reversed the routines of his previous powerfulness: he stopped the throngs of well-wishers, avoided companions and was rarely in the City, as if detained at home by adverse health or the study of wisdom" (*sed instituta prioris potentiae commutat, prohibet coetus salutantium, uitat comitantis, rarus per Vrbem, quasi ualetudine infensa aut sapientiae studiis domi attineretur*, 14.56.3). Although nothing has officially changed, Seneca curtails his participation in politics. Nero neither reprimands Seneca nor grants him retirement, but Seneca behaves as though he released him from his service (Koestermann 1963, *ad loc*). Seneca's de facto retirement is a nod to the discrepancy between Nero's professed wishes

12. The real/unreal opposition corresponds to one of Raskin's original script oppositions (1985, 114), which Tacitus uses repeatedly in his discussion of Nero.

13. Seneca supported Agrippina's murder at a critical moment (14.7.2–3), makes excuses to the Senate on Nero's behalf (14.11.1–3), and reluctantly permits Nero's chariot-racing antics (14.14.2).

and his actual desires. Although Nero claims that he relies on Seneca, Seneca understands that Nero does not want him to continue in politics. By retiring, Seneca disobeys Nero's explicit command, but obeys his implicit one, in accordance with the complex pretenses of Nero's principate.

Seneca's unofficial retirement also reinforces his own lies. Tacitus says he stayed away from politics "as if detained at home by adverse health or the study of wisdom," both of which were central excuses in his speech. Tacitus extends the sense of deception by saying Seneca did these things "as if" they were true, leaving open the possibility that they were a performance. Nero's authority has survived their meeting, but so has Seneca's request for retirement. Nero's influence on reality is shown to be imperfect (because Seneca's fabrications carry unequal but still considerable authority), but the details of reality do not matter much as long as Nero's actual, secret commands are obeyed.

Mockery as a Weapon of the Principate

Although it ends without harm, the exchange between Nero and Seneca marks the start of a new focus in Tacitus' narrative: the revenge that Nero takes on suspected dissidents. In treating this topic, Tacitus uses almost no humor but makes it clear that Nero had begun to leverage his ability to make reality absurd in order to mock and thereby control his enemies. Most strikingly, Tacitus narrates multiple instances in which Nero mocked the bodies of murdered enemies. In one example, Tacitus connects the deaths of Cornelius Sulla and Rubellius Plautus to Nero's dismissal of Seneca. Nero first has them removed from Rome by assigning them provincial governorships but continues to fear them for their distinguished backgrounds and their proximity to armies (14.57.1). Eventually, he decides to kill them.

Tacitus focalizes Sulla and Plautus' deaths through Tigellinus, who, he explains, played on Nero's fears to enhance his own standing. Although many of Tigellinus' arguments seem unjustified, famous ancestry and the potential to control armies are regular political concerns in Tacitus. Significantly, however, Tigellinus' case against Sulla and Plautus closes with accusations based on their appearance and performance. He calls Sulla "a simulator of sluggishness" (*simulatorem segnitiae*,[14] 14.57.3) and says that Plautus "was not even fabricating a

14. Wellesley's Teubner edition accepts *simulationem* rather than *simulatorem*, "pretense" rather than "imitator," although the second is listed as a variant. I have retained *simulatorem* here as it corresponds to Woodman's translation, and in any case the main idea of the sentence is not in question.

desire for inactivity but flaunted his imitations of the old Romans" (*ne fingere quidem cupidinem otii, sed ueterum Romanorum imitamenta praeferre* 14.57.3). Tacitus does not say which arguments convinced Nero to have them killed, but these are the last arguments that Tigellinus provides, and performance features conspicuously in Nero's method of exercising power, about which he may feel territorial, as another emperor would about the control of armies. Sulla pretends to be something he is not, displaying a skill in performance that might threaten an emperor whose power is based in performance. In contrast, Plautus has refused to pretend, an equally subversive act in Nero's principate, and has instead started to imitate traditional virtues, a subtle indictment of Nero's regime.

As Tacitus reports, Nero reacts to these charges by having Sulla and Plautus killed. Their heads are brought to Nero, who mocks them. In Plautus' case, Tacitus originally quoted Nero's exact words (14.59.3). The words have been lost in Tacitus, but they survive in Cassius Dio, who reports that Nero mocked Plautus' nose and implied that he would have spared his life had he known how ugly he was (epitome 62b.14.1). Nero's comment on Sulla has survived in Tacitus: "Nero mocked [Sulla's head] to the effect that with its premature greyness it was grotesque" (*relatum caput eius inlusit Nero tamquam praematura canitie deforme*, 14.57.4). Although Tacitus does not present this comment as humorous for his readers, it is humorous from Nero's perspective. *Inlusit* and *deforme* are both associated with humor in Latin.[15] Nero uses insulting humor against his slaughtered enemy, and Tacitus communicates that Nero meant the comment as a joke without encouraging readers to find it funny. Sulla's gray hair is not salient to his execution; Tacitus' Nero is excessively focused on superficial appearances. Nero's mockery of Sulla's severed head is simultaneously a sign of his superficiality and a tangible proof of his power over Sulla. Sulla's murder reasserts Nero's power, but it is mockery that puts Nero back in control of appearances. By mocking Sulla's head, Nero asserts his authority to decide what is and what is not important in Rome. Tacitus does not ask his readers to laugh at Nero's joke but rather considers it a point of historical importance that Nero's power depended on his control over what could and could not be understood as ridiculous.

After Sulla and Plautus are expelled from the Senate post mortem, Tacitus ends his discussion of their murders with a *sententia*: "the mockeries now being

15. Cicero infrequently uses forms of *ludere* in his discussion of humor, and it appears occasionally in connection to rhetorical humor more generally (e.g., *De Orat.* 2.238). Quintilian sometimes uses related words to refer to humor (e.g., 6.3.79). Both writers cite *deformitas* as one of the primary targets of humor (*De Orat.* 2.236, 2.239; *Inst.* 6.3.8). See also Corbeill on *deformis* (1996, 35–39).

more oppressive than the maladies" (*grauioribus iam ludibriis quam malis*, 14.59.4). Furneaux interprets this to mean "the mockery (of this condemnation of dead men) seeming even more revolting than the crimes" (1907, *ad loc*) but notes textual difficulties. Manuscript M reads *iam* as *tam*[16] meaning either "as great as was the crime, the mockery was yet greater" (which Furneaux does not support) or "'which sentence was however more grievous as a mockery than as a calamity' inasmuch as it could not hurt the dead" (Furneaux 1907, *ad loc*). Whichever reading is accepted, the passage compares crime to mockery. Crime and mockery are not quite opposed enough to form a joke,[17] but Tacitus explicitly discusses malicious humor (*ludibrium*).[18] Although the "injury" here is death, Tacitus suggests that mockery is even more serious or perhaps more difficult to deal with. "Mockery" seems to refer to Sulla's and Plautus' posthumous expulsion from the Senate. Depending on the reading of the text, their expulsion either didn't matter to them (because they were already dead) or its illegality paled in comparison to its audaciousness, but in either case mockery is prominent. Tacitus keeps humor out of his narration but points out that Nero, or Nero's cronies, used mockery alongside traditional punishments. This episode illustrates that mockery—the ability to control humor and maliciously direct it at a chosen target—was one means by which Nero wielded power, even on a par with the exercise of capital punishment.[19] Although Tacitus elsewhere points to places where Nero himself appeared absurd, in this instance humor and mockery represent the power of the emperor to shape reality as he pleases.

The Death of Octavia

Immediately after the murders of Plautus and Sulla comes the death of Octavia. This episode evokes humorous motifs but is dominated by tragedy.[20] Tacitus

16. Manuscript M reads *tam* (which could abbreviate *tamen*), *iam* is an emendation from M, and *tum* is a modern emendation from Halm (Furneaux 1907, *ad loc*).
17. Crime and mockery are substantially different, but they augment each other here, as in the English idiom "adding insult to injury." Besides, the scripts do not overlap because the phrase separates the two ideas instead of joining them.
18. As Plass notes, the meaning of *ludibrium* ranges from "joke" to "deception." Both senses appear in Tacitus (1988, 16).
19. Furneaux (1907, *ad loc*) and Woodman (2004, 303n111) compare 14.59.4 with 16.11.3, in which Nero adds mockery to the punishment of other enemies. Tacitus presents mockery as a significant part of Nero's reign in multiple *loci*.
20. The proximity of these episodes is no coincidence. Murgatroyd argues that the earlier murders set up an expectation that Nero, now confident in his ability to eliminate enemies, is prepared to murder everyone else he considers a threat (2008, 265).

portrays Octavia as a tragic heroine, a victim of the absurdity of the principate rather than a collaborator in it.[21] Tacitus does not make her a target for humor. Instead, he employs humor to describe the other characters involved in her death, especially its instigators, Poppaea and Tigellinus, whom he has already characterized as bad influences on Nero.

Tacitus blames Poppaea for instigating Octavia's downfall and benefiting from her death. Poppaea accuses Octavia of adultery with an enslaved Alexandrian singer and *tibicen* (14.60.2).[22] The accused adulterer, Eucaerus, has not been mentioned before, and his occupation is more suited to drama than history.[23] As I argue in chapter 4, Tacitus introduces Poppaea as a semi-comic figure and as an expert in uniting performance and concealment, two quintessential opposed scripts of Nero's principate. Here, Tacitus reminds readers that Poppaea stands in a limbo between concubine and wife.[24] Yet it is Tigellinus who is the most prominent target of humor in this episode. Tacitus reports that, when Octavia's accusers interrogated her slaves under torture to obtain corroboration of their charge, most denied it and, "one of them repl[ied] to Tigellinus' hounding that Octavia's womanly parts were more chaste than his mouth" (*ex quibus una instanti Tigellino castiora esse muliebria Octauiae respondit quam os eius*, 14.60.3).[25] This is one of the most obvious jokes in Tacitus. Its uncharacteristically scurrilous content sets up contrasts between chastity and hypersexuality, male and female, and genital and oral sex, uniting these oppositions in a strange chastity contest between Octavia and Tigellinus.[26] It also leaves the most salient

---

21. Ferri (1998) and Murgatroyd (2008) explore the episode's parallels to tragedy in detail.
22. Plass finds absurd humor in Tacitus' application of *designatur*, a legal term, to Poppaea's conclusion that the musician would make a likely scapegoat (1988, 65–66).
23. Woodman notes that "Eucaerus" means "opportune" or "timely" (2004, 303n112). The name could be another pun because he was convenient for Poppaea's purpose.
24. "[Poppaea] was long a concubine and powerful over Nero by adultery, then by marriage" (*ea diu paelex et adulteri Neronis, mox mariti potens*, 14.60.2). This is my translation, intentionally awkward to preserve the construction that bridges Poppaea's influence over Nero as a concubine and later as a wife.
25. Cassius Dio includes an almost identical joke, albeit in direct discourse: "My mistress' privy parts are cleaner, Tigellinus, than your mouth" (καθαρώτερον, ὦ Τιγελλῖνε, τὸ αἰδοῖον ἡ δέσποινά μου τοῦ σοῦ στόματος ἔχει, epitome 62b.13.4, trans. Cary and Foster). The similarity between these two jokes suggests that the joke format was an important part of this material. Although in both cases the humor originates with the character rather than the historian, this joke is a prime example of humor that serves a serious purpose.
26. In contrast to Tacitus' claim that few of Octavia's slaves gave evidence against her, Cassius Dio reports that all Octavia's slaves testified against her except for the speaker of the joke, whom he calls Pythias (epitome 62b.13.4). Tacitus emphasizes Octavia's innocence, while Dio highlights Pythias' bravery. Tacitus' focus on Octavia is typical of his sympathy for her and his disregard for characters of low social status. On the other hand, Tacitus relates several incidents in which subalterns display extreme courage in front of powerful people, including several that feature quips (Koestermann 1963, 14.60.3).

details for the punchline, even in Tacitus' indirect report. *Castiora esse muliebria Octauiae respondit* could be a complete sentence, after which the unexpected final clause adds a humorous comparison and includes a reference to Tigellinus at the very end. The phrase is calculated to produce both humor and insult and to highlight the *ancilla*'s bravery—hers was more than a simple denial of Octavia's guilt; she ran the risk of angering her interrogator—and to throw Nero's and Tigellinus' hypocrisy into vivid contrast with Octavia's virtue. The joke does not have much impact within the narrative, however. The opinion of an enslaved woman was too insignificant to damage Nero's fictions, even if it could be celebrated by historians.

Tacitus portrays Octavia as a perfect victim with an unimpeachably tragic aura while Nero and his supporters are characterized with humor. When rioters overturn Poppaea's statues in a gesture of support for Octavia (14.61.1), Nero takes the measured step of restoring the statues without inflicting punishment beyond the violence used to break up the riots. Poppaea, perhaps feeling threatened by the popular support for her rival, makes a speech that Tacitus reports in indirect discourse laced with humor. Poppaea makes no jokes, but, as when she persuaded Nero to marry her (13.46.1–3, discussed in chapter 4), Tacitus arranges her arguments so that they are completely unbelievable in context (Murgatroyd 2008, 269).[27]

Some of Poppaea's statements are humorous because of their obvious hyperbole, as when she claims her life has been threatened by Octavia's clients and slaves "who [. . .] dared in peacetime things which scarcely happened in war" (*ea in pace ausi, quae uix bello euenirent*, 14.61.2), a description patently at odds with Tacitus' description of the riot, which features shouting and vandalism from the crowd but no violence except by the soldiers sent to stop them. Tacitus also suggests that the riot was spontaneous, but Poppaea blames Octavia for starting it. Her complaints that Octavia is ready to remarry and march against Nero (14.61.4) are similarly unsupported by Tacitus.[28] As in Poppaea's

27. Murgatroyd interprets Poppaea as the cruel mastermind to Nero's bumbling dupe (2008, 264). Despite Murgatroyd's careful analysis, this interpretation gives Poppaea too much credit for competence, when she seems merely to egg Nero on to the same activities which he already intended, and too much credit for introducing cruelty into an environment where cruelty is commonplace.

28. Poppaea's argument parallels Agrippina's threat that she would throw her support behind Britannicus and obtain the principate for him (13.14.2–3). Tacitus does not suggest that Agrippina's threat was plausible, but it encouraged Nero to murder Britannicus. Koestermann notes that Poppaea emphasized the angle that Rome rioted against Nero where previously she had focused on the danger to herself (1963, 14.61.3). Schulz interprets Nero as actually convinced by Poppaea's argument that Octavia could rebel against him (2019, 110).

earlier speech, Tacitus frames her arguments to suggest that Poppaea was transparently lying (Murgatroyd 2008, 269). From Nero's perspective, however, Poppaea is either genuinely convincing or in such a position of favor that her words must be taken as true although they are obviously lies.[29]

One especially humorous phrase is Poppaea's rhetorical question, "Did the Roman people really prefer the offspring of an Egyptian flute-player to be introduced to the heights of the Commander's court?" (*malle populum Romanum tibicinis Aegyptii subolem imperatorio fastigio induci?* 14.61.4). The context for this statement is her claim that she is "about to present the hearth of the Caesars with true progeny" (*ueram progeniem penatibus Caesarum datura sit*, 14.61.4). Poppaea's insistence on her fertility accords with her earlier insistence on it (14.1.2) and the fact that infertility was the official grounds for Octavia's relegation to Campania (14.60.1). Poppaea may also have been pregnant by Nero at the time. Tacitus records the birth of their daughter at the start of the following year (15.23.1),[30] and she is right that Nero needs an heir. Tacitus, however, presents her argument as humorous. First, Octavia never committed adultery, as Nero and Poppaea must know from having tortured false confessions out of a very few of her slaves. Second, if Nero indeed believed Octavia was infertile, he could not truly fear that she was pregnant with someone else's offspring. Poppaea's claim about the *tibicen* is compatible with her earlier claim about an adulterous pregnancy, but it would obviously not be a credible accusation against a barren woman. Poppaea, however, seems to conclude that if either reason by itself would be grounds to divorce Octavia, then both together must be a truly excellent excuse. Reality is malleable for Poppaea and Nero. It matters little how they discredit Octavia as long as they agree that she should be disgraced, and others accept their reasoning. Nobody reasonable would believe the excuses they offer, yet these are the official reasons that Nero's subjects must acknowledge.

Finally, Poppaea compares Nero to Eucaerus the *tibicen*, perhaps intending to disturb Nero with the thought that a person of low status could take his place. Tacitus has prepared his readers to reflect that there are real similarities between Nero and Eucaerus. Nero will later show an interest in the lowly occu-

29. Koesterman attributes the logical failings in Poppaea's speech to female psychology (1963, 14.61.4). I suggest that in fact, Poppaea's arguments are founded on the knowledge that similar arguments have worked on Nero before, and that they are as appropriate to the tenor of Nero's principate as they are insane.

30. Tacitus will treat the birth, celebration, and prompt death of Nero's daughter with humor, too. Syme describes the disproportionate rejoicing as bathetic (1958, 349–50).

pation of musician (although not specifically *tibicen*),[31] and he has an excessive interest in foreign things.[32] Tacitus' readers are encouraged to see both Eucaerus and Nero as performers who practice a foreign art form. Poppaea's argument evokes humor because, although she believes her argument will appeal to Nero, the traits she conjures as illegitimate for an emperor are shared between Eucaerus and Nero.

Nero either believes Poppaea's absurd argument or doesn't believe it but chooses to act on it anyway. He comes up with a new excuse to get rid of Octavia, enlisting Anicetus to falsely confess to adultery with her. Tacitus reminds his readers that Anicetus was responsible for Agrippina's death (14.62.2),[33] and thereby puts the ridiculous plot of that episode in conversation with this one.[34] Anicetus plays his part even better than was necessary ("even more than had been ordered," *plura etiam quam iussum erat*, 14.62.4).[35] Tacitus does not say that any of Anicetus' contemporaries disbelieved him, but nor does he say that they genuinely believed him. For Tacitus' readers, the falsehood is obvious because Nero found Anicetus a suitable candidate to falsely attest to adultery with Octavia and then Anicetus did exactly that. The internal audience to this deception would not have been inclined to challenge Anicetus' story because they were "friends whom the princeps had assembled as if for a council" (*amicos, quos uelut consilio adhibuerat princeps*, 14.62.4). In a word, they were yes-men. Performance is still central to the plot, and still depends on the acting (lying) ability of courtiers who are the actors in the deception that Nero directs, but there is relatively little pressure to present a convincing story. Because Tacitus previously showed that Nero struggled to cope with public favor for Octa-

31. Nero's public musical debut (16.4.1–4) is discussed below.

32. Woodman argues that Tacitus evokes Alexandria as a dangerous foreign city when Tigellinus throws a decadent party (15.37.1–4, discussed further below) and that Nero's identification with Alexandria led him to plunder parts of Italy as if they were foreign (2012, 182–86). Mention of Eucaerus' native Egypt may be another subtle signal of what Nero has in common with him.

33. Woods argues that there were in fact two Anicetuses: one who was prefect of the fleet and drowned Agrippina and another who was Nero's freedman and slandered Octavia (2006, 643). The Anicetus who was prefect of the fleet could not have long survived Nero's downfall, while the Anicetus who slandered Octavia lived out his life peacefully in Sardinia. The prefect Anicetus might instead be identified with the Anicetus who helps proclaim a false Nero at *Histories* 3.47 (2006, 648). Woods' theory is naturally tenuous, but if Tacitus or his sources did combine multiple characters here, the combination demonstrates an even greater interest in drawing parallels between the deaths of Octavia and Agrippina.

34. In addition, both plots are instigated by Poppaea to do away with a rival imperial woman, and both are successful despite poor planning.

35. Anicetus' effective deception parallels Nero's effective performances at the murders of Britannicus and Agrippina (13.16.3 and 14.4.4).

via, it is even more striking that Tacitus does not emphasize the issue of popular opinion during this final campaign against her. Nero still supplies pretexts for his actions, but he appears to be confident that anything he says will be accepted.

In a final humorous jab, Tacitus asserts that Nero, "(quite forgetting his accusation of sterility a while before)," claimed "that [Octavia] had expelled a fetus in consciousness of her lusts" (*incusatae paulo ante sterilitatis oblitus, abactos partus conscientia libidinum*, 14.63.1). Tacitus calls this Nero's final excuse for sending her into exile.[36] Although this is blunt sarcasm by Tacitean standards,[37] it reiterates the humor of the contradictions in Poppaea's speech and transfers them from Poppaea to Nero himself. The contradiction supports one of the major points of the episode, that Nero was unafraid to flaunt the absurdity of his own commands once he felt secure in power. Tacitus shows that Nero had become so confident that he no longer provided coherent excuses for his behavior. Previously, performance and concealment were in tension with each other, but the frequent combination of the two has resulted in Nero's abandoning effective concealment in favor of simply layering one unconvincing performance on top of another. The doggedness and incompetence with which Nero puts forward such contradictory accusations lends an absurd cast to the whole event, because Nero's lies must be believed even when they are unbelievable. Tacitus heightens the contrast between what Nero professes and what is true by showing that the emperor stopped trying to create a convincing performance and merely expected that people would agree with a manifestly inconsistent lie (Schulz 2019, 111). As Nero becomes more secure in his principate, he neither hides nor openly owns his crimes. Instead, he continues to construct excuses, but he puts less effort into them. Tacitus treats this new strategy as a confirmation of Nero's power. Nero does not need to pretend to be a good emperor anymore. His reputation is irrelevant because he no longer has any serious rivals and is therefore not worried about threats to his power.

---

36. Scott cites this decree as so obviously false as to prove that Nero could no longer remember his own lies (1998, 15). I agree that this passage shows Nero in a very bad light, and Tacitus tells us that Nero indeed forgot on this occasion, but I suggest that Nero has never tried to keep his lies consistent (as we can see in earlier episodes, including in the murder of Agrippina). The truth of his utterances is less important than the fact that they must be treated as true.

37. Schulz sees this passage as an unusually clear example of an incredible excuse, perhaps even the nadir of Nero's attempts to find plausible reasons for his actions (2019, 110–11). It is also unusual because Tacitus frontloads the disconcerting element (that Nero had previously accused Octavia of infertility) although he mentioned it earlier and might have expected readers to pick up on the discrepancy without a reminder. In addition, Tacitus explicitly says that Nero forgot rather than that he lied, and this assertion is not typical in Tacitus, who frequently preserves the ambiguity of characters' thought processes.

Although Tacitus uses humorous motifs in this episode, Octavia's death is free from humor. There is irony, but it is tragic irony.[38] Octavia is an object of pity rather than mockery. Even after her death, when her severed head is brought to Rome, Tacitus reports that Poppaea looked at it but not that she said anything about it (14.64.2). Nero mocked the severed heads of his enemies (14.57.4, 14.59.3) but Tacitus does not allow Poppaea to humiliate Octavia in this way.[39]

Although the principate has become increasingly absurd under Nero's rule, and although Poppaea and other successful performers have elevated themselves according to Nero's absurd conditions, Octavia represents a pristine ideal that is incompatible with Nero's Rome. Tacitus does not allow the humor that pervades his narration to attach to her. Although Tacitus uses humor to show that the conspiracy arrayed against Octavia was absurd, he shields her from mockery. In that respect, this episode marks a shift from Tacitus pointing out how Nero benefited from the absurdity of his policies to demonstrating the contempt that virtuous people would have felt toward Nero for divorcing his blameless wife. As Nero leverages absurdity to maintain his power, Tacitus implies that absurdity is not always a winning strategy, and that it would alienate those who respected the traditional virtues.

Neronian Decadence

Tacitus continues to use humor to highlight how absurdity suffused Nero's principate. Tacitus cites a party thrown by Tigellinus as a paradigmatic example of Nero's bad behavior (15.37.1). Both disgust and humor feature in Tacitus'

38. Octavia's marriage is compared to a funeral and Acte is called "the [enslaved] maid, more influential than her mistress" (*ancilla domina ualidior*, 14.63.3). Comparing a funeral to a wedding and suggesting a slave overpowered an empress also introduces irony, but it is tragic irony, created by opposed scripts that do not overlap (Attardo 1994, 204). Although the funeral-as-wedding motif includes one literal and one metaphorical description of the same event, it was such a common nonhumorous motif in ancient literature that I doubt a Roman audience could have found it humorous. Murgatroyd interprets the wedding-funeral as a final note of pathos (2008, 271).

39. This episode is also a swan song for Poppaea. Tacitus never again describes her exerting political influence. When he comes to her death, Tacitus uses humor in his report (in indirect discourse) of Nero's speech at her funeral, saying that he praised her for her beauty and her child "and her other gifts of fortune—in place of virtues" (*aliaque fortunae munera pro uirtutibus*, 16.6.2). This last comment on Poppaea is Tacitus' punchline to her life (Plass 1988, 63). The joke is neither original nor insightful, but it reinforces the importance of humor in Tacitus' characterization of Poppaea and strongly contrasts her with Octavia.

description of the party. Its splendor (including an artificial lake, ships decorated in gold, and imported animals) ironically emphasizes its tawdry purpose.[40] The entire scene, as Tacitus describes it, is nothing but an elaborate environment for illicit sex, not a traditional topic for history nor a worthy project for a Roman emperor.[41] The clearest evocation of the contrast between exalted and sordid is Tacitus' description of "love-lairs filled with illustrious ladies, and, opposite, whores could be seen with naked bodies" (*lupanaria adstabant inlustribus feminis completa, et contra scorta uisebantur nudis corporibus*, 15.37.3). In normal circumstances, elite Roman women presented themselves differently from *scorta*.[42] Here, Tacitus distinguishes them by setting them on opposite sides of the artificial lake on which the party took place, physically separating the different orders of women.[43] By acknowledging the difference between these groups, Tacitus makes more of a surprise out of their similar appearance.[44] Identifying lustfulness in women of all statuses might be simple Roman misogyny on the model of Juvenal's sixth satire, but Tacitus emphasizes the meticulous organization of the debauched party, making it not merely an orgy but a reflection of the transgressive performances on which Nero's regime was built.[45] The juxtaposition of two separate

40. Elaborate structures built on water and gold combined with ivory are typical but ominous descriptions of luxury (Ash 2018, 15.37.2). Ash also calls the *exoleti* who row the ships on the lake "discordant with historiography's grandeur" and recognizes a "wry humor" in the fact that they are arranged as if for a military parade. Santoro L'Hoir compares the whole scene to an elaborate theatrical production (2006, 247–48).
41. Schulz notes that the setting—a celebration on boats—is reminiscent of the murder of Agrippina (2019, 72), another significant episode in which Tacitus uses humor.
42. The distinction would often but not always have been clear (Olson 2002, 397). Woodman comments that Tacitus depicts a break from normal social roles because the *scorta* are placed on display while the noblewomen remain inside (2012, 179). Although I agree that Tacitus indicates a disruption in the social order, I do not agree that this passage illustrates a simple reversal of roles. Woodman argues that aristocratic women would normally be displayed while *scorta* would be concealed, an opinion that may reflect historical reality but does not reflect the literary ideal of aristocratic female modesty. In addition, the separation of the groups of women does not hide the fact that all are at the party for the purpose of illicit sex. Tacitus elides the distinction between different orders of women to stir his audience's outrage (Ash 2018, 15.37.3). I apply Ash's nuance to Woodman's point to argue that Tacitus' description of the women illustrates not only a reversal of social norms but also the hidden truth that there is little practical difference between ordinary *scorta* and the libidinous aristocrats of Nero's court.
43. Although *scorta* is a gender-neutral term, Tacitus implies that the *scorta* are all or predominantly women through the parallel between them and the noblewomen (unambiguously identified as *feminae*) and because their male counterparts (*exoleti*) are rowing barges on the lake (15.37.2). *Scorta* could indicate a mixed-gender group, but that would jar with Tacitus' picture of ironically orderly debauchery.
44. Tacitus also draws, more subtly, on the contrast between obscenity and chastity, which is very common in jokes (Raskin 1985, 114).
45. Mader argues convincingly that Nero is also dramatizing an idealized relationship between him-

social groups creates an overlapping pair of opposed scripts; noble and ignoble combine in one promiscuous mass. Tacitus compares the conduct of the "illustrious ladies" to that of the "whores" while simultaneously underlining the distinction that ought to hold between them.

Next, Nero himself behaves inappropriately for a person of his class and gender by marrying a man, Pythagoras. Nero does not marry Pythagoras at Tigellinus' party, but Tacitus interlocks the two events by bridging Nero's behavior at the party and his marriage to Pythagoras in the same sentence (Schulz 2019, 125):[46] "after a few days [Nero] took one of that herd of perverts (his name was Pythagoras) in the fashion of a solemn espousal to be his husband" (*paucos post dies uni ex illo contaminatorum grege (nomen Pythagorae fuit) in modum sollemnium coniugiorum denupsisset*, 15.37.4). First, Tacitus refers euphemistically to the debauchery of the earlier party. Only in the last few words of the sentence does he reveal that Nero called his relationship with Pythagoras a marriage. Tacitus also identifies Pythagoras first as "one of that herd of perverts," a clause that delays the verb and creates a link to the party. Only at the end of the sentence is the reader informed that Nero "in the fashion of a solemn espousal was wed."[47] The last two words in the sentence step up its shock value. While it is not surprising that Nero would engage in illicit sexual activity, that he would marry one of Tigellinus' *exoleti* "in the fashion of a solemn espousal" presents a contrast between the seriousness of marriage and the reality that Nero's involvement with Pythagoras likely bore little resemblance to a marriage.[48] The script for "marriage" here overlaps with "illicit sex," which is typically opposed to marriage. Nero, however, attempts to legitimize his relationship with a man of low status, an arrangement completely incompatible with Roman elite matrimony.

Nero also violates elite gender norms. The verb, *denupsisset*, implies matrimonial solemnity but simultaneously reveals that Nero took the role of the

---

self and the Roman people, who have demanded that he not abandon Italy for Alexandria (2018, 392), so Nero probably believes that he is shoring up his power by throwing this party.

46. Ash argues that the distance of a few days makes the wedding more scandalous because it is a planned event rather than a spur-of-the-moment decision (2018, 15.37.4). I find Ash's argument plausible, but the grammar of the sentence better reflects Schulz's interpretation.

47. I have altered Woodman's translation to preserve the Latin word order (which is nearly impossible to do in a translation of the whole sentence) and to avoid Woodman's rendering of *denupsisset* ("took [. . .] to be his husband") which hints at the punchline earlier in the sentence.

48. Nero's behavior here reflects Messalina's at 11.26.3, discussed in chapter 3. Messalina, too, escalated her scandalous sexual behavior by marrying.

bride in his marriage to Pythagoras (Woodman 2012, 180).[49] While there is a considerable contrast between an *exoletus* and a spouse, the difference between an emperor and a bride is even greater. The idea that the emperor-as-bride would subject himself to the authority of an *infamis* husband heightens the incongruity of the scene. Two scripts (powerful emperor and submissive bride) overlap because Nero attempts to fulfill both. The final word in this sentence (*denupsisset*) resembles a punchline because it refocuses on the bridal script, which is particularly misaligned with the imperial script. The overlap between these scripts is even more vivid because Tacitus includes a list of bridal paraphernalia that figured in Nero's wedding. These include the *flammeum*,[50] a dowry, and wedding torches (15.37.4). All these fit with a bridal script, none with an imperial one, yet Nero is also emperor.

After he emphasizes gender contrasts at the wedding, Tacitus ties the humor of Nero's marriage to the established dynamic of performance and concealment that informs much of his characterization of Nero.[51] At the wedding of Nero and Pythagoras, "everything, in short, was observed which even in the case of a female is covered by night" (*cuncta denique spectata, quae etiam in femina nox operit*, 15.37.4). Nero turns out to be as imperfect a bride as he is an emperor because he does not possess the modesty appropriate for a bride. As with many of his crimes, Nero has decided that his priority is to show everyone that he is getting his way, even if that means he must reveal what would normally be concealed.[52]

Because of the script opposition (performance versus concealment) in Tacitus' treatment of Nero, Nero's behavior at his wedding to Pythagoras evokes the

49. The subject of *denubere* is always a bride (*OLD denubo*). The verb seems to have been uncommon, and therefore may not have been an obvious sign that Nero took the woman's role in this ceremony. The meaning of *denubere* is clarified in the next sentence.

50. Woodman sees the juxtaposition of *imperator* (a military title) and *flammeum* as "paradoxical" (2012, 180).

51. Femininity is not a central element in Tacitus' humorous criticisms of Nero. Although Roman elite men often used humor to criticize each other for effeminacy (Corbeill 1996, 151–73), Tacitus has not previously treated Nero's unmanly qualities as a matter for humor.

52. Possanza reinterprets this episode through the lens of a Pompeian graffito that may record a local reaction to the spectacle of Nero's public wedding night. Possanza compares Nero's performance on this occasion to antics in Petronius' *Satyricon*, Plautus' *Casina*, and mime performance and suggests that Nero intended to present a scandalous but delightful spectacle that was appreciated by local spectators (2023, 210–17). This interpretation is consistent with Champlin's contention that Nero's public performances were a considered strategy that would have increased his standing with the people (2003, 2–3), and it may have been true that the Pompeiians enjoyed this performance. Tacitus, however, does not see the benefit in Nero's disgraceful behavior and does not help us construct such a rational interpretation of the event.

same absurdity that has been central in Tacitus' treatment of his principate. Tacitus blames Nero for making the contrast between the emperor and a bride relevant to politics. If Nero had not decided to become a bride, then nobody would have had occasion to compare him to one, but he uses imperial power to pretend to be a bride even as imperial dignity ought to prevent him from doing so. Although the wedding does not directly impact Nero's government, Tacitus uses it to return to the idea that Nero blends together the use and misuse of power.

The Great Fire

Immediately after Nero's wedding to Pythagoras comes the great fire.[53] The first words of the next chapter shift the tone away from humor: "there followed a disaster" (*sequitur clades*, 15.38.1).[54] Nevertheless, details in this episode connect it to the warped reasoning of the principate that Tacitus has previously treated with humor. One such detail is the mysterious group of people that Tacitus says prevented others from extinguishing the fire, including some who "openly threw torches and shouted that they had authorization—whether to conduct their looting more licentiously or by order" (*alii palam faces iaciebant atque esse sibi auctorem uociferabantur, siue ut raptus licentius exercerent seu iussu*, 15.38.7).[55] This passage echoes an earlier one in which Nero dressed in disguise and wandered Rome doing random violence (13.25.1–4, discussed in chapter 4). Like the criminals who took advantage of Nero's behavior by assuming his

53. Waddell sees the fire as having an implied causal connection to Nero's marriage to Pythagoras. By describing Nero's scandalous marriage, Tacitus sets up the expectation that the gods will punish him for sacrilege, and the fire is an obvious example of divine retribution for an audience already primed to look for evidence of divine wrath (2013, 486–88).
54. Keitel (2010) discusses Tacitus' treatment of disasters at length. I agree with her observations that he focuses on the emperors' faults, encourages sympathy with the *vulgus*, and emphasizes social upheaval. None of these are conducive to humor.
55. This passage has interested scholars trying to reconstruct Tacitus' opinion on who set the fire. Furneaux and Griffin see Tacitus as only tentatively blaming Nero, unlike Suetonius and Cassius Dio, who blame him definitively (1907, *ad loc*; 1984, 132). O'Gorman points out that by reciting a poem about the destruction of Troy, Nero associates himself with the fire, literally performing it even if he has not literally caused it (2000, 171–73). Champlin notes that Tacitus is the only ancient source that does not hold Nero responsible for the fire (2003, 182). Schulz takes the episode as an example of Tacitean ambiguity, with suggestions of criminality but no confirmation of any single theory (2019, 144–45). The purported arsonists' claim that they have authorization evokes Nero whether they were truly acting on his orders or not. They presumably want *auctoritas* to be interpreted as an imperial command.

identity, the presumed arsonists take advantage of the possibility that Nero might plausibly have commanded them. Moreover, they do their burning openly (*palam*). If someone authorized them to burn Rome blatantly, that person must have been unconcerned about concealment, an oversight typical of Nero as Tacitus portrays him. Tacitus describes the alleged arsonists' motivations with a binary alternative; they either lied to make their crimes easier to commit (which would be consistent with the muggers at 13.25.2) or they were in fact ordered. The abruptness of *seu iussu*, at the end, makes the sentence slightly humorous. Although *siue* appeared earlier and expects a correlative (here supplied by *seu*), the bald command suggested by *iussu* is still a shock because it provokes the question of why an authority would want to set Rome on fire.[56]

I suggest that Tacitus includes these details to remind readers that the fire is highly Neronian, even if Nero himself is not responsible for it. An order to openly set Rome on fire must have come from someone who didn't care much about his reputation as long as his power was maintained, and Tacitus' Nero is just such a person, as he demonstrated by the murders of Agrippina and Britannicus. Tacitus shows that Nero's principate had fostered a society in which the safest way to commit crimes was not secretly, but openly, while claiming they were legal.[57] People besides Nero take advantage of the slippage between performance and reality, and as more people tell compelling falsehoods, reality becomes more difficult to discern. Most courtiers who encounter Nero understand that many of his claims are false and that they are required to pay lip service to his fictions but to act in a way that is also compatible with reality. Outside the court, people have less information on how to cope with Nero's behavior. Those who flee the fire try to untangle the fictions of Nero's principate but do not have enough information to understand who is responsible for the fire. There is less humor here because the situation is dire and the victims are average denizens of Rome, innocent in Nero's regime, unlike the courtiers against whom Tacitus often uses contemptuous humor. Nevertheless, this passage examines the implications of Neronian absurdity by demonstrating that his principate had arrived at such a height of absurdity that people could no longer tell if the emperor had ordered the city to be burned.

Tacitus does, however, use humor in describing Nero's reaction to the fire.

56. Cassius Dio claims that Nero desired to destroy as much of Rome as possible and was simply acting on that desire (epitome 62b.16.1–2). Suetonius agrees that Nero meant to destroy Rome but gives no particular reason why (*Nero* 38). Modern historians point out that burning Rome was against Nero's interests (e.g., Griffin 1984, 132). Tacitus leaves the question conspicuously open.

57. Tacitus does not claim that crimes were actually legal under Nero, but only that Nero's bad example was successfully followed by unscrupulous people.

Nero is not personally threatened by the fire, which makes him less pitiable than the Roman populace and therefore a better target for a joke. According to Tacitus, Nero returned from Antium when the fire approached one of his houses in Rome (15.39.1). Although not a joke in itself, Nero's motivation is a reminder of his disordered priorities, because he did not take notice of a major fire until it threatened his property. Despite an unpromising first reaction, Nero organized relief for those displaced by the fire by allowing them to shelter in public buildings and lowering the price of grain (15.39.1–2). The thing that makes an impression, however, is not Nero's fire relief policy (which Tacitus treats as genuinely helpful) but that "a rumor had spread that at the very time of the City's blaze he had actually mounted his domestic stage and sung of the extirpation of Troy, assimilating the present calamities to olden disasters" (*peruaserat rumor ipso tempore flagrantis Vrbis inisse eum domesticam scaenam et cecinisse Troianum excidium, praesentia mala uetustis cladibus adsimulantem*, 15.39.3). Tacitus does not confirm this rumor but leaves an impression that its transmission overrode Nero's attempts to help victims of the fire (Schulz 2019, 144–45). Tacitus again suggests that performance has usurped reality, but this time the audience is so large that the story spirals out of Nero's control.

The strongest point of thematic connection between this and other humorous passages is the emphasis on Nero as a performer rather than an emperor. Nero's alleged performance on a private stage demonstrates the tension between his public responsibilities as *princeps* and his personal desire to perform. Regardless of whether the rumor is true, it shows that Nero's penchant for substituting performance for reality was known by people outside the elite. Whereas before Tacitus focused on the effect of Nero's disconnection from reality among his court, here Nero's warping of reality is public knowledge. Tacitus rarely mentions the populace of Rome without upbraiding them for some flaw, so it is significant that he does not blame them for the misinterpretation. Nero's concern with performance has extended to affect the general population, not just people that he is personally in contact with, and it is such a powerful influence that they think about it even in the middle of a deadly crisis.

Nero takes this opportunity to cast himself in the role of poet, a role not entirely incompatible with that of emperor, but not appropriate, either. Strangely, Tacitus suggests that Nero's literary instincts are passable. Nero sings about the destruction of Troy as a parallel to the destruction of Rome (15.39.3).[58] Both historical and mythological events were typical subject mat-

58. Cassius Dio confirms that Nero sang the destruction of Troy (ἅλωσιν [. . .] Ἰλίου) to parallel the

ter in Roman epic.[59] The rumor, therefore, implies that Nero understood this poetic tradition.

Tacitus' focus on poetry distinguishes Nero's behavior from that of a good emperor. Although Nero appears halfway competent at selecting performance material, Tacitus subtly points out that poetic skill is irrelevant when leadership skill is required. He underscores the tension between Nero-the-emperor and Nero-the-performer by showing that Nero chooses to perform rather than to lead at a crucial moment. Tacitus emphasizes the inappropriateness of Nero's behavior by suggesting that because it was appropriate for a performer, it detracted from his credibility as an emperor.

Nero has misdirected people often enough that they have learned to focus on the performer and ignore the emperor. Performance has become such a major part of Nero's persona that his choice of song is considered significant to his reaction to the great fire. Nero's imperial response, which Tacitus presents first and as fact, is eclipsed by his rumored musical performance. Because Nero has often engaged in deceptive performances and expected people to respond to his fictions instead of to reality, his subjects have become habituated to respond to those fictions, sometimes to Nero's detriment. Tacitus implies that, although humor may have been a useful strategy for Nero while he consolidated his power, its utility decreased. Once Nero was in power, it was detrimental to his principate for him to be a laughingstock even though it kept all attention on him. That detriment became even more pronounced when he exercised his power in a setting broader than the imperial court.

The Pisonian Conspiracy

Tacitus suggests that Nero's behavior altered the standards by which elites evaluated the proper exercise of power. Although they rebelled against Nero's way of ruling, the Pisonian conspirators conceived of power on the same terms that Nero did.[60] Tacitus is indecisive about Piso's character: "he enjoyed a brilliant

---

destruction of Rome ([ἅλωσιν] Ῥώμης), which for Dio suggests Nero's glee in seeing Rome destroyed. Dio is certain that Nero caused the fire (epitome 62b.18.1).

59. A paradigmatic example, Vergil's *Aeneid*, treats both mythological events and contemporary politics. That epic also narrates the destruction of Troy. The combination of current events and the sack of Troy is therefore not necessarily a poetic crime, and Tacitus does not present Nero's choice of song as inherently objectionable.

60. Woodman (1993, 104) and Pagán (2004, 68–69) note that Tacitus gives the Pisonian conspiracy

reputation among the public for his virtue—or displays which resembled virtues" (*claro apud uulgum rumore erat per uirtutem aut species uirtutibus similes*, 15.48.2). Like Nero, Piso relies more on show than substance.[61] Tacitus is even less positive about the other conspirators.[62] Despite their opposition to Nero, they are creatures of a Neronian world. For instance, Lucan joined the conspiracy because Nero had suppressed his poetry out of envy (15.49.3). Unfair censorship could be a legitimate concern, but Tacitus represents the motive as pure poetic jealousy on both sides. Nero, unable to rival Lucan's poetry, curtails its distribution, and Lucan understands this as a political slight.

Other conspirators seem no better. Tacitus introduces Flavius Scaevinus and Afranius Quintianus with a backhanded compliment as having "belied their own reputations" (*contra famam sui*, 15.49.4) for agreeing to take part in such a dangerous endeavor. Tacitus associates Scaevinus with luxury and indolence and says Quintianus desired revenge against Nero for an insulting poem that Nero had written about him (15.49.4). Most of the conspirators are motivated to revolt by concerns that mirror Nero's obsessions. Like Nero, they consider appearance and performance to be dominant concerns in politics. Lucan and Quintianus display particularly Neronian preoccupations because they focus on poetry, one of Nero's characteristic obsessions. The opposed scripts, performance and reality, that Tacitus uses to describe Nero's principate, now inform the goals of a conspiracy against him. Because it is a conspiracy, appearance and reality are even more confused as the conspirators attempt to conceal their actual intentions beneath a façade of loyalty. For Nero, being the center of attention is synonymous with being the center of power, even when being the center of attention means being absurd. The Pisonian conspirators revile Nero but accept that the emperor must be the center of attention.

Tacitus stresses that the conspirators focused on reputation (*fama*) as much as injustice.[63] Quintianus is angry at being "defamed" (*diffamatus*), although by

---

much careful attention, perhaps more than it deserved. Pagán calls the conspiracy an "ample opportunity to develop the theme of disguise in a principate characterized by theatricality" (2004, 74). Even Rutledge, who reinterprets many alleged conspiracies as more serious than Tacitus admits, considers the Pisonians disorganized and slow to act (2001, 167).

61. Granted, Tacitus rarely gives Nero credit for "displays which resembled virtues," but the characters share a tendency to prioritize appearance over substance.

62. Tacitus approves of a few conspirators, namely Subrius Flavus and Sulpicius Asper, whose deaths he praises (15.49.2; 15.67.1–15.68.1), and Plautius Lateranus, who joined out of a selfless "love for the state" (*amor rei publicae*, 15.49.3). The rest are either subtly criticized or not described. The list of conspirators has repeatedly been likened to drama (Woodman 1993, 105n6 lists several such references).

63. As mentioned above, Lucan was annoyed at being unable to promote his poetry ("Nero [. . .] was

Tacitus' account he was already "infamous" (*infamis*, 15.49.4). *Fama* is markedly Neronian because it is twice connected to poetic rather than political accomplishments and because some sort of irrationality is necessary to explain why a secret conspiracy has been organized by people who want more attention. Tacitus continues to build on the idea that deception through performance is crucial to maintaining Nero's power and to suggest that although Nero used it to his advantage, this tool was equally available to his enemies. Here, it is Nero's frivolous accomplishments (suppressing and writing poetry) that stoke enmity against him.[64] According to Tacitus, the performative aspect of Nero's rule loomed large in the minds of the very conspirators who plotted his overthrow. Tacitus uses the conspirators to illustrate Nero's deleterious influence on the Roman elite and to demonstrate a nearly exclusive focus on public spectacle. Like Nero, the conspirators consider public performance to be an inextricable element of power.

Whether Nero was personally responsible for the decline of Roman values, or the Roman aristocracy was to blame for its own deterioration,[65] Tacitus does not say, but in either case Nero's methods of ruling influenced even those who wanted to overthrow him. The conspirators' reasoning grants legitimacy to the way Nero ruled even as they plot to overthrow him. Piso would not have been a different type of emperor but merely a different flavor of Nero. After the conspiracy was exposed, Tacitus reports a rumor that Subrius Flavus wanted to make Seneca emperor rather than Piso because "in terms of disgrace it made no difference if a lyre-player were removed and a tragedy-player succeeded him (since, just as Nero sang to the lyre, so did Piso in tragic costume)" (*non referre dedecori si citharoedus demoueretur et tragoedus succederet (quia ut Nero cithara, ita Piso tragico ornatu canebat)*, 15.65).[66] The comparison between emperor

---

trying to suppress the fame of his poems," *famam carminum eius premebat Nero*), while Scaevinus and Quintianus "belied their own reputations," (*contra famam sui*, 15.49.3–4).

64. Other grievances are invoked, and Nero has committed crimes worthy of resentment. In this passage, however, Tacitus highlights the conspirators' frivolous grievances.

65. Woodman characterizes the conspiracy as "responding to the emperor's pressure" in their tendency to perform and to spend time talking rather than making practical plans (1993, 107, 113, 121). Pagán sees this episode, especially the death of Epicharis, as a criticism of the cowardice of the senatorial class (2004, 81–82).

66. Piso probably did not perform in public, but he probably did perform. In private circumstances, tragic performance was suitable for Roman aristocrats (Furneaux 1907, *ad loc*; Griffin 1984, 113). Koestermann suggests that special occasions might have made even public performance acceptable (1963, 15.65). Woodman notes that Tacitus describes the lead role in the conspiracy as *primas partes* (15.53.2), a technical term for the main part in theater, which further associates the conspiracy with theatrical performance (1993, 106). Tacitus' readers would also have known that Seneca wrote tragedies, a complication to Subrius Flavus' professed desire to take theater out of the principate.

and actor is enough not only to liken Piso to Nero but also to reintroduce the contrast between Nero's performances and his real wishes.[67] Tacitus' characterization of Piso is fraught with the same appearance/reality script opposition that he uses with Nero. Although Piso says he aims to restore correct governance to Rome, Tacitus suggests that the conspiracy merely attempted to replace one actor with another and that it only pretended to be virtuous.

The humor that Tacitus uses in the introduction of the conspirators does not continue in the episode, and the conspirators' suicides are presented as serious consequences of Nero's cruelty.[68] The conspirators' motivations, however, confirm that their plans were an outgrowth of Neronian trends, not a true rebellion against them. In this way, the conspiracy confirms Nero's power. Not only is he still the best actor in Roman politics, but theatrical competition remains politically significant. Nero has set the terms of the contest for power so that performance and attention are crucial elements in both his rule and the conspirators' attempt to overthrow it.

The Bassus Episode (16.1–16.3)

In the surviving part of Book 16, Tacitus illustrates Nero's faulty approach to deception with an extreme example. Book 16 begins with the story of an apparently insane man, Caesellius Bassus, who convinces Nero that there is gold buried under his land near Carthage. There is, of course, no gold, but Nero sends a fleet to retrieve it. This episode would be odd anywhere and is an especially strange way to begin a book.[69] Bassus seems to have been otherwise insignificant, and this incident is not particularly outrageous by Neronian standards. Suetonius' version of the same episode makes Bassus (whom he identifies as an *eques*) a coda to Nero's massive spending. Suetonius claims that after the gold proved to be nonexistent, Nero was too poor to pay the army (*Nero* 31–32). Suetonius emphasizes the incident's political and economic implications, but he does not call Bassus insane.

Tacitus emphasizes the episode by putting it at the start of Book 16 and has

67. Tacitus introduces the comparison through Subrius Flavus and does not endorse Flavus' opinion. Nevertheless, Tacitus devotes attention to the idea that the emperor is like an actor, and the comparison reinforces the humorous strand that Tacitus has established previously.

68. Even in serious deaths, performance remains. Martin calls Seneca's suicide "almost histrionic," although he believes this does not detract from the seriousness of his death (1981, 184). Woodman agrees that Seneca kills himself in performative style (1993, 117–18).

69. Syme calls it "an extraneous interlude" (1958, 263).

more interest in Bassus' insanity than in economics. Tacitus' decision to open Book 16 with this episode sets an absurd tone. The episode is overtly humorous and deals directly with the conflict between reality and illusion. One major difference from earlier humorous episodes is that Nero is not in the leading role; Bassus is. Tacitus allows no ambiguity about Bassus' mental state. Bassus has a "disturbed mind" (*mente turbida*, 16.1.1) and his actions are so miscalculated that they could hardly be those of a sane person. Later, Tacitus says he had *uecordia* (16.3.2). The Bassus episode thus inserts mental illness into the ongoing contrast between reality and the illusions created by Nero's pronouncements.

Unlike other characters who have advanced false versions of reality, Bassus is not lying but believes his own deception because he is truly out of contact with reality.[70] All Nero's falsehoods and those of his courtiers were constructed either to deceive others or because they had been deceived by others. Bassus is the first manifestly insane man to navigate Nero's court.[71] His self-deception is neither willful nor beneficial for him. Because he believes his own wild claims, Bassus engages in a guileless act of deception when he convinces Nero that Dido's gold is buried under his land because he believes his story to be true. He is initially elevated and later ruined by telling the same "truth," which he never denies. Bassus is not the target of humor; his delusions are beyond his control and ruin his life.

The contrast between Bassus and Nero, however, creates humor. The first word of the book is *inlusit*, which connotes mockery and deception.[72] Tacitus says that "fortune" mocked Nero "owing to his own foolishness" (*per uanitatem ipsius*, 16.1.1) before Bassus appears. By blaming fortune for Nero's mistake, Tacitus detaches responsibility from Bassus. Although much deception so far has been done by Nero or at his behest,[73] here Nero is, for once, the victim of

70. At the end of the episode, Bassus insists that this is the first time his supposedly prophetic dreams have deceived him (16.3.2).

71. The distinction between mental illness and willful delusion is a difficult one. I argue that Tacitus treats Bassus as mentally ill insofar as he is ruled by his native delusions, something not common in the *Annals*. Nero occasionally behaves as if he were insane, but Tacitus suggests that Nero did so by choice, willfully deceiving himself rather than being deceived by a mental condition.

72. *Inlusit* can mean either "mock" or "deceive." The *Lexicon Taciteum* classifies this use of *inludere* as meaning *decipere*. The *OLD* entry for *illudere*, however, cites this same passage as an example of the usage that connotes mockery rather than deception. I suggest that here, mockery is at least as likely as deception because, according to the *Lexicon Taciteum*, there are at most only three uses of *inludere* to mean "deception" in Tacitus, whereas there are more than twice as many in which it indicates either mockery or physical harm. Tacitus is therefore considerably more likely to use *inludere* to mean mockery than deception. Where both meanings are possible, Tacitus may also have meant both to be considered.

73. One exception is the rumor that he lit the great fire, which seems to have originated independently of Nero.

someone else's distorted reality. Tacitus disrupts the pattern in which Nero usually controls deception.[74]

Tacitus emphasizes the humor here by suggesting that Nero was deceived by "fortune." Nero would not have believed Bassus' story if he had investigated it first. Bassus provides details that strike Nero as corroborative evidence (the large amount of gold, the forms in which it is stored, his theory that Dido hid the gold from the Numidians).[75] These same details, however, are absurdities from the perspective of Tacitus and his readers. The improbability of such a discovery is compounded by the amount of gold and by Bassus' fanciful explanation. In contrast to the skepticism that Tacitus encourages in his readers, Nero is credulous. He acted "without examining sufficiently the trustworthiness either of the author or of the business itself, and without sending inspectors to ascertain whether the news was true" (*non auctoris, non ipsius negotii fide satis spectata nec missis inquisitoribus, per quos nosceret an uera adferrentur*, 16.2.1). Nero could have assessed Bassus' claim, but he did not. This is an even greater oversight considering the transparency of Bassus' delusions.

Although Bassus did not intend to trick Nero, he produced a false impression that fooled Nero and those to whom Nero repeated the story. Tacitus exploits the contrast between the insane Bassus and the technically sane Nero to produce humor in the contrast between sane deception and insane honesty. Tacitus implicitly likens Nero to an insane man. In contrast to Bassus, Nero lives in his own personal reality by choice, and the encounter with Bassus juxtaposes Nero's enthusiasm for the fantasy of the gold with Bassus' delusional certainty. Generally, Tacitus portrays Nero's creative relationship with reality as humorous in order to make the point that Nero caused people to act in ways that were disconnected from reality. In this case, Tacitus suggests that Nero is subject to the same deceptions that his courtiers are. He cannot always recognize when others have manipulated reality. Where previously Tacitus blurred the distinction between what is true and what the emperor says is true, here he

74. In addition, Walker understands the first sentence of Book 16 as an indication that Nero's power was waning (1952, 43). Mendell understands it as an indication of Nero' descent into dramatic tyranny (1957, 164).

75. Braund argues persuasively that Bassus unwittingly made a well-tailored appeal. A discovery of hidden gold would have appealed to a Roman emperor as a sign of divine favor, gold evokes a Golden Age, and naming Dido as the treasure's original owner is a reminder of the Julio-Claudians' mythic ancestry (1983, 65–66). Griffin adds that Nero had written an epic about the Trojans and apparently believed the story of the miraculous discovery of another Trojan poem. He may therefore have been especially credulous about the gold (1984, 147). Bassus' story would have appealed to Nero's interest in presenting himself as both a legitimate ruler and an inspired poet.

compares the emperor who deceives on purpose with the insane man who deceives by accident. Where Bassus actually suffers from mental illness, Nero merely behaves as if he were insane. Like Bassus, Nero sets out to convince others once he is convinced of the absurd story. The soldiers of the fleet who are sent to receive the gold either believe in it or are bound to act as if they do; the people discuss the matter "with credulity" (*credulitate*); and panegyrical orators use the gold as material for their speeches (16.2.1–2).[76] Tacitus implicitly compares Nero's influence on his subjects with Bassus' influence on Nero. Just as Bassus can transmit a false belief to Nero, so Nero can do the same to many others. The obvious difference is that Bassus is convincing because he genuinely believes his delusions while Nero is convincing not because he believes the story but because he has the power to force people to act as though they believe him.

Nevertheless, Nero's belief in the Carthaginian gold is functionally indistinguishable from Bassus' belief in it. Tacitus compares Nero's credulity to Bassus' insanity,[77] adding another pair of opposed scripts: emperor/madman. Although there is no outright reason that an emperor cannot be insane, insanity is an undesirable trait in an emperor, and Tacitus emphasizes the overlap between Nero's power and his encouragement of delusions. Bassus, despite his insanity, gives the emperor instructions, and Nero, despite his ability to investigate Bassus' claim, believes the story as certainly as Bassus does. Without calling Nero insane, Tacitus shows that his behavior was more appropriate for a delusional person than for an emperor.

Jokes based on the opposed scripts of sanity and insanity have a history that reaches back to ancient Rome. A few Plautus characters are accused of madness or pretend to be insane to achieve their goals.[78] The closest parallel to the Bas-

76. Tacitus mentions that those who knew better (*prudentes*) did not believe the rumor and suggests (with the verb *fingebant*) that the panegyrical orators also knew that it was not true (16.2.1–2). Nero did not convince others to believe in the buried gold, but he widened the circle of people who must act as if they believed in it.

77. Tacitus does not portray Nero as a particularly discerning assessor of the truth. His grievances with Britannicus, Agrippina, Seneca, and the Pisonian conspirators are either imagined (as with Britannicus), stoked by third parties (as with Seneca and the conspirators), or based on correct but nonspecific knowledge of the offender's character (as with Agrippina). Tacitus' Nero does sometimes display an astute understanding of how to manipulate and deceive his subjects, but he has poorly developed his ability to comprehend the significance of others' behavior.

78. In *Casina*, the slave Pardalisca claims that the title character has gone insane as part of a gambit to prevent the lecherous *senex* Lysidamus from marrying her (621–629). In *Rudens*, the slave Trachalio briefly feigns insanity to intimidate his fellow slave Gripus into relinquishing a chest he has fished out of the sea (1006–1009). In both plays, the supposedly insane person offers violent threats that a sane person might not have been able to make without punishment.

sus episode occurs in *Menaechmi* when Menaechmus Sosicles, accused of insanity by his identical twin's wife and father, scares them away by playing to their expectations and claiming to hear the voices of Bacchus and Apollo commanding him to do violence (831–875). Menaechmus recognizes that being "insane" will serve him better than losing a rational argument. The humor hinges partly on his absurd, falsely insane behavior, but also on his canny decision to act insane for personal benefit. Being "insane" temporarily makes Menaechmus Sosicles powerful because he can frighten his twin's family with unfulfilled threats rather than convincing them that they have mistaken his identity.[79] Menaechmus Sosicles' choice to act insane is far more advantageous than it would be for him to attempt to appear sane before people who believe him to be crazy. Bringing the opposed scripts of sanity and insanity together, Plautus constructs a situation in which it is rational to act insane.[80]

The scene from *Menaechmi* demonstrates that joking about insanity can reflect on the irrationality of a group dynamic as much as on the insanity of a single character, an issue that is magnified in history, where an erratic ruler can force others into an abnormal "normalcy" (Plass 1988, 10, 75).[81] In Tacitus, the insane character is Bassus, whose insanity reflects on Nero's principate because Nero is sane but behaves similarly to Bassus. Tacitus emphasizes the similarities in their behavior despite the contrast in their mental health. Bassus acts as he does because he is coerced by his own delusions. Nero acts insane voluntarily,

79. Some modern jokes also play on a sane/insane opposition. Arthur Koestler cites several examples of what he calls the "lunatic story," jokes in which the target or a major character is insane (1949, 90–91). Koestler concludes that some of these jokes evince a repressed desire to do violence to their "lunatic" targets, but also that in interactions between "lunatics" and their sane interlocutors, the sane interlocutors are the ones who come off as out of touch. In one of these jokes, a sane journalist asks an insane man who is fishing in a washbasin whether he has caught anything, only to be rebuked: "Have *you* ever caught a fish in a washbasin?" (1949, 90). Koestler writes, "the [sane] journalist, by accepting the logic of illusion, is caught in his own trap, which increases our malicious pleasure" (1949, 90).

80. Bartsch cites Flavius Philostratus' comments on Nero in his life of Apollonius of Tyana (5.7) as an ancient example of the idea that an actor who attempted to remain in his role as a tyrant would appear insane and that a tyrant who attempted to be an actor could be perceived as insane even if he were not. Because Nero played tyrants and matricides on stage, the relationship between his real and fictive identities is especially complicated (Bartsch 1994, 36–40).

81. Alexei Navalny, writing during his final imprisonment, provided a strange modern parallel: a loud and irritating "psycho" was installed across from his punishment cell. Navalny initially suspected that the other prisoner was merely feigning insanity to torture him, but he concluded that nobody sane could keep up such energetic and persistent shouting. In that case, officials not only within the prison administration but "at the regional or federal level" took the initiative to source and transport the "madman" in order to bother Navalny. Such a plan, Navalny concluded, reveals the Putin regime as the true lunatics, people able to come up with punishments that "wouldn't occur to a bad-but-sane person" (Navalny 2024, 449–51).

because he hopes to benefit from doing so. Both are fooled or mocked. Nero is the object of *inlusit*, the first word in the episode, and Bassus wonders how he could have been deceived (*elusum*) by his dreams (16.3.2). By comparing Nero's poor judgment to Bassus' mental incapacity, Tacitus encourages humor by suggesting that Bassus' behavior, although similar to Nero's, can at least by explained by his mental illness.

His rhetorical use of humor does not prevent Tacitus from exploring the serious implications of an emperor behaving like a delusional person. Nero makes irresponsible financial decisions because he expects to be reimbursed by Bassus' treasure, to the point that he depletes public funds (16.3.1).[82] Unlike Bassus, whose delusions might not have harmed others had he not attracted Nero's attention, Nero causes damage by deciding that the buried treasure is real. Nero's mismanagement of resources is a serious scandal, not a joke, but Tacitus connects power to insanity because Nero makes an apparently rational decision based on a completely irrational premise (i.e., he spends money because he expects to be enriched by a buried treasure). Following descriptions of Nero's gullibility and the Senate's, people's, and panegyricists' praises of Nero, this description of Nero's financial policy brings the episode back to the consequences that Rome suffered because Nero believed Bassus.

Tacitus attributes to Bassus two possible exits (death or confiscation of property), either of which highlights the negative consequences of his actions. Tacitus does not, however, say if Nero suffered any personal consequences. This is a striking contrast to Bassus' downfall, which Tacitus describes in a long, winding sentence that catalogs Bassus' end in subordinate clauses that come before the main verb: "For Bassus dug up his land and the broad fields around about, all the time asserting that this or that was the place of the promised cavity, and followed not only by soldiers but by a veritable populace of rustics enlisted for carrying out the task; but, at last rid of his derangement, and saying in astonishment that his dreams had not been false before and that that was the first time he had been deluded, he escaped shame and dread only by a voluntary death" (*nam Bassus, effosso agro suo latisque circum aruis, dum hunc uel illum locum promissi specus adseuerat, sequunturque non modo milites, sed populus agrestium efficiendo operi adsumptus, tandem posita uecordia, non falsa antea somnia sua seque tunc primum elusum admirans, pudorem et metum*

82. Suetonius emphasizes the financial consequences even more strongly. In his version, Nero ran out of money to pay military *stipendia* (*Nero* 32).

morte uoluntaria effugit, 16.3.2). This sentence contrasts with the previous one, in which Tacitus describes the relatively minor financial consequences suffered by Nero. At first, it seems that Tacitus is building tension in the subordinate clauses that describe Bassus' fate and that he will conclude by addressing what happened to Nero when the gold failed to materialize. Instead, he never says how Nero reacted to the news that there was no gold. In contrast to Bassus' slow and painful realization that something is wrong, Nero moves straight from this incident to singing in public. Bassus, although insane, is forced to reckon with reality when it turns out that there is no buried treasure. Nero, in contrast, continued to act insane without acknowledging his mistake. The contrast between sane and insane is reversed. Because he does not have the power to impose his false reality on others, Bassus comes to grips with reality. Because Nero is powerful enough to ignore or alter any facts that conflict with his preferred reality, he walks away from this incident without acknowledging that there was no gold. Tacitus' readers may see cracks in Nero's façade, but that weakness does not register with Nero, who still considers himself too powerful to care about reality.

Nero as Musician

Nero is so unruffled by the Bassus incident that he immediately decides to commit to a musical performance at the upcoming Quinquennial Games. The Senate, apprehensive about the performance, attempts to mitigate the damage of Nero's performance by awarding him a new crown for "eloquence" (*facundiae*, 16.4.1).[83] The Senate hopes to prevent a display of *ludicra deformitas*, a concept difficult to render in English. Woodman translates it as "disfiguring performance," which is correct but cannot capture all its connotations. *Ludicrum* has a connotation related to public games, and *deformitas* has connotations related to physical ugliness and social stigma (*OLD ludicrum, deformitas*). Ugliness

83. "Meanwhile, with the five-yearly contest now near, the senate, to avert disgrace, offered the Commander the victory in singing and added the crown for eloquence, by which a disfiguring performance might be screened" (*interea senatus, propinquo iam lustrali certamine, ut dedecus auerteret, offert imperatori uictoriam cantus adicitque facundiae coronam, qua ludicra deformitas uelaretur*, 16.4.1). I have changed Woodman's translation of *facundia* from "fluency" to "eloquence" because it seems just as accurate and less obscure. Woodman comments that the sentence *is* obscure because it does not explain what effect the Senate hoped this honor would have (2004, 342n4). I interpret it to mean that the Senate wanted to reduce Nero's interest in performing at the contest by eliminating the last veneer of competition.

and spectacle are both associated with humor. Ugliness is considered a primary spur to laughter by both Cicero and Quintilian.[84] In a delicious irony, the Senate offers Nero prizes for singing and eloquence to discourage him from singing and speaking.

Of course, Nero performs anyway, and Tacitus describes Nero's performance in humorous terms. Nero insists (*dictitans*) that he does not need the Senate's awards and will win the competition on his own merits (16.4.2). When he performs, the people (*uulgus, plebs*) are enthusiastic, and Nero makes a show of obeying all the rules observed by regular performers, right down to displaying a "fabricated panic" (*ficto pauore*, 16.4.4) at the judges' assessment. Tacitus underlines the contrast between the performer-emperor and the other competitors by pointing out how closely and how needlessly Nero followed their practices. Nero's determination to act like any other competitor and earn his prizes is shown to be absurd by the contrast between what Nero needs to do to win (nothing; he has already won by senatorial decree) and what he actually does. Tacitus' description of Nero's performance brings together the opposed scripts of the powerful emperor and the nervous musician. By performing in the contest instead of claiming an unearned prize, Nero apparently intends to make his victory more real, although he presumably knows that his victory is assured even in an apparently fair contest.[85] Nero's victory is inevitable from the start of the contest, where Tacitus enumerates the rules that Nero chose to follow, the same rules that all the other competitors must have followed as a matter of course. Nero's participation in the contest is conspicuously on his own terms.

Nero's initial objection to the interference of the Senate is significant because it begins a sentence and includes political terminology. Nero comments that he does not need the support of the Senate, which suggests an explicitly political disagreement, not one about a musical competition. Nero claims that he needs neither their canvassing nor their power (*ambitus* and *potestas*, 16.4.2), both political terms that here refer to the contest prizes in an understated pun. In a different context, Nero might have used the same words to dismiss the Senate's political authority, and Tacitus reinforces his character-

84. See footnote 15 above for references to *deformitas* as an element of humor in Cicero and Quintilian.

85. His "fabricated panic" is evidence that he knew this because it was "fabricated" (16.4.4). The detail that Nero pretended to be afraid is absent from the parallel tradition (other authors imply Nero's fear was real), which makes it even more pointed (Bartsch 1994, 27).

ization of Nero as a tyrant through his disregard for the Senate. The main point of contention, however, turns on performance, which Nero still seems to consider a major support to his power. Tacitus makes the source of Nero's power seem even more absurd because Nero is supported by the *uulgus* instead of the Senate.[86] Tacitus attributes no clear motivation to the *uulgus*. Perhaps they find Nero's antics entertaining. Tacitus does, however, make a serious point in his illustration of the relationship between Nero, the elite, and the common people. At the same time, he uses humor to illustrate Nero's turn from a powerful emperor into an apparently terrified lyre player. Although Nero wins public support by competing in the contest, he appears less powerful than he is, a departure from the effect of performance earlier in his reign. Here, Nero's former strategies have become predictable and have ceased to be effective.

Tacitus heightens the humor of the musical contest by describing the requirements imposed upon competitors. These include restrictions to do with sweat and "emissions from mouth or nostrils" (*sudorem* and *oris aut narium excrementa*, 16.4.3). Tacitus' careful periphrasis for mucus and saliva underscores his opinion that these fluids are beneath the dignity of history and should not have been the object of the emperor's public concern. I argue that Tacitus includes these details to emphasize the humorous contrast between emperor and lyre player.[87] The mundane physical requirements of competing in a musical contest are important for professional lyre players, but they should not be political concerns. In comparison, Suetonius describes the physical regimen that Nero underwent to improve his voice, but he focuses on different details, many of which are related to voice training and would presumably have been done in private (*Nero* 20). His public performances are as spectacular for a simultaneous earthquake and a cadre of professional applauders as for Nero's personal behavior (*Nero* 20). Cassius Dio provides few physical details but focuses on Nero's musical taste, the quality of his voice, and the sycophantic adoration of the audience (epitome 62a.20.1–5).[88] By concentrating on Nero's

86. Tacitus says that the *plebs* were "importuning [Nero] that he should communicate to them the complete range of his enthusiasms (these were the words they spoke)" (*flagitante uulgo ut omnia studia sua publicaret (haec enim uerba dixere)*, 16.4.3). Because the whole *uulgus* could not have said the same thing, this is a very improbable claim of exact words that nevertheless emphasizes the *uulgus*' responsibility for encouraging Nero's performances. The crowd may not be entirely sincere, but they seem enthusiastic about watching Nero perform (Bartsch 1994, 29).

87. Lyre playing was not necessarily incompatible with being emperor. Augustus associated himself with Apollo *citharodos*, but Nero took what had been a low-key affiliation and increased its prominence to an unreasonable degree (Fantham 2013, 21–22).

88. Fantham argues that Tacitus includes fewer details of Nero's performance because he is con-

attention to these rules, Tacitus shows how far Nero would depart from his imperial dignity in service of his desire to perform. Nevertheless, Nero either could not or did not want to abandon his imperial status. If the emperor pretends to be a regular lyre player, all he accomplishes is to demonstrate that emperors sweat.

Tacitus finishes the episode with a description of Nero's fans among the plebs: "For its part the plebs of the City, accustomed as it was to encourage the gestures of actors too, resounded with regular rhythms and organized applause. You would have believed them delighted—and perhaps they were delighted, in their indifference to public outrage" (*et plebs quidem Vrbis, histrionum quoque gestus iuuare solita, personabat certis modis plausuque composito. crederes laetari, ac fortasse laetabantur per incuriam publici flagitii*, 16.4.4). Tacitus implicitly likens Nero to an actor because the plebs responds as if he were one.[89] Not only the emperor and the aristocracy but also the plebs have deteriorated morally. They are "accustomed" to praise actors.[90] Tacitus first evinces doubt about their joy (*crederes laetari*), then admits that perhaps they were happy because disgrace did not matter to them. The final words of the sentence, *per incuriam publici flagitii*, are a punchline. The crowd's happiness, which was ambiguous at first, is confirmed and identified as the result of "indifference to public outrage," a significant moral flaw. Tacitus shows that Nero's subjects, from senators to the plebs, either go along with his lies or adapt their realities to support whatever disgraceful or false thing he does or says. Because Tacitus leaves this information to the end of the sentence, like a punchline, it takes on a humorous tone that resonates with Tacitus' humorous treatment of this motif in earlier episodes.

Conclusion

Because Book 16 breaks off midsentence, it is not known how Tacitus might have concluded his humorous treatment of Nero.[91] In the surviving Neronian

cerned about violations of decorum, not about the particulars of how decorum was violated (2013, 24). Tacitus' approach to the details of Nero's performance is unusual among ancient historians.

89. Koestermann draws a compelling parallel between this passage and *Hist.* 1.36.3, in which Otho blows kisses to the Roman crowd to win their support (1963, 16.4.4). In both incidents, an emperor debases himself for attention and Tacitus describes the incident with humor.

90. At *Histories* 2.90.1–2, the plebs cheer for Vitellius with "the usual flatteries" (*solitas adulationes*) even though Vitellius has no good qualities. In both passages, Tacitus criticizes the crowd for its unmerited praise.

91. The remaining text includes a few more references to humorous motifs. 16.11.3 contains a cursory

books, Tacitus employs humor in his narration to illustrate how Nero acquired power, and how Nero's imperial absurdities were refracted through the senatorial class and the urban plebs. Tacitus shows that Nero's performances could backfire on him because, although performance reinforces his power and encourages people to treat his fictions as truths, it also makes him seem absurd. Tacitus does not rely on a single script opposition with Nero, but he frequently plays on the contrast between Nero as an emperor and Nero as a performer. Tacitus also frequently discusses the difference between reality and imperial fictions.[92] Tacitus' use of humor is not merely an expression of disapproval (although it is often that), but a comment on the way Nero exercised power and how certain mechanisms of power became more central during his principate. In Tacitus' portrayal, Nero acted as more of a laughingstock than an emperor and in doing so forced the Roman elite to acknowledge his power and to conform to his manner of ruling, in which public performance was central. Performance was traditionally humiliating for Roman aristocrats, who suffered under Nero's rule and would not tolerate it forever. Nevertheless, some of them became inured to the idea that performance was central to imperial power, even as it was also a marker of the emperor's unsuitability. Emperors had always courted public opinion, but none so disruptively as Nero.

The first part of Nero's reign, in Tacitus' view, was characterized by ridiculous behavior that Nero's contemporaries treated as entirely serious. Tacitus does not clarify whether Nero made himself ridiculous on purpose at this early stage, but he highlights the absurdity of Nero's behavior to demonstrate Nero's power by showing that he could bend perceptions to his advantage. Once Nero has attained a stable position of power, Tacitus is more explicit about Nero's purposeful use of mockery. The emperor continues to act ridiculous by pursuing his artistic passions, but just as often mocks his enemies to decrease the threat they pose to him. In the final part of Tacitus' discussion of Nero, it becomes clear that many have accepted performance as a central part of imperial power, but many also see Nero's power as ridiculous and embarrassing and,

reference to Nero inflicting "mockery" (*ludibria*) on his dead enemies. Antistius Sosianus is exiled for writing insulting poetry about Nero (16.14.1), and Curtius Montanus is accused of a similar crime (16.28.1).

92. The senators' reaction to Nero's musical performance suggests growing aristocratic discontentment about Nero's performances. Many nonurban Italians also disapproved of Nero's performances (16.5.1) and Subrius Flavus, one of the Pisonian conspirators, criticized Nero for behaving like an actor (15.65). Suetonius records anti-Nero slogans that criticize his penchant for singing and acting (*Nero* 39). Cassius Dio mentions one of the same insults (epitome 62a.16.2). Tacitus may have been setting up Nero's performances as part of his downfall.

crucially, capable of being usurped by another performer. In short, Tacitus uses humor to comment on the trajectory of Nero's power, characterizing him as both a corruptor who made performance a more important part of the principate than it should have been and as a poor strategist who, by making politics a performance, weakened his own power.

Tacitus could, of course, have explained Nero's rise and fall without using humor. Often, however, he uses humor to link power, performance, and perception. When Tacitus makes Nero the target of humor, he vividly demonstrates that Nero equated being powerful to being the center of attention, even when being the center of attention meant being an object of ridicule. Tacitus' use of humor constitutes both a criticism of Nero's use of power and a demonstration of why a performative display of power could effectively keep Nero powerful. The combination of absurdity and power reveals that Nero's authority in Rome amounted to a kind of mind control. Tacitus magnifies the dissonance between the realities that Nero expects his subjects to engage with and the ones that he expects them to profess. Nero not only controlled what people did, but also sought to control what they thought. Tacitus' use of humor showcases multiple perspectives instead of cementing a single interpretation in a reader's mind. The contradictions that Nero demands are humorous by Tacitus' standards, but further reveal the complex set of perspectives that people in Nero's time had to sort through in order to understand the ruler under whom they lived. Furthermore, these contradictions seem to have eventually proved too much for Nero as he had to justify an increasingly nonsensical principate.

Conclusion

As I have argued, Tacitus employs rhetorical and literary techniques of humor as tools of his historical narrative. He uses humor to emphasize serious points, to enhance character portrayals and criticisms, and to outline the hypocrisy that he perceives at all levels of Roman society. Tacitus' use of humor is entwined with what Develin called his "techniques of insidious suggestion" (1983) and it often springs from irony, *variatio*, and the delay of pertinent information to the ends of sentences. Techniques that foster humor form a significant part of Tacitus' distinctive style, and Tacitus employs these techniques to make and elaborate upon historical points, creating the strong yet elusive impressions that distinguish his works.

Tacitus' style of humor generally conforms to the principles laid out by Cicero and Quintilian. He applies humor more often to shameful than to heinous crimes, uses humor to support his character-drawing rather than to entertain, and criticizes bad behavior without reveling in its description. Tacitus persuades differently than an orator might, and his humorous motifs have more space to develop, but he shares with the orators a sense of decorum (none of them descend into bawdy humor) and oratorical techniques of implication. The use of a joke structure can fix a significant detail in an audience's mind or imply moral judgment and would have been useful in both rhetoric and historiography. By using rhetorical techniques that foster humor, Tacitus directs readers' attention toward significant plot and character details and makes those details more memorable. Tacitus' humor is ironic and understated because it serves a purpose other than entertainment, and the purposeful use of humor is equally suited to serious as to cheerful material.

In my close readings, I have shown both that humor is present in Tacitus and that its use is calculated to subtly influence readers' perceptions of history. Tacitus does not generally use humor to introduce new information, nor does he add details for the purpose of being humorous, nor does humor always attach to any single type of historical event. Rather, Tacitus uses humor to outline his perspective on events while avoiding a clearer expression of opinion. This technique is part of what makes Tacitean insinuation so persuasive yet so difficult to ground in the facts of the narrative. Because humor brings together disparate ideas, it underlies the inferences to which Tacitus leads his readers, especially when Tacitus has not provided a factual basis for those inferences.

For example, Tacitus does not introduce Otho as a man torn between the appearance of authority and the reality of his dependence on his supporters, but this problem becomes characteristic of Otho, and Tacitus establishes the conflict through humor. Tacitus' consistent employment of the same humorous motif provides a powerful yet brief characterization of Otho that supports the narrative of *Histories* 1. Tacitus uses a consistent set of opposed ideas to illustrate Otho's powerlessness, a method that both crystalizes the problem with his reign and makes Otho the object of readers' contempt.

Tiberius may be the least ridiculous emperor discussed in Tacitus' surviving works. Although he, like Otho and Nero, thrives in an atmosphere of falsehood, Tiberius is too cryptic, or too consistently in control of information, to be a frequent target of Tacitus' humor. Indeed, he may be too competent a villain to be an acceptable target for humor. Libo Drusus, however, is incompetent enough to be mocked. Tacitus treats his trial as a gross injustice without ever actually declaring Libo innocent (in fact, without presenting a conclusive argument against his guilt). Instead, he creates the impression that Libo was harmless by employing humor to characterize him as pathetic. The main takeaway from that episode, however, is not about Libo (a minor figure) but about Tiberius' *maiestas* trials and the injustice that they encouraged. Tacitus' use of humor in this episode establishes a sense of injustice for later trials in which he does not use humor. Libo's incompetent conduct powerfully demonstrates the irrelevancy of the person accused when his harmlessness is compared to the incentives for delation.

In contrast to the cold observation of Tiberius, Claudius' obliviousness is buffoonish. Beneath his unwatchful eye, the imperial court becomes a farcical household, complete with influential mistresses and *liberti callidi*, elements imported from comedy. Claudius' wife Messalina shows more imperial ambition than he does, but her gender and poor planning make her ridiculous as well. At Messalina's wedding to Silius, Tacitus presents the couple's actions as highly absurd, but his humor aims at the ineffectiveness of the emperor as much as at Messalina's or Silius' personal conduct. Most of the central characters of the episode are portrayed as humorously incompetent, but Tacitus' use of humor also points to the failure of the Roman elite to govern the lower orders and perhaps even themselves.

Tacitus' use of humor becomes more extensive in his treatment of Nero, whose rise and fall are tied to an absurd dynamic of pretended credulity that Nero fosters but ultimately cannot control. This dynamic is ridiculous to those who stand outside it (including Tacitus and his readers) but deadly serious for Nero and his court. Nero's ability to control others is demonstrated by the bizarreness of the falsehoods he requires his subjects to believe, and conversely his control over Rome loosens as the system is usurped by his allies, rivals, and even one Caesellius Bassus. Throughout, Nero's rule is a cruel joke at which Rome is forbidden to laugh.

Tacitus applies more diverse humorous motifs to Nero than he does to other characters, and he emphasizes humor in major episodes. Tacitus' account of Nero's plot to have Agrippina killed, for example, hardly varies in substance from accounts given by Cassius Dio and Suetonius, yet Tacitus emphasizes a theme of concealed performance that shapes readers' impressions. Although Tacitus makes Nero responsible for the frequency and dominance of performance during his reign, he applies the humorous theme of performance to Nero's followers and occasionally his victims as well.

Most of the figures and events that Tacitus characterizes with humor are objects of his contempt. Granted that a great many historical figures are objects of Tacitus' contempt, his use of humor marks these characters out as abnormally unworthy. The humor in these passages is perhaps compromised by the fact that many of Tacitus' targets of humor behave reprehensibly and commit acts worthy of condemnation, which runs counter to the advice of Cicero and Quintilian, who both opine that serious crimes should be condemned with condign gravity (*De Orat.* 2.237, *Inst.* 6.3.31). Nevertheless, Tacitus tends not to center humor on heinous acts, but rather on the ridiculous excuses that their perpetrators create, as when Otho justifies his coup, Tiberian prosecutors justify the trial of Libo Drusus, or Nero justifies his mother's murder. Messalina's wedding reverses the pattern in that it is a laughably ramshackle power grab that leads to a near-usurpation by a freedman, such that Tacitus turns from humor to horror instead of the other way around. The distinction between humor and crime is maintained, however. There is nothing funny in, for example, the murder of Galba or Octavia, but there is humor in the justifications given by Otho and Nero. These examples actually augment the moral force of the victims' deaths by portraying the emperors as clownishly unworthy of the power they abuse.

Tacitus applies a similar humorous logic to larger groups, including the Roman people and the Senate. These groups, like Tacitus' individual targets of humor, are treated as contemptible, especially when they prefer to secure their immediate interests rather than to pursue long-term or laudable goals. Otho's soldiers, for example, provide essential support for his coup and are in turn targeted by the humor that Tacitus uses to characterize Otho. The soldiers' behavior is less ridiculous than Otho's because they have less dignity to lose, but their power and outrageous behavior are key elements of the joke centered on Otho. Tacitus' famous jab at astrologers (*Hist.* 1.22.1) serves a similar function on a smaller scale. I have focused on Tacitus' tendency to use humor in reference to specific historical figures in part because Cicero and Quintilian advise that a prudent orator should not target broad groups of people in his jokes, because jokes that apply to a broad range of people appear premeditated and undignified (*De Orat.* 2.245, *Inst.* 6.3.32), but written humor (and history) must have different standards for premeditation. Historians do not need to persuade a jury or assembly and may therefore write with a self-selected audience in mind. Tacitus' quips targeting the *vulgus*, astrologers, and other people of low status may therefore offer evidence of a different kind of Roman elite humor, perhaps a more private one than Cicero or Quintilian recommend.

Tacitus also spreads out his humorous passages for maximum effect. Often, the most humorous moments emphasize the climax of a character or narrative arc. Agrippina's death, for example, marks the end of a power struggle between her and Nero, and Tacitus emphasizes the strange circumstances of her death to demonstrate the triumph of Nero' s absurdity. Elsewhere, however, Tacitus adopts a gravely offended tone in discussions of Agrippina, and her threat is treated as real. Agrippina and Nero are dangerous, yet her death is ridiculous. The emperor's ability to turn the world upside-down on a whim makes him dangerous, and illustrating his crime in lurid, humorous detail emphasizes the danger alongside the absurdity. Additionally, Agrippina is a singularly unsympathetic victim (unlike, for example, Octavia) whose death is significant not for its tragedy but for the freedom it grants Nero. In this example, Tacitus applies a high concentration of humor to mark this turning point in Nero's reign.

Although Tacitus is not usually associated with humor, I wish to stress the continuity between my observations on humor and previous scholarly work on Tacitean style. In addition to studies like Plass' *Wit and the Writing of History* (1988), which puts humor at the forefront, plenty of scholarship on Tacitus refers to humorous elements,[1] yet rarely is humor treated as an integral, significant, and meaning-making part of Tacitus' work, probably because of his justified reputation as a Very Serious Author. Although Tacitus did not rely primarily on humor, humor was one tool available to him, and he availed himself of it, just as Cicero and Quintilian recommended. Similar uses of humor have been documented also in Cicero's rhetorical works, especially the *Pro Caelio*.[2] Given that two of our most influential sources on Latin oratory not only mention but even recommend the use of humor in texts that are primarily intended to make serious points, it is productive to study the humorous elements as humor, not simply as irony or *variatio*, but as part of a deliberate program of humor.

Tacitus' style is unique, but other serious Roman historical writers may have used humor as well. A prime candidate is Sallust, whose work predates Quintilian's advice and who might not have aligned with Cicero's, but whose tone and style frequently include the same elements that Tacitus uses to create humor. Another is Suetonius, whose style is distinctly different from Tacitus', but who includes absurd details frequently. There is also Seneca, whose sententious style fosters a clipped irony.[3] More generally, if we accept the possibility that humor is present even in serious works of Latin literature, we can avoid the temptation to downplay its manifestations as insignificant. Small deviations from complete seriousness are accepted as typical in modern works, and this phenomenon is present also in ancient texts.

Finally, it does not escape me that most examples of humor that I have found in Tacitus focus on extremes of power. Modern scholars doubt that political humor can reliably influence the real world, although it can influence our interpretations of reality.[4] Tacitus' use of humor accords with this theory, in part because he is a historian, writing about events that literally cannot be changed because they have already occurred. I contend, however, that the ways

1. Syme found irony, sarcasm, and even "gaiety" and "parody" in Tacitus (1958, 539). In a less famous but equally typical example, N. P. Miller introduced a commentary on *Annals* 1 by quoting a limerick to illustrate the effect of Tacitus' style (1959, 16). This example, like others I have cited throughout, demonstrates that humor is a useful, offhand parallel for important aspects of Tacitus' style.
2. See in the Introduction, footnote 10.
3. Margaret Graver has recently summarized previous work on humor in Seneca and made substantial contributions (2023, 222–38).
4. See in the Introduction, footnote 15.

in which Tacitus employs humor demonstrate its power to change the interpretation of events. Humor is not the only tool that Tacitus uses to evince contempt for his subject matter, but it is the only one that conveys both the impossibility and reality of the ways in which power was exercised by Roman emperors. The uses of humor that I point to in Tacitus are not, therefore, isolated examples, nor are they a temporary and accidental solution to the problem of portraying power. Tacitus' use of humor is instead an example in a long tradition that employs humor to capture the paradoxes that extreme political power imposes upon the world.

Bibliography

Apte, Mahadev. 1985. *Humor and Laughter: An Anthropological Approach.* Cornell University Press.

Ash, Rhiannon. 1999. *Ordering Anarchy: Armies and Leaders in Tacitus' "Histories."* University of Michigan Press.

Ash, Rhiannon. 2007. *Tacitus "Histories" Book II.* Cambridge University Press.

Ash, Rhiannon. 2017. "Rhetoric and Historiography." In *The Oxford Handbook of Rhetorical Studies*, edited by Michael J. MacDonald. Oxford University Press.

Ash, Rhiannon. 2018. *Tacitus "Annals" Book XV.* Cambridge University Press.

Attardo, Salvatore. 1994. *Linguistic Theories of Humor.* Mouton de Gruyter.

Attardo, Salvatore. 2001. *Humorous Texts: A Semantic and Pragmatic Analysis.* Mouton De Gruyter.

Attardo, Salvatore, Christian F. Hempelmann, and Sara Di Maio. 2002. "Script Oppositions and Logical Mechanisms: Modeling Incongruities and Their Resolutions." *Humor* 15 (1): 3–46. https://doi.org/10.1515/humr.2002.004

Attardo, Salvatore, and Victor Raskin. 1991. "Script Theory Revis(it)ed: Joke Similarity and Joke Representation Model." *Humor* 4 (3–4): 293–347. https://doi.org/10.1515/humr.1991.4.3-4.293

Baar, Manfred. 1990. *Das Bild des Kaisers Tiberius bei Tacitus, Sueton und Cassius Dio.* Teubner.

Baldwin, Barry. 1977. "Tacitean Humor." *Wiener Studien* 11: 128–44.

Barbe, Katharina. 1995. *Irony in Context.* John Benjamins.

Bartsch, Shadi. 1994. *Actors in the Audience: Theatricality and Doublespeak from Nero to Hadrian.* Harvard University Press.

Batstone, William W., trans. 2010. *"Catiline's Conspiracy," "Jugurthine War," "Histories."* By Sallust. Oxford University Press.

Benario, Herbert W. 1983. *Tacitus "Annals" 11 and 12.* University Press of America.

Bhatt, Shreyaa. 2017. "Useful Vices: Tacitus' Critique of Corruption." *Arethusa* 50 (3): 311–33. https://dx.doi.org/10.1353/are.2017.0011

Bittarello, Maria Beatrice. 2011. "Otho, Elagabalus, and the Judgement of Paris: The Literary Construction of the Unmanly Emperor." *Dialogues d'histoire ancienne* 37 (1): 93–113. https://doi.org/10.3917/dha.371.0093

Bonner, Stanley F. 1977. *Education in Ancient Rome: From the Elder Cato to the Younger Pliny*. University of California Press.

Borzsák, Stefan, ed. 1992. *Cornelii Taciti Libri Qui Supersunt: Ab Excessu Divi Augusti Libri I-VI*. Teubner.

Braester, Marlena. 1992. "Du 'signe ironique' à l'énonce ironique." *Semiotica* 92 (1–2): 75–86. https://doi.org/10.1515/semi.1992.92.1-2.75

Braund, David. 1983. "Treasure-Trove and Nero." *Greece & Rome* 30 (1): 65–69. https://www.jstor.org/stable/642745

Brugnola, Vittorio. 1896. *Le facezie di Cicerone*. S. Lapi.

Cassius Dio. 1925. *"Roman History," Volume VIII: Books 61–70*. Translated by Earnest Cary and Herbert B. Foster. Loeb Classical Library 176. Harvard University Press.

Caviglia, Franco. 2010. "Seneca e Nerone: Un dialogo squilibrato (Tac. *Ann.* XIV 53–56)." *Aevum Antiquum* 10: 333–42.

Celotto, Giulio. 2021. "The Escalating Repetitiveness of Civil War: Lucanian Allusions in Tacitus' Account of the Conflict Between Otho and Vitellius in *Historiae* 1–2." *Classical World* 114 (2): 171–99. https://dx.doi.org/10.1353/clw.2021.0001

Champlin, Edward. 2003. *Nero*. Harvard University Press.

Chlopicki, Wladyslaw. 1997. "An Approach to the Analysis of Verbal Humor in Short Stories." *Humor* 10 (3): 333–48.

Chlopicki, Wladyslaw. 2000. "Linguistic Analysis of Humour in Short Stories." In *Świat Humoru*, edited by Stanislaw Gajda and Dorota Brzozowksa, 513–24. University of Opole.

Christenson, David. 2016. "All's Well That Ends Well? Old Fools, Morality, and Epilogues in Plautus." In *Roman Drama and Its Contexts*, edited by Stavros Frangoulidis, Stephen J. Harrison, and Gesine Manuwald. De Gruyter.

Connolly, Joy. 2016. "A Theory of Violence in Lucan's *Bellum Ciuile*." In *Wordplay and Powerplay in Latin Poetry*, edited by Philip Mitsis and Ioannis Ziogas. De Gruyter.

Corbeill, Anthony. 1996. *Controlling Laughter: Political Humor in the Late Roman Republic*. Princeton University Press.

Corbier, Mireille. 1995. "Male Power and Legitimacy Through Women: The *Domus Augusta* Under the Julio-Claudians." In *Women in Antiquity: New Assessments*, edited by Richard Hawley and Barbara Levick. Routledge.

Cowan, Eleanor. 2016. "Contesting *Clementia*: The Rhetoric of *Severitas* in Tiberian Rome Before and After the Trial of Clutorius Priscus." *Journal of Roman Studies* 106: 77–101. https://www.jstor.org/stable/26346751

Cramer, Frederick H. 1954. *Astrology in Roman Law and Politics*. American Philosophical Society.

Damon, Cynthia. 2003. *Tacitus "Histories" Book I*. Cambridge University Press.

Damon, Cynthia. 2007. "Rhetoric and Historiography." In *A Companion to Roman Rhetoric*, edited by William Dominik and Jon Hall. Blackwell.

Dawson, Alexis. 1969. "Whatever Happened to Lady Agrippina?" *Classical Journal* 64 (6): 253–67. https://www.jstor.org/stable/3296108

Develin, R. 1983. "Tacitus and Techniques of Insidious Suggestion." *Antichthon* 17: 64–95. https://doi.org/10.1017/S0066477400003075

Dews, Shelly, Joan Kaplan, and Ellen Winner. 1995. "Why Not Say It Directly? The Social Functions of Irony." *Discourse Processes* 19 (3): 347–67. https://doi.org/10.1080/01638539509544922

Dickison, Sheila K. 1977. "Claudius: Saturnalicius Princeps." *Latomus* 36 (3): 634–47. https://www.jstor.org/stable/41530377

Drinkwater, John F. 2019. *Nero: Emperor and Court*. Cambridge University Press.

Edwards, Catharine. 2007. *Death in Ancient Rome*. Yale University Press.

Eisterhold, Jodi, Salvatore Attardo, and Diana Boxer. 2006. "Reactions to Irony in Discourse: Evidence for the Least Disruption Principle." *Journal of Pragmatics* 38 (8): 1239–56. https://doi.org/10.1016/j.pragma.2004.12.003

Fagan, Garrett G. 2002. "Messalina's Folly." *Classical Quarterly* 52 (2): 566–79. https://www.jstor.org/stable/3556420

Fantham, Elaine. 2004. *The Roman World of Cicero's "De Oratore."* Oxford University Press.

Fantham, Elaine. 2013. "The Performing Prince." In *A Companion to the Neronian Age*, edited by Emma Buckley and Martin T. Dinter. Blackwell.

Feldherr, Andrew. 1998. *Spectacle and Society in Livy's History*. University of California Press.

Ferri, Rolando. 1998. "Octavia's Heroines: Tacitus *Annales* 14.63–64 and the *Praetexta Octavia*." *Harvard Studies in Classical Philology* 98: 339–56. https://www.jstor.org/stable/311347

Fraser, Cora Beth. 2007. "Otho's Funny Walk: Tacitus, *Histories* 1.27." *Classical Quarterly* 57 (2): 621–31. https://www.jstor.org/stable/27564098

Furneaux, Henry, ed. 1896. *The "Annals" of Tacitus Volume I Books 1–6*. 2nd ed. Revised by H. F. Pelham and C. D. Fisher. Oxford University Press.

Furneaux, Henry, ed. 1907. *The "Annals" of Tacitus Volume II Books 11–16*. 2nd ed. Revised by H. F. Pelham and C. D. Fisher. Oxford University Press.

Fyfe, W. H., trans., and D. S. Levene, rev. 1997. *Tacitus: "The Histories."* Oxford University Press.

Galtier, Fabrice. 2011. *L'image tragique de l'Histoire chez Tacite: Étude des schèmes tragiques dans les "Histoires" et les "Annales."* Collection Latomus 333. Éditions Latomus.

Galtier, Fabrice. 2014. "Le motif du rivage dans l'épisode de la morte d'Agrippine (Tac., *Ann.*, 14.1–10)." In *Neronia* IX. *La villégiature dans le monde romain, de Tibère à Hadrien:* Actes du IXe congrès de la SIEN. Scripta antiqua 62, 309–16.

Gärtner, Thomas. 2010. "Drusus Libo als Exempel für einen wohlüberlegten Selbstmord (Sen. epist. 70, 10)." *Klio* 92 (2): 411–20.

Geffcken, Katherine. 1995. *Comedy in the "Pro Caelio": With an Appendix on the "In Clodium et Curionem."* Bolchazy-Carducci.

Goodyear, F. R. D. 1981. *The "Annals" of Tacitus Books 1–6.* Cambridge University Press.

Grant, Michael, trans. 1996. *The Annals of Imperial Rome.* Penguin.

Graver, Margaret. 2023. *Seneca: The Literary Philosopher.* Cambridge University Press.

Griffin, Miriam. 1984. *Nero: The End of a Dynasty.* Routledge.

Griffin, Miriam. 1986a. "Philosophy, Cato, and Roman Suicide: I." *Greece & Rome* 33 (1): 64–77. https://www.jstor.org/stable/643026

Griffin, Miriam. 1986b. "Philosophy, Cato, and Roman Suicide: II." *Greece & Rome* 33 (2): 192–202. https://www.jstor.org/stable/643257

Griffin, Miriam. 1990. "Claudius in Tacitus." *Classical Quarterly* 40 (2): 482–501. https://www.jstor.org/stable/639107

Haiman, John. 1990. "Sarcasm as Theater." *Cognitive Linguistics* 1 (2): 181–205. https://doi.org/10.1515/cogl.1990.1.2.181

Harris, B. F. 1962. "Tacitus on the Death of Otho." *Classical Journal* 58 (2): 73–77. https://www.jstor.org/stable/3294672

Harvey, Tracene. 2020. *Julia Augusta: Images of Rome's First Empress on Coins of the Roman Empire.* Routledge.

Haynes, Holly. 2003. *The History of Make-Believe: Tacitus on Imperial Rome.* University of California Press.

Haynes, Holly. 2012. "Tacitus' History and Mine." In *A Companion to Tacitus*, edited by Victoria Emma Pagán. Wiley Blackwell.

Haynes, Holly. 2022. "Tacitus' Tragic Touch: Vespasian's Healing Miracles at *Histories* 4.81–83." In *Tacitus' Wonders: Empire and Paradox in Ancient Rome*, edited by James McNamara and Victoria Emma Pagán. Bloomsbury.

Heubner, Heinz. 1963–1982. *P. Cornelius Tacitus: "Die Historien."* Heidelberg: Carl Winter Universitätsverlag.

Hughes, Joseph J. 1997. "Inter Tribunal et Scaenam: Comedy and Rhetoric in Rome." In *Roman Eloquence: Rhetoric in Society and Literature*, edited by William J. Dominik. Routledge.

Hughes, Lisa A. 2007. "Unveiling the Veil: Cultic, Status, and Ethnic Representation of Early Imperial Freedwomen." *Material Religion* 3 (2): 218–41. https://doi.org/10.2752/175183407X219750

Jorgensen, Julia. 1996. "The Functions of Sarcastic Irony in Speech." *Journal of Pragmatics* 26 (5): 613–34. https://doi.org/10.1016/0378-2166(95)00067-4

Joseph, Timothy A. 2023. "Agrippina's (Un-)Augustan Anger: Tacitus, *Annals* 12.22.3 and Ovid, *Tristia* 2.127." *Classical Quarterly* 73 (1): 320–27. https://doi.org/10.1017/S0009838823000228

Keeline, Thomas J. 2018. *The Reception of Cicero in the Early Roman Empire: The Rhetorical Schoolroom and the Creation of a Cultural Legend.* Cambridge University Press.

Keitel, Elizabeth. 1987. "Otho's Exhortations in Tacitus' 'Histories.'" *Greece & Rome* 34 (1): 73–82. https://www.jstor.org/stable/642973

Keitel, Elizabeth. 1991. "The Structure and Function of Speeches in Tacitus' *Histories* I–III." *Aufstieg und Niedergang der römischen Welt* II 33 (4): 2772–94.

Keitel, Elizabeth. 1992. "*Foedum Spectaculum* and Related Motifs in Tacitus *Histories II–III*." *Rheinisches Museum für Philologie* 135 (3/4): 342–51. https://www.jstor.org/stable/41233873

Keitel, Elizabeth. 2006. "*Sententia* and Structure in Tacitus *Histories* 1.12–49." *Arethusa* 39 (2): 219–44. https://www.jstor.org/stable/44578919

Keitel, Elizabeth. 2010. "The Art of Losing: Tacitus and the Disaster Narrative." In *Ancient Historiography and Its Contexts: Studies in Honour of A. J. Woodman*, edited by Christina S. Kraus, John Marincola, and Christopher Pelling. Oxford University Press.

Koestermann, Erich. 1963. *Cornelius Tacitus "Annalen."* Carl Winter Universitätsverlag.

Koestler, Arthur. 1949. *Insight and Outlook: An Inquiry into the Common Foundations of Science, Art and Social Ethics*. Macmillan.

Koestler, Arthur. 1964. *The Act of Creation*. Macmillan.

Leeman, A. D. 1963. *Orationis Ratio: The Stylistic Theories and Practice of the Roman Orators, Historians and Philosophers*. Adolf M. Hakkert.

Leeman, Anton, Harm Pinkster, and Edwin Rabbie. 1989. *M. Tullius Cicero, "De oratore" libri III: Kommentar*. 3. Band. *Buch II.99–290*. Carl Winter Universitätsverlag.

Leigh, Matthew. 2004. "The *Pro Caelio* and Comedy." *Classical Philology* 99 (4): 300–335. https://doi.org/10.1086/429939

Leigh, Matthew. 2017. "Nero the Performer." In *The Cambridge Companion to the Age of Nero*, edited by Shadi Bartsch, Kirk Freudenburg, and Cedric Littlewood. Cambridge University Press.

Levene, D. S. 2009. "Speeches in the *Histories*." In *The Cambridge Companion to Tacitus*, edited by A. J. Woodman. Cambridge University Press.

Levick, Barbara. 2013. "The Conspiracy of Libo Drusus—and What Follows from It." *Politica Antica* 3 (1): 43–50. https://doi.org/10.7381/73905

Luke, Trevor. 2013. "From Crisis to Consensus: Salutary Ideology and the Murder of Agrippina." *Illinois Classical Studies* 38: 207–28. https://www.jstor.org/stable/10.5406/illiclasstud.38.0207

Mader, Gottfried. 2018. "Nero Playing 'Nero': Programme Notes on Tacitus, *Ann.* 15.36." *Latomus* 77 (2): 383–94. https://www.jstor.org/stable/48741822

Maiuri, Arduino. 2012. "*Occultae notae*. Linee evolutive del trattamento del reato di magia negli *Annales* di Tacito: profilo giuridico e puntualizzazioni lessicali." In *Contesti magici-Contextos mágicos*, edited by Marina Piranomonte and Francisco Marco Simón. De Luca editori d'arte.

Malloch, S. J. V. 2009. "Hamlet without the Prince? The Claudian Annals." In *The Cambridge Companion to Tacitus*, edited by A. J. Woodman. Cambridge University Press.

Malloch, S. J. V. 2013. *The "Annals" of Tacitus: Book 11*. Cambridge University Press.

Marchetta, Antonio. 2004. *Studi tacitiani*. Casa editrice Universitá La Sapienza.

Martin, Ronald. 1981. *Tacitus*. University of California Press.

Márványos, Krisztián. 2015. "Some Aspects of Tiberius' Trials from the Viewpoint of the Libo Drusus Case." In *Sapiens Ubique Civis: Proceedings of International Conference on Classical Studies (Szeged, Hungary, 2013)*, edited by János Nagyillés, Attila Hajdú, Gergö Gellérfi, Anne Horne Baroody, and Sam Baroody. ELTE Eötvös József Collegium.

May, James M., and Jakob Wisse, eds. and trans. 2001. *Cicero: "On the Ideal Orator."* Oxford University Press.

Mayer, Roland, ed. 2001. *Tacitus: "Dialogus de Oratoribus."* Cambridge University Press.

Melounová, Markéta. 2014. "*Crimen Maiestatis* and the *Poena Legis* During the Principate." *Acta Antiqua Academiae Scientiarum Hungaricae* 54 (4): 407–30. https://doi.org/10.1556/068.2014.54.4.5

Mendell, Clarence W. 1957. *Tacitus, the Man and His Work*. Yale University Press.

Miller, N. P., ed. 1959. *Tacitus: "Annals" Book I*. Methuen.

Milnor, Kristina. 2009. "Women in Roman Historiography." In *The Cambridge Companion to the Roman Historians*, edited by Andrew Feldherr. Cambridge University Press.

Murgatroyd, Paul. 2008. "Tacitus on the Death of Octavia." *Greece & Rome* 55 (2): 263–73. https://www.jstor.org/stable/20204213

Nappa, Christopher. 2010. "The Unfortunate Marriage of Gaius Silius: Tacitus and Juvenal on the Fall of Messalina." In *Latin Historiography and Poetry in the Early Empire: Generic Interactions*, edited by John F. Miller and Anthony Woodman. Brill.

Navalny, Alexei. 2024. *Patriot*. Translated by Arch Tait and Stephen Dalziel. Knopf.

Nicolson, Frank W. 1893. "The Use of HERCLE (Mehercle), EDEPOL (Pol), ECASTOR (Mecastor) by Plautus and Terence." *Harvard Studies in Classical Philology* 4: 99–103. https://www.jstor.org/stable/310401

Oakley, S. P. 2009. "Style and Language." In *The Cambridge Companion to Tacitus*, edited by A. J. Woodman. Cambridge University Press.

Obrdlik, Antonin J. 1942. "'Gallows Humor'—a Sociological Phenomenon." *American Journal of Sociology* 47 (5): 709–16. https://www.jstor.org/stable/2769536

O'Gorman, Ellen. 2000. *Irony and Misreading in the "Annals" of Tacitus*. Cambridge University Press.

Olson, Kelly. 2002. "*Matrona* and Whore: The Clothing of Women in Roman Antiquity." *Fashion Theory* 6 (4): 387–420. https://doi.org/10.2752/136270402779615352

Oring, Elliott. 1992. *Jokes and Their Relations*. University Press of Kentucky.

Oring, Elliott. 2011a. "Parsing the Joke: The General Theory of Verbal Humor and Appropriate Incongruity." *Humor* 24 (2): 203–22. https://doi.org/10.1515/HUMR.2011.013

Oring, Elliott. 2011b. "Still Further Thoughts on Logical Mechanisms: A Response to Christian F. Hempelmann and Salvatore Attardo." *Humor* 24 (2): 151–58. https://doi.org/10.1515/HUMR.2011.009

Oring, Elliott. 2016. *Joking Asides: The Theory, Analysis, and Aesthetics of Humor*. Utah State University Press.

Oring, Elliott. 2019. "Oppositions, Overlaps, and Ontologies: The General Theory of Verbal Humor Revisited." *Humor* 32 (2): 151–70. https://doi.org/10.1515/humor-2018-0066

Pagán, Victoria. 2004. *Conspiracy Narratives in Roman History*. University of Texas Press.

Pearce, Celia. 2010. "Banqueting in Tacitus' *Annals*." *Ancient History* 40 (1): 58–67.

Perkins, Caroline A. 1993. "Tacitus on Otho." *Latomus* 52 (4): 848–55. https://www.jstor.org/stable/41536785

Pettinger, Andrew. 2012. *The Republic in Danger: Drusus Libo and the Succession of Tiberius*. Oxford University Press.

Phang, Sara Elise. 2008. *Roman Military Service: Ideologies of Discipline in the Late Republic and Early Principate*. Cambridge University Press.

Plass, Paul. 1985. "An Aspect of Epigrammatic Wit in Martial and Tacitus." *Arethusa* 18 (2): 187–210. https://www.jstor.org/stable/44578152

Plass, Paul. 1988. *Wit and the Writing of History: The Rhetoric of Historiography in Imperial Rome*. University of Wisconsin Press.

Plass, Paul. 1995. *The Game of Death in Ancient Rome: Arena Sport and Political Suicide*. University of Wisconsin Press.

Pomeroy, Arthur J. 2006. "Theatricality in Tacitus' *Histories*." *Arethusa* 39 (2): 171–91. https://www.jstor.org/stable/44578917

Possanza, D. Mark. 2023. "Imperial Nuptials at Pompeii: *CIL* IV.1261, an Obscene Take on the Marriage of Nero and Pythagoras." *Classical Journal* 119 (2): 189–224. http://doi.org/10.1353/tcj.2023.a914589

Quintilian. 2001. *The Orator's Education*, Volume III: *Books 6–8*. Translated by Donald A. Russell. Loeb Classical Library 126. Harvard University Press.

Ramage, Edwin S. 1973. *Urbanitas: Ancient Sophistication and Refinement*. University of Oklahoma Press for the University of Cincinnati.

Raskin, Victor. 1985. *Semantic Mechanisms of Humor*. D. Reidel.

Rhetorica ad Herennium. 1954. Translated by Harry Caplan. Loeb Classical Library 403. Harvard University Press.

Ridley, Ronald T. 2017. "The Case of the Missing Sense of Humour: The Historian Livy." *Ancient Society* 47: 87–117. https://www.jstor.org/stable/26773304

Ripat, Pauline. 2011. "Expelling Misconceptions: Astrologers at Rome." *Classical Philology* 106 (2): 115–54. https://www.jstor.org/stable/10.1086/659835

Rives, J. B. 2011. "Magicians and Astrologers." In *The Oxford Handbook of Social Relations in the Roman World*, edited by Michael Peachin. Oxford University Press.

Robinson, O. F. 2007. "The Role of Delators." In *Beyond Dogmatics: Law and Society in the Roman World*, edited by John W. Cairns and Paul J. du Plessis. Edinburgh University Press.

Rogers, Robert Samuel. 1952. "A Tacitean Pattern in Narrating Treason-Trials." *Transactions and Proceedings of the American Philological Association* 83: 279–311. https://www.jstor.org/stable/283391

Rutledge, Steven H. 2001. *Imperial Inquisitions: Prosecutors and Informants from Tiberius to Domitian*. Routledge.

Ryberg, Inez Scott. 1942. "Tacitus' Art of Innuendo." *Transactions and Proceedings of the American Philological Association* 73: 383–404. https://www.jstor.org/stable/283558

Santoro L'Hoir, Francesca. 1994. "Tacitus and Women's Usurpation of Power." *Classical World* 88 (1): 5–25. https://www.jstor.org/stable/4351613

Santoro L'Hoir, Francesca. 2006. *Tragedy, Rhetoric, and the Historiography of Tacitus' "Annales."* University of Michigan Press.

Scafuro, Adele. 1989. "Livy's Comic Narrative of the Bacchanalia." *Helios: Journal of the Classical Association of the Southwest* 16 (2): 119–42.

Schmitzer, Ulrich. 2005. "Der Tod auf offener Szene. Tacitus über Nero und die Ermordung des Britannicus." *Hermes* 133 (3): 337–57. https://www.jstor.org/stable/4477663

Schulz, Verena. 2019. *Deconstructing Imperial Representation: Tacitus, Cassius Dio, and Suetonius on Nero and Domitian*. Brill.

Scott, James Morgan. 1998. "The Rhetoric of Suppressed Speech: Tacitus' Omission of Direct Discourse in His *Annals* as a Technique of Character Denigration." *Ancient History Bulletin* 12: 8–18.

Scott, R. T. 1968. *Religion and Philosophy in the Histories of Tacitus*. American Academy in Rome.

Seager, Robin. 2005. *Tiberius*. 2nd ed. Blackwell.

Severy, Beth. 2003. *Augustus and the Family at the Birth of the Roman Empire*. Routledge.

Shannon, Kelly. 2012. "Memory, Religion and History in Nero's Great Fire: Tacitus, *Annals* 15.41–7." *Classical Quarterly* 62 (2): 749–65. https://www.jstor.org/stable/23470136

Shanz, Martin, and Carl Hosius. 1959. *Geschichte der Römishcen Literatur: Bis zum Gesetzgebungswerk des Kaisers Justinian*. Vol. 2. 4th ed. C. H. Beck'sche Verlagsbuchhandlung.

Shochat, Yanir. 1981. "Tacitus' Attitude to Otho." *Latomus* 40 (2): 365–77. https://www.jstor.org/stable/41532078

Shotter, D. C. A. 1972. "The Trial of M. Scribonius Libo Drusus." *Historia: Zeitschrift für Alte Geschichte* 21 (1): 88–98. https://www.jstor.org/stable/4435247

Späth, Thomas. 2012. "Masculinity and Gender Performance in Tacitus." In *A Companion to Tacitus*, edited by Victoria Pagán. Wiley Blackwell.

Suetonius. 1997. *Lives of the Caesars*. Translated by J. C. Rolfe. Loeb Classical Library 38. Harvard University Press.

Sumi, Geoffrey S. 2005. *Ceremony and Power: Performing Politics in Rome between Republic and Empire*. University of Michigan Press.

Sumner, G. V. 1970. "The Truth About Velleius Paterculus: Prolegomena." *Harvard Studies in Classical Philology* 74: 257–97. https://www.jstor.org/stable/311010

Syme, Ronald. 1958. *Tacitus*. Clarendon Press.

Syme, Ronald. 1981. "Princesses and Others in Tacitus." *Greece & Rome* 28 (1): 40–52. https://www.jstor.org/stable/642481

Treggiari, Susan. 1991. "Divorce Roman Style: How Easy and How Frequent Was It?" In *Marriage, Divorce, and Children in Ancient Rome*, edited by Beryl Rawson. Clarendon Press.

Tsakona, Villy, and Diana Elena Popa, eds. 2011. *Studies in Political Humor: In Between Political Critique and Public Entertainment*. John Benjamins.

van Hooff, Anton J. L. 2002 [1990]. *From Autothanasia to Suicide: Self-Killing in Classical Antiquity*. Routledge.

Vessey, D. W. T. C. 1971. "Thoughts on Tacitus' Portrayal of Claudius." *American Journal of Philology* 92 (3): 385–409. https://www.jstor.org/stable/292801

Volpe, Michael. 1977. "The Persuasive Force of Humor: Cicero's Defense of Caelius." *Quarterly Journal of Speech* 63 (3): 311–23. https://doi.org/10.1080/0033563770938 3391

Von Albrecht, Michael. 1989. *Masters of Roman Prose from Cato to Apuleius*. Translated by Neil Adkin. Francis Cairns.

Von Stackelberg, Katharine T. 2009. "Performative Space and Garden Transgressions in Tacitus' Death of Messalina." *American Journal of Philology* 130 (4): 595–624. https://www.jstor.org/stable/20616210

Waddell, Philip. 2013. "Eloquent Collisions: The *Annales* of Tacitus, the Column of Trajan, and the Cinematic Quick-Cut." *Arethusa* 46 (3): 471–97. http://muse.jhu.edu/journals/arethusa/v046/46.3.waddell.html

Walker, B. 1952. *The "Annals" of Tacitus: A Study in the Writing of History*. Manchester University Press.

Weinrib, E. J. 1968. "The Family Connections of M. Livius Drusus Libo." *Harvard Studies in Classical Philology* 72: 247–78. https://www.jstor.org/stable/311081

Wellesley, Kenneth, ed. 1986. *Cornelii Taciti Libri Qui Supersunt: Ab Excessu Divi Augusti Libri XI–XVI*. Teubner.

Wellesley, Kenneth, ed. 1989. *Cornelii Taciti Libri Qui Supersunt: Historiarum Libri*. Teubner.

Whitehead, David. 1979. "Tacitus and the Loaded Alternative." *Latomus* 38 (2): 474–95. https://www.jstor.org/stable/41531206

Whitmarsh, Tim. 2006. "'This In-Between Book': Language, Politics and Genre in the *Agricola*." In *The Limits of Ancient Biography*, edited by Brian McGing and Judith Mossman. Classical Press of Wales.

Wilkins, Augustus S., ed. 2002. *Cicero "De Oratore" I–III*. Bristol Classical Press.

Willett, Cynthia. 2008. *Irony in the Age of Empire: Comic Perspectives on Democracy and Freedom*. Indiana University Press.

Woodman, A. J. 1988. *Rhetoric in Classical Historiography: Four Studies*. Routledge.

Woodman, A. J. 1993. "Amateur Dramatics at the Court of Nero: *Annals* 15.48–74." In *Tacitus and the Tacitean Tradition*, edited by T. J. Luce and A. J. Woodman. Princeton University Press.

Woodman, A. J. 1998. *Tacitus Reviewed*. Clarendon Press.

Woodman, A. J., trans. 2004. *The Annals*. By Tacitus. Hackett.

Woodman, A. J. 2012. "Nero's Alien Capital: Tacitus as Paradoxographer (*Annals* 15.36–7)." In *Oxford Readings in Tacitus*, edited by Rhiannon Ash. Oxford University Press.

Woodman, A. J., and R. H. Martin. 1996. *The "Annals" of Tacitus. Book* 3. Cambridge University Press.

Woods, David. 2006. "Tacitus, Nero, and the «Pirate» Anicetus." *Latomus* 65 (3): 641–49. https://www.jstor.org/stable/41544211

Wyke, Maria. 2002. *The Roman Mistress: Ancient and Modern Representations*. Oxford University Press.

Index Locorum

CASSIUS DIO
Roman Histories
48.34.3: 52n19
55.5.4: 63n45
61a.31.1–2: 77n26
61a.31.3: 75n18
61a.31.5: 90
61b.1.1: 102n28
61b.9.3–4: 112
62a.11.1: 116n71
62a.12.1: 116n71
62a.12.2: 126n102
62a.13.3: 122n93
62a.16.2: 167n92
62a.20.1–5: 165
62b.13.1: 116n71
62b.13.4: 142n25, 142n26
62b.14.1: 140
62b.16.1–2: 152n56
62b.18.1: 153–54n58
62b.28.1: 116n71
63.13.2: 44n83

CICERO
De Oratore
1.183–184: 87n49
2.220: 7
2.221: 8
2.236: 140n15
2.237: 5, 24, 47n2, 103, 171
2.238: 140n15
2.239: 140n15
2.244–245: 7n20
2.245: 172
2.250: 4, 7, 13
2.251: 5n11
2.252: 7
2.256–257: 24n27
2.257: 7
2.262: 5, 7n19
2.267: 17n6
2.268: 7
2.269: 7, 7n16, 18n12
2.270: 7n17
2.272: 7, 7n19, 31, 105n37
2.274: 22–23
2.277: 24
2.289: 7
3.220: 7n17
Pro Rege Deiotaro
1.3: 63n45
Tusculan Disputations
4.17–18: 17n8

HERODOTUS
Histories
9.108–113: 75n19

LIVY
Ab Urbe Condita
1.46: 74n15

LUCAN
Pharsalia
2.531–533: 40n76

MARTIAL
Epigrams
6.32: 44n83

OVID
Amores
3.9.55–58: 74n14

PLAUTUS
Asinaria
920–940: 74
884–889: 75n19
Casina
621–629: 160n78
Menaechmi
130–134: 75n19
831–875: 161
Rudens
1006–1009: 160n78

PLUTARCH
Life of Otho
3.5: 33n58, 34n59
3.7: 34

PROPERTIUS
Carmina
4.8: 74n13

QUINTILIAN
Institutio Oratoria
6.3.1: 8n22
6.3.3: 8
6.3.8: 7, 140n15
6.3.26: 4
6.3.26–28: 8
6.3.28: 24
6.3.31: 5, 47n2, 171
6.3.32: 172
6.3.47–49: 7
6.3.53–54: 7
6.3.62: 7
6.3.63: 6
6.3.70: 18n12
6.3.79: 140n15
6.3.99: 23
6.3.112: 24n27
9.2.3: 7n17
9.2.14: 18n12

Rhetorica ad Herennium
1.10: 8n22
4.67: 7n17

SALLUST
Bellum Catilinae
10.5: 29n45
25.3: 73, 114n61

SENECA
Epistulae Morales
70.10: 61–62n41

SUETONIUS
Augustus
25: 38n68
Caesar
67: 38n68
Caligula
12: 100n21
Nero
7: 99n18
20: 165
31–32: 157
32: 162n82
33: 103n30, 104, 108, 110
34: 121n90, 128n110
35: 116n71
38: 152n56
39: 167n92
43: 35n65
49: 64n47
Otho
3: 19n14
8: 34n59
Tiberius
25: 49n10, 56, 62n42

TACITUS
Annales
1.7.1: 31n48
1.10.5: 136
1.54.1–2: 136n7
1.72.1–3: 66n54
2.26.2–4: 48
2.26.5: 48
2.27.1: 49
2.27.1–2: 48
2.27.2: 50

2.28.1: 54
2.28.2: 54–55, 59
2.28.2–3: 56
2.29.1: 57
2.29.2: 58–59
2.30.1: 56, 60–61, 76n23
2.30.2: 62
2.30.3: 63
2.30.4–2.31.1: 63
2.30.4: 67
2.31.1: 64–65
2.31.2: 65
2.31.3: 67
2.32.1–2: 68
2.32.2: 68
2.39.1: 56n28
2.82.1–2.83.5: 100n20
3.75.1: 7–8n21
4.1.1–3: 49n6
4.13.2: 60n37
4.22.1–2: 49n6
4.28.1–3: 60n37
4.29.1: 60n37
4.29.2–3: 60n37
4.30.1: 60n37
4.31.4: 51n11
6.20.2: 51n15
11.2.1–2: 72
11.5.3: 72–73
11.5.3–11.6.2: 72
11.7.4: 72n4
11.11.2: 97, 103
11.11.3: 98
11.12.1: 72
11.12.2: 72–73, 76, 78n28, 83, 86n48
11.12.3: 74, 85
11.26.1: 76, 78
11.26.1–2: 77n25, 83
11.26.2: 77, 86n48
11.26.3: 77–78, 149n48
11.27: 78–82
11.28.1: 81–82, 86n48
11.28.2: 83
11.29.3: 84
11.30.1: 84–85
11.30.2: 75, 85–86
11.31.1: 87–88, 91
11.31.2: 88
11.31.2–3: 88
11.31.3: 89
11.32.1: 89
11.32.2: 89
11.33: 89
11.34.1: 90
11.34.2–3: 91
11.35.1: 91
11.35.2: 89
11.36.4: 92n63
12.3.1: 73n11
12.3.1–2: 99
12.3.2: 99
12.5.1: 73n11
12.7.3: 91n61
12.22.1: 51n15
12.22.3: 51n15
12.25.1: 73n11
12.26.1: 7–8n21
12.41.1: 100–101
12.41.3: 101
12.52.3: 24n25
13.3.1: 137
13.3.1–3: 101n26
13.3.3: 103n30
13.5.1: 72n5
13.13.1: 118n75
13.14–13.15: 52n17
13.14.1: 101–2n27
13.14.2–3: 101, 143n28
13.15.1: 104n34
13.15.2: 102–3, 104n34
13.15.3: 56n28, 104n33, 105n37
13.15.1–3: 102
13.15.4: 105, 106n41
13.15.5: 105–6
13.16.1: 106
13.16.3: 107–8, 145n35
13.16.3–4: 102
13.16.4: 106, 108–9, 119n81
13.17.3: 110n53
13.19.2–3: 73n12, 74n15
13.25.1: 111
13.25.2: 111, 128n109, 152
13.25.3: 113n58
13.25.1–4: 151
13.44.1–5: 114n60
13.45.1: 114
13.45.2: 114
13.45.3: 114, 116n70, 119n78

TACITUS
Annales (*continued*)
13.45.4: 115
13.46.1: 115
13.46.1–3: 143
13.46.2: 83n38, 116–18
13.46.3: 18n11, 19n14
14.1.1: 120
14.1.2: 118n77, 120, 144
14.1.3: 120
14.2.1: 73n11
14.2.1–2: 120, 120n84
14.3.1: 120, 120n84
14.3.2: 121n88
14.3.3: 121, 129n113
14.4.1: 122, 122n92
14.4.4: 122, 145n35
14.5.1: 122, 124n99
14.5.1–3: 123
14.5.2: 123
14.5.3: 123–24
14.6.1: 126
14.6.2: 126
14.7.2: 128
14.7.2–3: 138n13
14.7.4: 129n111
14.7.6: 128
14.8.1: 126–27
14.8.5: 130n115
14.9.3: 130n115
14.10.1: 130
14.10.3: 122n94
14.10.3–14.11.1: 131
14.11.1–3: 131, 138n13
14.11.2–3: 131n116
14.11.3: 132
14.13.1: 131
14.14.1: 134n3
14.14.1–2: 134
14.14.2: 134, 138n13
14.52.1–3: 135
14.52.3: 135–36
14.55.1: 137
14.56.3: 137n10, 138
14.57.1: 139
14.57.3: 139–40
14.57.4: 140, 147
14.59.3: 140–41, 147
14.59.4: 141
14.60.1: 18n11, 144
14.60.2: 56n28, 142
14.60.3: 142
14.61.1: 143
14.61.2: 143
14.61.4: 118n77, 143–44
14.62.2: 145
14.62.4: 145
14.63.1: 146
14.63.3: 147n38
14.64.2: 147
15.23.1: 144
15.35: 83n37
15.37.1: 147
15.37.1–4: 145n32
15.37.3: 148
15.37.4: 149–50
15.38.1: 151
15.38.7: 151
15.39.1: 153
15.39.1–2: 153
15.39.3: 153
15.44.4: 136
15.48.2: 155
15.49.1: 49n6
15.49.2: 155n62
15.49.3: 155
15.49.3–4: 155–56n63
15.49.4: 155–56
15.57.1–2: 73n11
15.60.4: 64n49
15.62.1–2: 64n49
15.65: 156, 167n92
15.67.1–15.68.1: 155n62
16.1.1: 158
16.2.1: 159
16.2.1–2: 159–60
16.3.1: 162
16.3.2: 76n23, 158, 162–63
16.4.1: 136n7, 163
16.4.1–4: 145n31
16.4.2: 164
16.4.3: 95n2, 165
16.4.4: 164, 166
16.5.1: 167n92
16.6.2: 147n39
16.7–8: 52n17
16.8.1: 51n13
16.11.3: 141n19, 166n91

16.14.1: 166–67n91
16.19.1–3: 64n49
16.28.1: 166–67n91
Agricola
2.4: 7–8n21
Dialogus de Oratoribus
11.1: 7n21
Historiae
1.6: 53n22
1.10: 53n22
1.13.2: 16
1.13.3: 17–18, 25n30, 118n73
1.13.4: 19
1.16.1: 86n46
1.21.1: 20, 22, 88n53
1.21.2: 21
1.22.1: 22–23, 26, 172
1.22.2: 25, 56n28
1.22.3: 25
1.25.1: 26
1.25.2: 26
1.27: 26n34
1.27.1: 56n28
1.29.2: 38n68
1.30.1: 39n70
1.30.2: 38n68, 39n70
1.31.2: 38n68
1.35.2: 38n68
1.36.3: 27, 166n89
1.37.1: 27–29, 38
1.44.1: 32n55, 109n51
1.45.1: 30–31
1.45.2: 31
1.46.1: 32n54
1.52: 53n22
1.78.2: 26n34, 116n69
1.80.1: 33, 34n63
1.81.1: 33
1.81.2: 33
1.82.1: 34–35
1.82.3: 36
1.83–84: 39
1.83.1: 29n44, 37, 39
1.83.2: 37–38
1.84.3: 39–40, 109n48
1.84.4: 41–42
1.85.1: 36, 40n75
1.90.3: 43
2.33.3: 34n60
2.47.1: 44
2.48–49: 44
2.49.4: 44
2.68.1: 33n56
2.70.4: 109n51
2.77–78: 53n22
2.90.1–2: 166n90
2.93.2: 7–8n21
3.47: 145n33

TERENCE
Hecyra
750–760: 74

THUCYDIDES
Histories
3.82.3–4: 29n45

VELLEIUS PATERCULUS
Roman History
2.129.2: 49n10
2.130.3: 49n10

General Index

absurdity, 3; at Messalina's wedding to Silius, 80–81, 85, 87, 89–92; in the trial of Libo Drusus, 53, 61, 66–68; of Nero and his principate, 9, 14, 19, 95–97, 100–101, 104–9, 112–13, 115–17, 119, 121, 124–26, 130–39, 142, 145–47, 151–52, 158–61, 164–68, 171–73; of Otho and his principate, 29, 36, 39
Acerronia (freedwoman of Agrippina), 122–26
Acte (mistress of Nero), 83n38, 84n43, 118–19, 147n38
Agerinus (freedman of Agrippina), 128–29
Anicetus, 121, 127, 129, 145
ambiguity (as a spur to humor), 7, 12, 28, 30
Agrippina the Younger, 72, 91–92n61, 97, 99-106, 108, 110, 143n28; murdered by Nero, 9–10, 14, 119–32, 134, 138, 145, 148n41, 155, 171–72
appendix sentence, 1, 13n35, 31
Augustus, 6, 38n68, 52, 63n45, 72n5, 97n11, 100n22, 136, 165n87

Britannicus, 72n6, 77, 97, 99; murder by Nero, 10, 101–11, 119, 125, 129, 132, 134, 143n28, 145n35
Burrus, Sextus Afranius (praetorian prefect), 97, 102, 128, 129n111, 133–35

Caesellius Bassus, 76n23, 157–63
Calpurnius Piso, C. (conspired against Nero), 155–57
Calpurnius Piso, Cn. (accused murderer of Germanicus), 64
Calpurnius Piso Frugi Licinianus, L. (heir of Galba), 39n70, 109n51
Claudius, 14, 71–73, 76–78, 82–93, 99, 170
comedy, 3, 7n20, 9, 14, 40n74, 53, 71, 73n11, 75–76, 79–80, 82, 85–86, 93, 115–16, 119, 170; New Comedy, 8. *See also* theatricality
contradiction, 12, 14–20, 23, 27–28, 43–45, 54, 59, 61, 91, 96, 112, 115, 125, 146, 168
contrast (element of humor), 2, 6, 8–10, 12, 15–20, 22, 25, 27, 32, 35–36, 39, 42–44, 48, 51, 53–54, 57–60, 62, 64, 68, 72, 75, 77, 80–82, 86, 89–91, 105n36, 106–13, 121–24, 128–29, 131–32, 138, 142–43, 146, 148–51, 157–59, 161–65, 167
Cornelius Sulla (consul 52 CE), 139–41

deception, 7, 10, 18n12, 28, 31, 34, 58, 96, 112–13, 116–18, 123–24, 128–31, 134, 136, 138–39, 145, 156–60
delatores, 53n21, 48, 54, 56–62, 68–69, 84, 92n62. *See also entries for individual delatores*
Drusus Libo. *See* Libo Drusus

Firmius Catus, 49n10, 50–57, 60, 68
Fonteius Agrippa, 60
freedpeople, 14, 64, 73n11, 93, 101–2n27, 118, 128; Otho's freedmen, 21–24, 26, 44; Claudius' freedmen, 71, 76, 82–84, 87, 89–91, 93, 171. *See also entries for individual freedpeople*
Fulcinius Trio, 49n10, 56, 60

Galba, 17, 19–21, 29–31, 38n68, 86n46
Germanicus, 48
great fire of Rome, 151–54

hypocrisy, 1, 10, 22, 25, 30–31, 37–41, 59, 63, 67, 69, 76, 143, 169

inconcinnitas, 3n6, 24
incongruity, 6, 16n3, 21–22, 30, 39, 54, 60, 78–81, 91, 137, 150; appropriate incongruity, 11
inconsistency, 13, 20, 67
irony, 1–3, 6n14, 7–8, 10, 12, 19, 27n40, 30–32, 38n59, 65, 67–68, 78, 89, 102, 105n37, 114, 122, 130n115, 136–37, 147, 164, 169, 173; dramatic irony, 28, 63, 118n74, 122, 126, 136

joke, 3–5, 11–13, 16n3, 22, 24–25, 26n34, 27, 36, 78, 92, 101–2n27, 102n29, 124, 125n100, 127, 140, 141–43, 147n39, 153, 160–62, 169, 171–72
Julius Caesar, 38n68, 52, 67
Julius Montanus, 111–13, 128n109
Junia Silana, 72–74

Libo Drusus, 14, 47–50, 68–69, 76n23, 77, 83n37, 170–71; consultation of diviners, 50–51; family background, 51–53; accused of treason, 53–58; tried for treason, 58–64; suicide, 64–67
Livia Augusta, 52, 136
loaded alternative. *See* weighted alternative
Locusta, 56n28, 105, 109–10
logical mechanism, 10–11n28, 24, 87n50, 102n29, 106n40, 123n97
Lucan, as an epic poet, 40n76, 95n2; as a member of the Pisonian conspiracy, 155
lying. *See* deception

maiestas, 49n8, 53–54, 63n45, 64n48, 170; Tiberian *maiestas* trials, 14, 49n8, 49n10, 53–54, 55n23, 56, 59, 170
Messalina, 71, 170–71; relationship with G. Silius, 72–76; marriage to G. Silius, 14, 76–89, 115n65, 149n48; consequences of marriage to G. Silius, 89–93
mockery, 3, 48, 103, 104n35, 120, 133, 136, 139–41, 147, 158, 167
mutiny, of Otho against Galba, 26n34, 27–28n40, 29n42, 30; of Otho's troops against their officers, 15, 32–37, 39, 42

Narcissus (freedman of Claudius), 84–87, 89–93
Nero, 9–10, 14, 59, 64n47, 72, 78n27, 83n38, 95–97, 166–68, 170–72; accidental deception by Caesellius Bassus, 157–63; debate over Seneca's retirement, 135–39; early public appearances, 97–101; marriage to Pythagoras, 147–51; mockery of enemies, 139–41; murder of Agrippina, 119–32; persecution of Octavia, 141–47; petty crimes, 111–13; Pisonian conspiracy, 49n6, 154–57; public performances, 133–35, 163–66; relationship with Otho, 16–20, 23, 25–26, 35n65, 43, 45; relationship with Poppaea, 114–20, 130; response to the great fire, 151–54; rivalry with and murder of Britannicus, 52n17, 101–10

Octavia (daughter of Claudius), 18n11, 99, 102, 108, 109n49, 119, 120n82, 172; death, 141–47
Ofonius Tigellinus, 66n54, 135, 139–40, 142–43, 147, 149
Otho, 12, 13–16, 53, 64, 76n21, 83n37, 88n53, 109, 166n89, 170–72; decision to usurp Galba, 20–26; defeat and death, 42–45; relationship with Nero, 16–19, 115–18; relationship with Poppaea, 17–18, 25, 115–18, 120; subservience to partisans, 26–32, 36–42; suppression of nighttime mutiny, 32–36
opposed scripts. *See* script opposition
overlap. *See* script overlap

Pallas (freedman of Claudius), 101–2n27
performance, 37; theatrical, 57n30, 79n29, 80n31; in Nero's principate, 9, 96–99, 101, 103–8, 110, 112, 114–15, 118–26, 128, 130, 132–40, 142, 145–48, 150, 152–57, 163–68, 171
Piso. *See under* Calpurnius Piso
Pisonian conspiracy, 154–57
Poppaea Sabina, 114–15, 142–47; relationship with Nero, 114–20, 130; relationship with Otho, 17–18, 25, 115–18
punchline, 2–3, 24, 26–27, 31–32, 62, 80–81, 102, 109, 112, 114, 124, 127, 143, 147n39, 149, 150, 166
pun, 7n21, 142n23, 164

Rubellius Plautus, 139–41

sarcasm, 1, 7n18, 24, 86, 146
satire, 1, 3, 9n25
Scribonia (first wife of Augustus), 48, 50, 52
script opposition, 10–12, 16, 47–48, 54, 64, 72, 74–75, 96, 108, 110n52, 111n54, 113–15, 119, 123, 125n100, 127, 129–30, 138n12, 142, 147n38, 149–50, 155, 157, 160–61, 164, 167
script overlap, 10–12, 16, 22, 48, 107, 113, 116, 125n100, 129, 137, 147n38, 149–50
script theory of humor, 10–13, 16, 24, 106n40; scripts, 102n29, 125n100, 132n119. *See also* script opposition; script overlap
Senate, 39–42, 58–59, 86, 131, 163–65; criticized by Tacitus, 62–64, 67–69, 172
Silius (C., Messalina's concurrent second husband), 14, 171; introduction, 71–74; marriage to Messalina, 74–90, 92–93
sententia, 3, 24, 26, 140
subabsurda, 7, 22–23
Subrius Flavus (member of Pisonian conspiracy), 156, 157n67, 167n92

theatricality, 9–10, 66, 79, 85, 88, 95, 105, 121, 126n102, 129–30, 157. *See also* comedy; performance; tragedy
Tiberius, 9, 14, 47–48, 49n10, 51–56, 58–59, 60n37, 63, 65–68, 77, 100, 170
Tragedy, 8–10, 89, 141–42, 172
treason, 14; trials in the reign of Tiberius, 47–58, 68–69. *See also maiestas*

variatio, 1, 8, 169, 173
Vibius Serenus (Caius), 60, 68n60
Vitellius (emperor), 26n33, 33n56, 40, 42–43, 166n90
Vitellius (L., cos. 34, 43, 47), 90–91

weighted alternative, 21, 115n64